KANDAHAR TOUR

KANDAHAR TOUR

The Turning Point in Canada's Afghan Mission

Lee Windsor
David Charters
Brent Wilson
Gregg Centre for the Study of War and Society

John Wiley & Sons Canada, Ltd.

The photograph sections in this book are dedicated in memory of MCpl Darrell Priede, Image Technician from 3 Area Support Group, CFB Gagetown, killed in action in southern Afghanistan on 30 May 2007. Many of the DND Combat Camera photos herein were his.

Library and Archives Canada Cataloguing in Publication Data

Windsor, Lee A., 1971–
    Kandahar tour : the turning point in Canada's Afghan mission / Lee Windsor, David Charters, Brent Wilson.

Includes bibliographical references and index.
ISBN 978-0-470-15761-9
    1. Afghan War, 2001—Participation, Canadian. 2. Canada—Armed Forces—Afghanistan.
3. Canada—Military policy. I. Charters, David II. Wilson, Brent III. Title.

DS371.412.W55 2008   958.104'7   C2008-903716-2

Production Credits
Cover and interior text design: Michael Chan
Typesetting: Thomson Digital
Cover photo: Rifleman from India Company, 2nd Battalion, Royal Canadian Regiment on dawn patrol in Zharey District, June 2007. (Sgt Craig Fiander DND/Combat Camera).
Map of Afghanistan South: used with permission of Land Forces Command, Department of National Defence.
Printer: Friesens

John Wiley & Sons Canada, Ltd.
6045 Freemont Blvd.
Mississauga, Ontario
L5R 4J3

Printed in Canada

1 2 3 4 5 FP 12 11 10 09 08

There is little time for Canadian soldiers to grieve for fallen comrades in Kandahar. Once the aircraft ramp closes, they must press on with their mission. This book is dedicated to Canadians that returned safe to help remember great accomplishments and friends lost on the way.

Table of Contents

Canada in Kandahar
Mission Components and Principal Leaders
to August 2007

TF 107, Roto 3

Joint Task Force Afghanistan Headquarters: Brigadier-General Tim Grant

Kandahar Provincial Reconstruction Team: Lieutenant-Colonel Bob Chamberlain

> Foreign Affairs Section: Gavin Buchan
>
> Correctional Services of Canada Team: Louise Garwood-Filbert
>
> Civilian Police Section: Superintendent David Fudge, Royal Canadian Mounted Police
>
> Civil-Military Co-operation Team: Major Sean Courty
>
> Military Police Platoon
>
> Engineer Troop
>
> Force Protection Company: composite of the Royal 22^e Regiment (R22eR)

Battle Group based on 2nd Battalion, Royal Canadian Regiment (2RCR): Lieutenant-Colonel Rob Walker

> Infantry Companies
>
> > Hotel Company, 2RCR: Major Alex Ruff
> >
> > Hotel Company, 2RCR: Major David Quick
> >
> > Charles Company (Parachute), 3rd Battalion, Princess Patricia's Canadian Light Infantry (3PPCLI): Major Chris Henderson
>
> Reconnaissance and Surveillance Squadron
>
> > "A" Squadron, Royal Canadian Dragoons & Reconnaissance Platoon 2RCR: Major Stephan Graham
>
> Armored Squadron
>
> > "A" Squadron, Lord Strathcona's Horse (Royal Canadians): Major David Broomfield
>
> Artillery Battery
>
> > "D" or "Dragon" Battery, 2nd Royal Canadian Horse Artillery: Major Dan Bobitt

Engineer Squadron
41 Field Squadron, 4 Engineer Support Group: Major Jake
Galuga

*Operational Mentoring and Liaison Team with 1 Brigade, 205ᵗʰ Corps, Afghan
National Army: Lieutenant-Colonel Wayne Eyre*

*National Support Element, composite group of combat service support sol-
diers from across Canada, based primarily on 3 Area Support Group in CFB
Gagetown: Lieutenant-Colonel Charles Mathe:*
Logistics Operation Centre
Supply and Transportation Company
Maintenance Company
Force Protection Company
Contracts Management Section
Civilian employees of the Canadian Forces Personnel
Support Agency

Health Services Support Company

List of Abbreviations

Canadian Forces Ranks

Gen	General
LGen	Lieutenant-General
MGen	Major-General
BGen	Brigadier-General
Col	Colonel
LCol	Lieutenant-Colonel
Maj	Major
Capt	Captain
Lt	Lieutenant
2Lt	Second Lieutenant
RSM	Regimental Sergeant-Major
CSM	Company Sergeant-Major
SSM	Squadron Sergeant-Major (Royal Canadian Engineers and Royal Canadian Armoured Corps)
BSM	Battery Sergeant-Major (Royal Canadian Artillery)
CWO	Chief Warrant Officer
MWO	Master Warrant Officer
WO	Warrant Officer
Sgt	Sergeant
MCpl	Master Corporal
Cpl	Corporal
Pte	Private

Canadian Forces Vehicles and Kit

Badger	RCE heavy armoured engineering vehicle
Bison	Wheeled armoured personnel carrier
C-7, C-8	Standard issue Canadian rifle and carbine, respectively
C-9 LMG	Standard issue Canadian section level light machine gun
C-6 GPMG	Standard issue Canadian medium or general purpose machine gun
Coyote	Armoured reconnaissance and surveillance vehicle

LAV-III	Light armoured infantry fighting vehicle
Leopard C1 & C2	RCAC main battle tank
M-777	Towed 155mm Howitzer
RG-31	Nyala South African-built mine-hardened 4x4 armoured car
T-LAV	Tracked LAV based on rebuilt M-113 APCs

General Abbreviations

2i/c	Second-in-command
ADZ	Afghan Development Zone
ANA	Afghan National Army
ANDS	Afghan National Development Strategy
ANP	Afghan National Police
AO	Area of Operations
AOR	Area of Responsibility
APC	Armoured Personnel Carrier
ASG	Area Support Group
CCF	Commander's Contingency Fund
CDC	Community Development Council
CEFCOM	Canadian Expeditionary Force Command
CF	Canadian Forces
CFB	Canadian Forces Base
CFPSA	Canadian Forces Personnel Support Agency
CIDA	Canadian International Development Agency
CIMIC	Civil-Military Co-operation
CMTC	Canadian Manoeuvre Training Centre
CNS	Camp Nathan Smith
DAG	Deployment Assistance Group
DCO	Deputy Commanding Officer
DFAIT	Department of Foreign Affairs and International Trade
DFID UK	Department for International Development United Kingdom
DND	Department of National Defence
DRA	Democratic Republic of Afghanistan
DSC	Deployment Support Centre

EOD	Explosive Ordnance Disposal
FATA	Federally Administered Tribal Area (Pakistan)
FOB	Forward Operating Base
FOO	Forward Observation Officer (artillery)
GMFRC	Gagetown Military Family Resource Centre
GOA	Government of Afghanistan
HIG	Hezb-e-Islami Gulbuddin
HLVW	Heavy Logistics Vehicle Wheeled
ICRC	International Committee of the Red Cross
IED	Improvised Explosive Device
IMF	International Monetary Fund
IO	Information Operation, Information Officer
ISAF	International Stability and Assistance Force
ISI	Inter-Services Intelligence Agency (Pakistan)
ISTAR	Intelligence, Surveillance, Targeting, and Acquisition
JPCC	Joint Provincial Co-ordination Centre
JTF2	Joint Task Force 2
JTFA	Joint Task Force Afghanistan
KAF	Kandahar Airfield
KMNB	Kabul Multinational Brigade
KPRT	Kandahar Provincial Reconstruction Team
LAV	Light Armoured Vehicle
LFAA	Land Forces Atlantic Area
LSH	Lord Strathcona's Horse
LUVW	Light Utility Vehicle Wheeled
MBT	Main Battle Tank
MFRC	Military Family Resource Centre
MND	Minister of National Defence
MP	Member of Parliament, Military Police
MRRD	Ministry of Rural Rehabilitation and Development (Afghanistan)
NATO	North Atlantic Treaty Organization
NCO	Non-commissioned Officer
NCM	Non-commissioned Member
NGO	Non-Governmental Organization
NSP	National Solidarity Program

NSE	National Support Element
OGD	Other Government Departments
OMLT	Operational Mentoring and Liaison Team
OSI	Operational Stress Injury
OSISS	Operational Stress Injury Social Support
OTSSC	Operational Trauma and Stress Support Centre
PM	Prime Minister
POMLT	Police Operational Mentoring and Liaison Team
PPCLI	Princess Patricia's Canadian Light Infantry
PRT	Provincial Reconstruction Team
PSTC	Peace Support Training Centre
PTSD	Post-traumatic Stress Disorder
QIP	Quick Impact Project
QRF	Quick Reaction Force
R22eR	Royal 22e Regiment
RCA	Royal Canadian Artillery
RCAC	Royal Canadian Armoured Corps
RCD	Royal Canadian Dragoons
RCE	Royal Canadian Engineers
RCHA	Royal Canadian Horse Artillery
RCIED	Radio-Controlled Improvised Explosive Device
RCMP	Royal Canadian Mounted Police
RCR	Royal Canadian Regiment
RNBR	Royal New Brunswick Regiment
RPG	Rocket-propelled Grenade
SAT	Strategic Advisory Team
SIED	Suicide Improvised Explosive Device
SSR	Security Sector Reform
TCCC	Tactical Combat Casualty Care
TFA	Task Force Afghanistan
TLD	Third Location Decompression
TPT	Tactical Psychological Operations Team
UAV	Unmanned Aerial Vehicle
UFSR	Unit Family Support Representative
UN	United Nations
UNAMA	United Nations Assistance Mission to Afghanistan
UNCOHA	United Nations Co-ordinator of Humanitarian Assistance

UNESCO	United Nations Educational, Scientific, and Cultural Organization
UNHCR	United Nations High Commission for Refugees
UNODC	United Nations Office on Drugs and Crime
UNWFP	United Nations World Food Programme
USAF	United States Air Force
USAID	United States Agency for International Development
USPI	United States Protection and Investigations
VAC	Veterans Affairs Canada

On the afternoon of Easter Sunday 2007, the unmistakable sound of trouble crackled over the radio in the battalion headquarters at Kandahar Airfield: "Zero, this is Two-Niner Alpha contact: Two-Two Bravo hit an IED. More to follow, over." The message came from Lt Ben Rogerson's Light Armoured Vehicle (LAV). His platoon was conducting a move across an ancient underground aqueduct north-west of the company leaguer in Maywand—three LAVs carrying 30 officers and men travelling across a dusty plain in central Asia, on the lookout for Taliban.

Ben Rogerson had just seen the vehicle in front of him thrown into the air by a massive explosion, and watched as it crashed back down. He felt the heat and blast wave across his face. As the dust and smoke settled, Rogerson saw two of his men on the ground, and he knew there were other casualties. Instinctively Rogerson ordered Rick Yuskiw, his Platoon Warrant Officer, to clear a medevac helicopter landing zone of any more IEDs and then leapt from his vehicle. He ran forward alone, unwilling to risk another life in case the Taliban had buried a secondary bomb to catch rescuers. When he was sure the site was safe, Rogerson motioned for help and especially for his medic, Cpl Rob Wickens. Once the situation was clearer, he sent a curt update to the battalion's LAV Captain, Dave Nixon: "Confirm Two-Two Bravo has struck IED. Cas rep and nine-liner to follow. Out." For the battlegroup commander, LCol Rob Walker, and his staff in Kandahar, anxious moments followed. Gradually the grim reality filtered through, and the nine-line format for ordering a medevac helicopter told the tale. Call-sign 22B had been totally destroyed in a powerful explosion. Sgt Don Lucas and five men of his section died instantly: the vehicle's driver, gunner, and one rear sentry were seriously wounded. All were victims of an IED in a counter-insurgency operation half a world away from home.

When the news of the incident broke the next day, Canadians were already deeply involved in a solemn act of remembrance for their war dead. 9 April 2007 marked the 90th Anniversary of the battle of Vimy Ridge, the iconic Great War victory which cost

Canada nearly 4,000 dead during several days of fierce fighting on the Western Front. That dreadful toll had quickly been reconciled in Canada's collective consciousness as the critical founding moment of Canadian nationhood: when all four divisions of the Canadian Corps fought shoulder to shoulder for the first time, and won a victory that had eluded our allies for years. After decades of neglect, the Vimy Memorial had been completely rebuilt, and on that April day in 2007, the nation was focused on the rededication ceremony and the meaning of that distant and bloody conflict. Canadians, it seems, understood what Vimy was about. But the news that six more Canadian soldiers had died on a foreign battlefield raised old and puzzling questions: What was to be achieved by sending thousands of Canadians to a shattered and utterly foreign country in central Asia? Was not Canada a nation of peacekeepers, not war-fighters? Why did Sgt Lucas and his men die?

These questions, in regard to Afghanistan, were not new, and dated back to Canada's first operational deployment there in 2001. Curiously, with Canadians totally absorbed in the sponsorship scandal that embroiled the federal ruling party, the announcement in 2005 that Canada was to deploy combat forces to southern Afghanistan occasioned little public debate. As a result, when Canadian combat operations in that country produced heavy casualties and intense media coverage in 2006, Canadians seemed suddenly dismayed that this latest peacekeeping mission looked a lot like a war. After months of dormancy on the Afghan question through the winter of 2006–07, media frenzy and public debate flared again on 9 April. Critics insisted that combat efforts against Taliban insurgents ought to be curtailed in favour of reconstruction, and that Afghans should shoulder their own security burden. Many Canadians trying to understand Afghanistan through the popular press sensed an imbalance between making war and rebuilding that country.

Ironically, the reconstruction effort demanded by mission critics was well underway by early 2007, with little fanfare and even less media attention. On the day that Sgt Lucas and his men were killed, Canada's Provincial Reconstruction Team (PRT) in Kandahar carried out a full slate of tasks, chief among them co-ordinating road and bridge repairs; the restoration of the war-ravaged, millennium-old irrigation system; the massive challenge of re-generating provincial and municipal government services from scratch; and even reforming the prison system.

Meanwhile, Canadian soldiers embedded as mentors to an Afghan National Army Kandak (battalion) patrolled and trained in Panjwayi District, near the newly built Afghan Army base located at the District Centre at Ma'Sum Ghar. From that ground, the Canadian-mentored 2nd Kandak, 1st Brigade of 205th "Hero" Corps of the Afghan National Army, germinated Afghan government professionalism and law and order after years of war, chaos, and police corruption. The new base at Ma'Sum Ghar stood as a symbol of United Nations (UN), Afghan government, and NATO's commitment to support the restoration of civil society right in the heart of Taliban country.

Perhaps the best indication of positive change in the Kandahar region on 8 April 2007 was the half-marathon held in downtown Kandahar City that day. Under the protection of North Atlantic Treaty Organization troops, based at Kandahar Airfield to the east, and an Afghan Army unit at Ma'Sum Ghar in the west, the event was sponsored by the Bayat Foundation and a local television station. Canada's Provincial Reconstruction Team helped with security, and its commander sat in the stands as a guest of honour with the governor of Kandahar. Hundreds of boys ran through crowds of cheering spectators in the kind of community sporting event not witnessed there in decades. The run revealed a sense of hope that life was gradually returning to normal in the city of a half-million people. According to local media and community leaders, Kandaharis were outraged when reports trickled in from 2nd Battalion of the Royal Canadian Regiment (2RCR) that six of its soldiers were dead. Many understood that the Canadian battlegroup's fight in the remote rural parts of the province kept the populated districts relatively secure, and that the Canadian lives just spent had helped purchase this hope-filled day.

Most importantly, Canada's effort to rebuild Kandahar was in full swing by April 2007. While the Taliban gravitated toward NATO and Afghan Army posts and patrols, a small army of 1,400 UN workers, Afghan civilian government officials, and independent aid agency staff laboured in the agricultural heartland of the Arghandab Valley, in remote mountain villages, and amid squatter slums on the outskirts of the city to rebuild a civil society. They worked to establish municipal councils and manage the first public works projects that rural Kandaharis had seen in decades, if ever. Many of these were funded by the Canadian International Development Agency (CIDA). This low-profile activity, called the National Solidarity Program (NSP), was more than a mere pot of money for drilling wells or digging canals. The NSP was designed to re-generate local village councils and their ability to work for a common purpose, something sorely lacking after 25 years of focus on basic self-preservation. Ideally, as each council grew, power shifted away from drug lords and Taliban chieftains and back to Afghans. Rebuilding community trust in the power of good government, in particular, required time and patience, two things westerners seem to lack.

In the spring of 2007 Canadians were largely unaware of the NSP and their country's non-combat efforts in southern Afghanistan. Media coverage fixated on casualties and ramp ceremonies and, when these were not available, on scandal and corruption within the Afghan government, or errors made in Ottawa. Little front-page attention went to reconstruction and diplomatic elements: ditch digging and public service training is either too tedious to read about or will not make a good photo-op. In such an information void, the deaths of Sgt Lucas and his men seemed pointless—as did the deaths of all the other Canadians in Afghanistan before them.

The objective of this book is to help Canadians make sense of their mission in Afghanistan. The province of Kandahar, where Canada's efforts were focused in 2007, was the most impoverished and traumatized of Afghanistan's 34 provinces. It was also the birthplace of the Taliban movement, the focal point for its resurgence, and thus is the strategic key to restoring health to the entire nation. In short, this is the story of what Sgt Donald Lucas and his section were doing, and how the security they were establishing enabled reconstruction efforts to at last reach full speed, when a massive Taliban-laid bomb took their lives.

* * *

The story is told here through the eyes of one six-month rotation of Canadian soldiers and civilian government officials: Task Force 1-07 deployed to Afghanistan from February to August 2007. TF1-07 was based on 2RCR and other units from CFB Gagetown, New Brunswick, backed by reservists from militia units across Atlantic Canada, and augmented by units from across Canada. Land Forces Command allowed the Gregg Centre at the University of New Brunswick to follow the battalion as it trained for the mission, to visit it while in theatre, and to access official war diaries and after-action reports. This has enabled us to write a rich and comprehensive account of the fight against bomb-making cells and drug gangs, which occurred simultaneously with the dramatic but unsung effort to establish a stable government. The latter involves an often frustrating struggle with corruption, as well as a desperate battle against crippling drought, disease, malnutrition, poverty, and a Taliban-driven opium economy.

The Canadian Forces' (CF) name for the deployment to south Asia is Joint Task Force Afghanistan (JTFA). As with earlier extended operations, troops are rotated through the mission in six-month tours, dubbed "Rotos." The technical term for the rotation which forms the focus of this book is Task Force 1-07, the first Roto of 2007. The nomenclature gets a little more confusing, however, since the 2RCR Battlegroup (which was comprised of soldiers from many units, as we shall see) was the third battlegroup to rotate through the operation in Kandahar province, so it is often described as "Roto 3." All of this can be confusing to the uninitiated, but the important point is that JTFA included all CF personnel deployed in the country, including soldiers, civilian officials, the battlegroup, the PRT, the mentoring and liaison teams, and the supporting base troops from the base at Kandahar Airfield. This book focuses on the exploits of TF 1-07, especially the 2RCR Battlegroup, as a vehicle for understanding the larger mission of JTFA.

In the event, the deployment of TF 1-07 to Kandahar in early 2007 marked a turning point in the international assistance effort in Afghanistan. Only five months earlier, Canadian soldiers had defeated a small Taliban army that massed near Kandahar City. Working alongside Afghan, Danish, Dutch, and American troops, Canadians of TF 3-06 fought an unanticipated conventional battle against approximately 2,000 Taliban fighters and local recruits who sought to smash the Afghan rebuilding effort before it could truly start. Six months later, hard-core Taliban and foreign fighters were scattered in small groups to remote parts of the province, or had been driven to neighbouring Helmand Province, where British, Estonian, and Danish troops hunted for them during the winter.

The result of these battles in 2006 was that, in Kandahar province, people returned to their farms on the promise that Canada, NATO, and their own army would provide security. Fortunately, normal rainfall during the winter of 2006–07 brought an end to the drought and gave farmers hope and opportunity. TF 1-07 and the Afghan National Army were able to push the security and development zone far and wide in early 2007, allowing UN, NATO, and Afghan restoration operations to function as intended, gaining momentum. Most importantly, chronically underfunded, poorly organized, and often corrupt Afghan National Police—a key part of the Afghan government's credibility problem—began to turn around with help from Canadian soldiers, police, and officials from Foreign Affairs and CIDA. When small Taliban units returned to Kandahar in the warm months of 2007, they found a population largely unwilling to rise up with them. They often found themselves as fugitives on the run from NATO's International Security and Assistance Force, and Afghan soldiers and police. Taliban violence in Kandahar was by no means finished, but it had changed since 2006.

Progress in Kandahar went largely unreported in Canada. Detailed accounts are now available of the unexpected battle of Pashmul in 2006, known as *Operation Medusa*, and of the seemingly insurmountable hurdles encountered that year. These works record some parts of the political decision process, the realities of Canadian soldiers facing combat, and the mess Canadians uncovered when they took over Kandahar; but they do not tell the subsequent story of how those same Canadians rose to meet those challenges. Most Canadians understood the origins and purpose of the Afghan mission as part of a continuum of late 20th-century peacekeeping operations. These deployments immediately conjured cherished images of smiling, blue-bereted Canadians manning quiet, if tense, checkpoints, standing stalwartly between former enemies who were learning to live peacefully side by side. International "aid and development" evoked only slightly less familiar images of civilian aid workers delivering food, medical care, water, and building materials to refugees in a largely benign, post-conflict environment. Canadians and others in the west became conditioned to the notion that war-fighting, peacekeeping, and aid delivery were separate functions.

The daily reality of the UN Assistance Mission to Afghanistan (UNAMA), and the NATO military effort that protected it in 2007, was that war-fighting, peacekeeping, and aid delivery occur simultaneously. Each day, soldiers sought out and often battled Taliban fighters, drug gangs, and other criminal elements. When it happened, the shooting war was small in scale—involving a hundred or only dozens of soldiers—but there are no "small wars" at the section level. For the Canadian infantry soldier, reloading his weapon while enemy bullets lashed the mud wall above his head, or the tanker, swinging the turret around to blast the Taliban rocket launcher before it blasts him, the experience was intense. Yet, Afghanistan in 2007 was a small war, and the distinction is highly relevant to understanding what this war was all about, because no NATO or Afghan leader expected to win with military power alone.

By early 2007, Canadian and international troops were patrolling areas of Afghanistan where peace had been restored, and where diplomats assisted Afghan officials in building relationships with former insurgents, warlords, and mistrustful neighbouring nations. These activities resembled traditional peacekeeping and involved a daily surge of thousands of Afghan and international aid workers across the country. They worked to restore basic services and the rule of law in a nation ripped apart by three decades of war, poverty, hunger, drought, and lawlessness. The simple fact that all these efforts occurred simultaneously, and that each function depended on the other to succeed, was lost on many in the West. This was the new reality of war—and peacekeeping.

The uncertainty and complexity that plagued recent international missions in the former Yugoslavia and in Somalia were also felt in Afghanistan by 2007. What was certain was that the Soviet war and the subsequent civil war, combined with drought and a Taliban government that lacked the will or ability to run the country, destroyed the social and economic structure of Afghanistan. What grew in its place was an ad hoc system of criminal gangs, refugee camps, and pockets of extremist Taliban supporters all directly manipulated by the international terrorist network of al-Qaeda. That latter relationship, by inviting US coalition attack on the already weak Taliban government, worsened the social-economic devastation. The UN and, later, NATO were left to pick up the pieces.

Canada's mission to Afghanistan and especially Kandahar, therefore, came as part of a new pattern of overseas operations in support of the UN and the international community. In the post-Cold War world, these have been less often the comfortable Chapter VI UN operations intended to help warring parties who want peace find a way to establish it. Rather, western states have been drawn into more challenging Chapter VII UN missions to enforce a peace where none exists, such as in the Balkans, Somalia, and Darfur. The mission to Afghanistan seemed especially controversial, in large part because of doubt over its potential for success, and whether it was a job worth doing in the first place—the same doubts and anxieties which have plagued many overseas missions since 1989.

Canada's JTFA, TF 1-07, arrived in Kandahar province at a critical time. The previous year saw the UN and NATO prove to Afghans in the south that they would stand alongside their fledgling government, army, and police. Moreover, western countries demonstrated that they would fight those who opposed the restoration of civil society and fundamental human rights. By early 2007, the stage was set for rebuilding to begin in earnest in Kandahar Province, even if that rebuilding was still threatened by hard-core militants and had to be defended by Canadian, Afghan, and other international soldiers in small, easily forgotten battles. Meanwhile, the network of diplomats, aid workers, and other civilian government officials laboured away on the largest, most difficult, and comprehensive international development mission ever undertaken.

This book seeks to fill a void in our understanding of the Canadian role in Afghanistan by describing the various mission elements after *Medusa*, through the eyes of the men and women of TF 1-07. We are mindful that this remains very much a first draft of history. A great deal remains unsaid due to on-going security requirements and we have made no attempt to play "armchair generals"—nit-picking about failures of training, equipment, intelligence, and doctrine. Our object was simply to capture the story in all its complexity within the limits imposed by time and circumstance, and to inform Canadians that their mission in Afghanistan in 2007 was about much more than war-fighting.

Perhaps the greatest limitation imposed on us is that at the time of writing, the final result of the Canadian mission to Kandahar remains unknown. For many, including those who have served in a series of rotations (though not for the Canadian media) the future looks guardedly promising. It is perhaps worth remembering that in 1993–95 critics of the international mission in the former Yugoslavia urged a withdrawal from that hopeless place because, they argued, the hatred and violence there ran too deep to be averted. How different Sarajevo, Dubrovnik, and Drvar look today. It is also important to realize that no matter what happens in Kandahar's next decade, the story of TF 1-07 is one of extraordinary Canadians performing noble tasks to the highest standards and traditions of their professions, and in service to their country. Perhaps, by the end of this book, the reader will understand why, on another Easter Sunday and half a world away, Canadian soldiers once again laid down their lives.

SEPTEMBER MORN

The story of Joint Task Force Afghanistan (JTFA) TF 1-07 began on a beautiful September morning in 2001. Out of a sunlit, cloudless sky four crowded American airliners laden with fuel were hijacked by al-Qaeda terrorists, and turned into missiles. Two were flown into the World Trade Center in New York City and one into the Pentagon in Washington, DC. A fourth, also en route to the US capital, crashed in a field in Pennsylvania following a struggle between the hijackers and the passengers.[1] Nearly 3,000 people, including 24 Canadians, died in the attacks, which caused hundreds of billions of dollars in damage and economic disruption. It was the biggest, most dramatic, most costly terrorist attack in history.

The Economist magazine described 9/11 as "The Day the World Changed."[2] Whether it truly did or not will be debated for decades to come. But for many in positions of authority it was a day that rapidly transformed their jobs. As one senior Canadian official said later, "My world changed on 9/11."[3] At a minimum, it set in motion the events discussed in this book.

LCol Rob Walker, then deputy commanding officer (DCO) of 2nd Battalion, Royal Canadian Regiment (2RCR), was one of those whose career and life was to be changed dramatically by the events of that day, although he did not realize how much at the time. That morning, 2RCR was on exercise at Camp Petersville in the Base Gagetown training area. LCol Walker recalled

> being in an orders group conducted by the Commanding Officer, LCol Jon Vance, when Capt James Price came into the tent and informed us about . . . passenger planes that had struck the World Trade Center. Our initial thought was that it

had to be some sort of an accident. The orders group soon broke up and we went over to the dining tent to see the latest report from CNN on this developing situation, which was by this time being described as an attack on the United States. . . . We were joined by a number of newly arriving platoon commanders . . . straight out of the infantry school. The Commanding Officer welcomed them to the battalion and a number of us returned to Base Gagetown . . . to start preparations for our standup as the LFAA [Land Forces Atlantic Area] Immediate Reaction Unit for a potential deployment to either conduct security tasks or to assist the civilian authorities manage the stranded [airline] passengers.[4]

Five and a half years later, LCol Walker was a battalion commanding officer (CO), and 2RCR was in Kandahar, Afghanistan, helping to rebuild a "failed state" and fighting a small war to make that possible. James Price was there too, part of a training team with the Afghan National Army (ANA). How they came to be there, what they experienced, and their accomplishments, are discussed in the chapters that follow. But before we get to that, it is essential first to set the story in its historical context. For neither 9/11 nor the Kandahar Tour of the 2RCR Battlegroup are events isolated from each other or from the continuum of Afghan history.

AFGHANISTAN IN HISTORY

Task Force Afghanistan TF 1-07 occurred in a social and political setting that is as complex as it is difficult to operate in. Like the rest of the Middle East and central Asia, Afghanistan has been shaped as much by external forces as internal ones. Its territory was contested for many centuries by rival empires: Greek, Indian, Persian, Arab, Turkish, British, and Russian. The last of the imperial contests—the "Great Game" between Britain and Russia in the 19th century—defined the modern boundaries of Afghanistan. This history left a dual legacy. First, Afghans resisted every foreign incursion and gained a fearsome reputation as tough, unbeatable guerrilla fighters. Empires have come and gone; Afghans have endured and ensured their independence from foreign rule. And second, Afghanistan became a multi-ethnic society, with loyalties defined largely by local ethnicity and geography, which limited the authority of any central

Afghan government over its subjects. During the 20th century, Afghan experiments with democracy and constitutional monarchy were unsuccessful; the country was ruled by small elites and strongmen. However, more than any national government, tribal loyalties and traditions and an abiding faith in Islam command the allegiance of most Afghans. Yet neither tribe nor faith has served as a unifying force.[5]

Ironically, while Afghanistan did not develop an effective state apparatus, its people developed a very strong national identity. A common understanding of being Afghan grew from shared experience in resisting foreigners and from the country's locus that both isolates it and makes it a commercial bridge between continents. Chris Alexander, former Canadian Ambassador to Afghanistan and later United Nations (UN) Deputy Special Representative there, observed that Afghans "share a bond and vision of nationhood based on a desire to avoid being victimized by their powerful neighbours." These unifying elements, Alexander says, "create strong cohesiveness among the population"[6] which allowed a tribal federation to function until the Cold War.

Afghanistan worked because no ethnic group commanded a clear majority of the population. The smaller groups range from the Hazara in the centre, through the Turkmen, Uzbek, Tajik, and Kirghiz across the north, to the Nuristani in the north-east. The Pashtun, at about 40 percent, constitute the largest minority and occupy a huge slice of the country from the Pakistan border in the east across the south-west almost to the border with Iran. The ancient Afghan capital of Kandahar lies squarely within Pashtun territory. But even the Pashtun are divided between the dominant Durrani tribe and their principal rivals for power, the Ghilzai.

Nevertheless, their numbers and location make the Pashtun the one group with the potential to make or break Afghanistan's recovery from centuries of internal and external conflict. The Durrani Pashtun dominated the political leadership of Afghanistan for more than 200 years (until 1978). So, the selection of a Durrani, Hamid Karzai, as the interim president of Afghanistan in 2001 was expedient; someone from one of the smaller minorities could not have been chosen. The Taliban leadership also draws from the Durrani tribe, which gives them a natural constituency among people in the south-east. Equally important, the Pashtun span the porous border with Pakistan, where their kin occupy the North West Frontier Province and the Federally Administered Tribal Agencies (FATA), and where the authority of the Pakistani government is the weakest. This is where the Taliban and al-Qaeda find sanctuary.[7]

Finally, the trans-border character of the Pashtun community has given Pakistan considerable influence within Afghanistan. The "Pashtunistan" issue—a long-standing conflict between Afghanistan and Pakistan over their tenuous border—has plagued relations between the two countries since Pakistan gained its independence in 1947. Overmatched in its prolonged hot/cold war with India, Pakistan has long regarded Afghanistan as its "backyard"—territory that provides Pakistan with the "strategic depth" it otherwise lacks. Thus, it has a strategic interest in the internal affairs of Afghanistan and has engaged in covert political and military activity within its neighbour. Indeed, some see the Taliban as simply a Pakistani "Trojan Horse."[8]

The seeds of the current conflict were sown in the 1950s, during the first regime of Mohammed Daoud Khan. Daoud moved Afghanistan closer to the Soviet Union militarily, economically, and politically. This eroded the stability of Afghanistan. Some of the officers and troops trained in the USSR operated as pro-Soviet moles in the armed forces, while the Soviet Union helped to create openly pro-Soviet parties, whose Marxist beliefs offended devout Muslims. By the 1970s, militant Islamists were clashing with the communists. The state's immature democratic political institutions could not survive the subversion and instability undamaged. When Daoud tried to reduce Soviet influence and develop closer ties with Muslim Middle Eastern states in the mid-1970s, he was overthrown and killed in a bloody coup in April 1978 by pro-Soviet Afghan military units.[9]

The pro-Soviet People's Democratic Party of Afghanistan seized power in the wake of the coup, proclaiming it the "Saur Revolution." Led by former publisher Nur Mohammed Taraki, the new government soon launched a social reform program along Soviet lines, and immediately found itself internally divided and at odds with much of the population. Some of the proposed reforms, such as those intended to liberate women and to reform education, were not radically different from those being implemented by the Karzai government and the international community a generation later. But, then as now, they challenged traditional values and upset the social structure, especially in rural areas. Other reforms were attempted with little thought, planning, or local consultation. The plan to reduce the dominance of the Pashtu language obviously did not find favour with the country's largest ethnic group. The land reform program was launched hastily without proper study or management because many experienced officials had been eliminated during the coup. As a result, agriculture suffered. And to add insult to injury, the government proclaimed that it would "clean up" Afghani Islam, and replaced the green flag of Islam with the red flag of socialism. [10]

These reforms not only failed, they created widespread popular resistance. That prompted the government to enforce its programs with repression which, in turn, stimulated a burgeoning insurgency. By the fall of 1979 the situation in Afghanistan had deteriorated drastically. Insurgents controlled about half of the country, and had massacred Soviet advisers in Herat. Large portions of the Afghan army had defected to the insurgents. Following pleas from Taraki, Moscow reluctantly sent small numbers of troops to assist his regime, but these were unable to stabilize the situation. In September 1979, Taraki was overthrown and killed in a coup by rival Hafizullah Amin. But Amin proved to be even more incompetent and repressive than Taraki, deepening the crisis. By December 1979, the USSR was confronted with two bad choices: either cut its losses and get out, letting a pro-Soviet government fall and losing face in the process; or intervene on a major scale to save the regime. The geriatric leaders in Moscow, lacking critical analysis and probably fearing the fallout from the emergence of a second Islamic regime on the Soviet Central Asian border (the first being in Iran earlier that year), chose to intervene. On Christmas day 1979 the Soviet Union invaded Afghanistan. Some 100,000 Soviet troops spent a decade fighting the insurgency, at a cost of about 15,000 Soviet combat fatalities and nearly a half-million wounded, before withdrawing in 1989. [11]

The punitive 10-year war had four major impacts on Afghanistan, whose cumulative effect after 1989 was an unstable, devastated, failed state, vulnerable to internal factional fighting and foreign subversion and manipulation. First, the war largely destroyed the infrastructure of the country; homes and villages, government services, buildings, roads, and agriculture were devastated by Soviet "scorched earth" tactics. Second, that approach killed, wounded, or starved over a million Afghans and drove about one-third of the population into exile, mostly to Pakistan.[12]

Third, because of its strategic location and its acceptance of refugees, Pakistan was able to assert its role as the power-broker in Afghanistan, both during and, more importantly, after the war. During the war, the United States had launched the largest and most success-ful covert operation in its history in arming and training the Afghan *mujahideen*. But this required the co-operation of Pakistan, which limited the scale of American aid and insisted that it be channelled through Pakistani sources, especially the Inter-Services Intelligence Directorate (ISID). This suited the United States, which wanted to maintain "plausible deniability" about its role in the operation. So, the Central Intelligence Agency (CIA) presence in Pakistan was small and had limited contact with the insurgents. The consequence of this deal was that the ISID controlled the allocation of aid to the mujahideen, and it gave the most support to those groups that suited its strategic agenda. Their preferred choice was the Pashtun Gulbuddin Hekmatyar's Hizb-i-Islami, the most extreme of the Islamist militias.[13]

Pakistan was able to exercise this freedom of action in part be-cause its support for the Afghans did not depend solely on American funding. Saudi Arabia eventually provided about $1 billion and en-couraged other Gulf states to donate to the cause. Wealthy Muslims also did so individually or through charities, essentially privatizing the war against the Soviets. Muslim states also sent many of their young men, especially Islamist dissidents, to serve in the *jihad,* and funded their participation. When the war ended some of them re-mained in Afghanistan.[14]

One Saudi who had heeded the call to *jihad* was Osama bin Laden. The devout son of a wealthy, well-connected Saudi businessman, he had been radicalized by the Islamist preacher Abd'Allah Azzam, and was both encouraged and frustrated by a failed Islamist uprising at the Grand Mosque in Mecca in November 1979. The Soviet invasion of Afghanistan was the last straw for bin Laden. By the early 1980s he was working in the Makhtab al-Kidmat (MAK), the "Services Bureau" which Azzam had set up in Peshawar, Pakistan. The MAK served as a contact point, recruiting centre, and funding organization for non-Afghans joining the *jihad*. Bin Laden used family money and resources from his father's company to build bases for the mujahideen in the Tora Bora Mountains along the Afghan–Pakistan border. He also was wounded in combat with the Soviets, giving him credibility as a dedicated *jihadi*. In 1989, Azzam was killed by a car bomb, and bin Laden inherited the leadership of the non-Afghan mujahideen. Among them were many who, because of their militant pasts and now their combat experience and training, would not be welcome in their home countries. Bin Laden fused these fighters and the MAK into a new organization: al-Qaeda, "the Base."[15]

After the Soviet withdrawal, the Afghan mujahideen—who never had been a unified movement—fought amongst themselves over who would wield power in post-Soviet Afghanistan. When they finally captured Kabul in April 1992, they proclaimed an Islamic state and established new councils to govern the country. For the first time in several centuries, the Pashtun had lost control of Kabul. However, under Hekmatyar's leadership they fought back, bombarding the city until a peace deal and power-sharing agreement was reached the next year. Factional disputes continued, however, and by 1994, the already war-torn country was again wracked by civil war among the rival groups. In the south, including Kandahar, former mujahideen-turned-warlords looted, raped, and plundered at will.[16] State institutions and the tribal governance systems that maintained social cohesion collapsed and chaos ensued. It was as if Thomas Hobbes's theoretical "state of nature," in which humanity is locked in a "war of all against all," had become the terrifying reality.

Enter the Taliban

It was at this time that the Taliban emerged as a political and military force in, and around, Kandahar. The *Talib*, meaning "student," had long been a fixture within the Pashtun community, serving as local itinerant preachers of Islam. But as a political movement the Taliban had incubated, during and after the Soviet war, in the Afghan refugee camps in Pakistan. There young men had been educated in *madrassas*,

Islamic schools funded by Saudi Arabia that taught the strictest theologies of Islam: Wahhabist and Deobandi Salafism. There are several versions of the story of the Taliban's emergence in Afghanistan in 1994. In all of them cleric Mullah Omar, a former mujahideen commander from the Panjawayi area of Kandahar province, and his Taliban movement are presented as heroes. They easily took Kandahar, where they restored order by imposing strict Islamic rule. With their status as heroes, they captured the popular imagination—and a dozen more provinces—over the next three months. Two years later, in September 1996, the Taliban marched into Kabul and proclaimed the Islamic Emirate of Afghanistan.[17] By 2001, only a small sliver of the north, held by the famous Tajik mujahideen commander Shah Ahmad Massoud, remained outside Taliban control. Throughout the rest of the country, the Taliban had restored peace, but it was peace purchased at the point of a sword and at the price of widespread and massive human rights violations.[18]

The Taliban movement was not entirely home-grown, and it did not come to power without outside help. Pakistan provided military training, weapons, and supplies, and may have even sent troops to fight alongside the Taliban. It provided funds to pay the salaries of the new regime's officials. Ordinary Pakistanis volunteered to fight with them. The movement received financial support from the merchant/trucking/smuggling industry in the south, and from Saudi Arabia. In 1996, even before the Taliban captured Kabul, Osama bin Laden returned to Afghanistan from Sudan, where he had been living in exile. He brought with him fighters and funds, which he placed at the Taliban's disposal to assist its conquest of Afghanistan. In return, bin Laden was allowed to use Afghanistan as a base for al-Qaeda.

While the Taliban shared al-Qaeda's ideological outlook and served as its state-sponsor, theirs was an unequal relationship. Bin Laden's group had much greater financial resources, which ultimately underwrote the regime's budget. His trained fighters assassinated their rival, Massoud, two days before 9/11. So, the Taliban regime, recognized by only three countries, was beholden to al-Qaeda. Even if it had wanted to sever its ties with the group, it could not have done so and survived. In the end, it did not survive as a regime anyway. Having hosted al-Qaeda while the group was planning and carrying out the 9/11 attacks, the Taliban was attacked, defeated, and over-thrown in October-November 2001 by the US-led coalition. The remnants fled to the FATA in Pakistan where, largely ignored by Pakistani security forces, they regrouped, re-armed, and prepared to counterattack.[19]

The UN and human rights groups had been watching, and raising red flags about, the repressive rule of the Taliban regime long before 9/11.[20] The Americans knew Osama bin Laden was using it as a base for his self-declared global "Jihad Against Jews and Crusaders." In fact, the US had attacked terrorist bases there in 1998, after al-Qaeda had bombed American embassies in Africa.[21] But, in a world awash in post-Cold War conflicts and humanitarian crises from the Balkans to Africa and Southeast Asia, Afghanistan was a low priority. And few outside the US intelligence community even knew or worried about bin Laden and his al-Qaeda movement. It took the 9/11 attacks to spur the international community into action over Afghanistan.

Devastated by more than 20 years of war, Afghanistan in 2001 was a failed state. One of the world's poorest nations, its citizens lacked the basic necessities of life. Its infrastructure—roads, schools, medical facilities—lay in ruins. Even while faced with massive chal-lenges of poverty, hunger, and homelessness, the Taliban had purged the public service of experienced non-Pashtu personnel, rendering most government ministries inoperable and leaving the country in a shambles. The Taliban was both incapable of and unwilling to manage the economy or food production and distribution. In fact, until 1999 they insisted that they were only an interim government. Mullah Omar himself had remained in seclusion in Kandahar where, uninterested in the mundane details of governance, he issued only sweeping decrees to govern Islamic life. These defined his quest to transform the country into an ultra-Islamic society "by force and violence." The only public service the Taliban had provided was the harshest form of law and order to enforce Omar's bizarre decrees. The only reason many Afghans survived at all in such conditions was thanks to aid programs and food handouts provided by the UN and other agencies.[22] Thus, to most Afghans, *Operation Enduring Freedom* (*OEF*), the 2001 invasion that toppled the regime, seemed like a great blessing.

To Rescue a Failed State

OEF was about capturing and punishing the perpetrators of 9/11 and their hosts. But, given the conditions in that country, international intervention could not end with the military defeat of al-Qaeda and the Taliban. Professor Ramesh Thakur, one of the world's leading authorities on UN assistance to failed states and a principal author of the *Responsibility to Protect* doctrine, argued that the UN-authorized invasion came with a "responsibility to rebuild what is broken."[23] As harsh and violent as they were, the Taliban could not be tossed out leaving 30 million people in even worse chaos. Furthermore, many diplomats and scholars believed that the West owed a debt to Afghanistan for its role in bringing down the Soviet Union and ending the Cold War.[24] Promises to rebuild in the early 1990s were broken when the Gulf War and the collapse of Yugoslavia turned the international community's attention farther west.

Therefore, 2001 provided the opportunity to make good on broken promises, end Afghanistan's cycle of fragmentation and violence, and to put the country back together. Of course, those nations, including Canada, which came forward to help, did so not just for the good of Afghanistan but for global security. "International support galvanized around the need for Afghanistan to recover from its status as a failed state, so it would never again become a breeding ground to threaten the world."[25] It would be the toughest mission ever undertaken by the UN.

The process got underway in December 2001 at the UN-sanctioned Bonn Conference, where the international community agreed to rebuild Afghanistan. Hamid Karzai, a politically acceptable Pashtun, was appointed interim president while a new constitution was drafted and elections held. The UN established an International Security Assistance Force (ISAF) to help stabilize the capital. In March 2002, the UN Assistance Mission in Afghanistan (UNAMA) was created to direct all humanitarian, relief, and reconstruction activities in Afghanistan.

Canada's involvement in Afghanistan started with *OEF*. Canadian warships and aircraft deployed immediately to secure the airspace and sea lanes in the region. They were followed by a detachment of Special Forces from Joint Task Force 2 (JTF2). LCol Pat Stogran's 3rd

Battalion, Princess Patricia's Canadian Light Infantry (3PPCLI) arrived in February 2002. Their first job was to protect the American airfield built up around the old Kandahar airport. This they did in typical Canadian fashion by talking with local leaders, playing soccer with children, and starting with small rebuilding projects in the battle-ruined area. JTF2 and 3PPCLI also participated in the hunt for remnants of al-Qaeda and the Taliban.[26] However, Canadian participation in that purely military effort ended after only one six-month rotation and the loss of four soldiers in a tragic friendly-fire incident.

Canadian participation in the reconstruction process began at the same time with much less fanfare. Eileen Olexiuk was Canada's first Foreign Service Officer (FSO) on the ground in Kandahar in 2001. Her job was to monitor the implementation of the Bonn Agreement on rebuilding the Afghan state structure. There had been some Canadian diplomatic and development work in Afghanistan in the 1970s, but that ended with the Soviet invasion. Ottawa, therefore, had very little expertise on the country prior to 9/11. As a result, Olexiuk recalls, the strategy for reopening diplomatic and aid ties with Afghanistan had to be made up on the fly.[27]

By 2002 the magnitude of the rebuilding task became clearer. What the first Canadians found when they arrived in Afghanistan was massive devastation and a people desperate for all kinds of help. If the UN mission was to work, the trickle of foreign assistance had to dramatically increase. For this reason, Canada's and NATO's commitments to Afghanistan grew in 2003. The UN gave NATO responsibility for ISAF in Kabul, and Canada, having agreed to wind down its commitment in the former Yugoslavia, took command of the force, supporting it with a commitment of over 1,400 soldiers.

In February 2003, Canada's Department of Foreign Affairs (DFAIT) sent a team to Kabul after Canada announced that it would build an embassy there, establishing a diplomatic presence in Afghanistan for the first time. Canada's first ambassador, Chris Alexander, arrived in August. Nepa Banerjee, a senior official from the Canadian International Development Agency (CIDA), arrived a month later. Their jobs were to help make the Bonn Process and Afghanistan itself work. Like so many other Canadian military and peacekeeping operations of the previous century, from Vimy Ridge to Sarajevo, it was a noble cause, but came with little direction on how to make it succeed. And just as in those previous efforts, the vision for success came from the people faced with the reality on the ground.

Janice Stein and Eugene Lang suggest in their important book *The Unexpected War: Canada in Kandahar*[28] that Canada's decision to lead ISAF resulted from the Chretien government's desire to avoid committing Canadian troops to the US invasion of Iraq. Maintaining good relations with the United States while staying out of the unpopular war undoubtedly played a role in Chretien's decision. But this narrow view overlooks decades of multilateral Canadian foreign policy initiatives, and the facts that Canada was both a signatory to the Bonn Agreement and a full voting member of NATO, the alliance that chose collectively to take on the Afghan task on behalf of the UN. But it is equally clear that Canada's commitment to stay in Afghanistan after the Taliban regime fell was also shaped by a century of foreign policy that favoured maintaining international rule of law and a long tradition of Canadians assisting people in need. Fortunately, the Canadian soldiers and diplomats who went to Afghanistan took with them a decade of recent experience in nation-building and security sector reform from the Balkans, Africa, the Caribbean, and Southeast Asia.

THE TRANSFORMATION OF PEACEKEEPING

Just as TF 1-07's mission cannot be separated from Afghanistan's history, neither can it be understood in isolation from the recent operational history of the Canadian Forces. For *Operation Athena* (the official code-name for Canada's commitment to ISAF) is simply the most recent in a long series of post-Cold War missions that have transformed the Canadian approach to peace support operations. It is part and parcel of Canada's "Road to Kandahar."

Even before the Cold War ended, the "Pearsonian" model of peacekeeping that Canadians most readily recognize was an anachronism. Few of the UN missions that Canadians participated in after 1956 matched the post-Suez UN Emergency Force (UNEF) model: lightly armed, blue-helmeted soldiers patrolling a clearly defined cease-fire line between two national armies that had agreed to stop fighting. In fact, many of the post-UNEF operations were observer missions only, with mandates limited to reporting on cease-fire violations. Furthermore, from Lebanon to the Congo, Cyprus, Central America, and Cambodia, UN peacekeepers deployed into internal, civil wars between militant political factions and their armed, often brutal, and ill-disciplined militias. There were no front lines and cease-fires were fragile. The UNEF model was the exception, not the rule.[29]

That trend continued and accelerated with the end of the Cold War. Animosities old and new, previously held in check by the superpowers and their alliances, erupted violently in a wide range of conflicts across the globe. The most striking feature of these post-Cold War conflicts was that of "state failure." In Yugoslavia, Somalia, Haiti, and Afghanistan, the state "withered away," leaving only chaos in its wake.[30] Throughout the 1990s, the international community got a tough education in "the transformation of war"[31] and its classroom was the failed state. It experienced a steep—and at times bloody—learning curve as it tried to develop new techniques to contain violence and restore functioning, civil societies.

The UN initially tried to deal with the crisis in Yugoslavia by inserting peacekeepers guided by the traditional rules, such as requiring the consent of the host nation to intervene. But in the Balkans, there was no authority able to grant and uphold consent, no factions willing to play by the rules, no Green Line to be patrolled, and in fact, no peace for the UN to keep. Unable to stop violence that in some cases, such as the massacre at Srebrenica, reached proportions of genocide, UN peacekeepers found themselves serving as nothing more than aiming points and "bullet traps."[32]

Clearly, a new approach was needed. One of the most dramatic—and controversial—changes surrounded the use of lethal force. Under the "old rules" UN peacekeepers could use deadly force only in self-defence. But the chaotic situation in Former Yugoslavia showed those rules of engagement to be irrelevant. They did not protect the peacekeepers from attack and did not deter armed gangs from attacking aid efforts or conducting atrocities. So, on some occasions even the Blue Berets had to fight to uphold their mandate. Nothing symbolized that change more than the Battle of the Medak Pocket.

In September 1993 the UN, acting to implement a cease-fire agreement, had ordered LCol Jim Calvin's 2PPCLI to enter and secure a small piece of disputed ground in Croatia known as the Medak Pocket. But the Croatian forces were determined to keep them out. The result was an intense 15-hour firefight: the largest, longest battle Canadian troops had fought since the Korean War. It continued until the next day when Calvin faced down the Croatian commander at a roadblock in front of a media scrum. Shamed by the publicity, the Croatians allowed the UN force to advance and complete its mission. But it was a pyrrhic victory for the UN. The area they inherited was devoid of life and reeking of death and destruction.[33]

The Medak incident had demanded a rapid shift from peace-keeping to peace-enforcement and back, exploiting the full range of the Canadian soldiers' capabilities from mechanized mobile combat to negotiation. 2PPCLI had started the operation under traditional peacekeeping rules, but then had used deadly force when Croatian soldiers defied the UN. However, when the fighting had stopped and the Croatians had backed down, the Canadians immediately reverted to their role as impartial peacekeepers in their dealings with troops who, only hours before, had been trying to kill them.[34] That the battalion could do so was a testament to the professionalism and skill of the Canadian Army.

But it was more than that. The lesson of that battle was that peacekeeping forces had to be able to make that rapid tactical transition. It meant they had to be trained, equipped, and prepared for combat just as much as they were for peacekeeping. This was not news to Canadian soldiers, who always trained for war first. But for peacekeeping practice generally, it was an epiphany.

The Battle of the Medak Pocket was only one example of Canadian soldiers calling upon their war-fighting skills to manage chaotic situations around the world. They have shown themselves to be particularly good at balancing those skills with peacekeeping and diplomacy. The need to shift rapidly from peacekeeping to combat or to conduct such actions simultaneously has since come to inform the doctrine known as "the Three-Block War."[35]

While post-Cold War peacekeeping missions became more dangerous, and thus required more military power than most pre-1989 operations, they were also more inclusive. They were no longer about military power alone, largely because post-Cold War collapsing states needed comprehensive assistance. Starting with the UN operation in Cambodia and continuing with missions in the Balkans, Somalia, and Haiti, peacekeeping morphed into peace-building. The UN and other bodies recognized that simply separating combatants was not enough. International organizations would have to take a direct and active role in helping nations rebuild national institutions, representative political processes, and social and economic infrastructure. The role of peacekeeping forces was to provide a safe environment for those activities and to help establish responsible law-enforcement agencies through security sector reform.[36] The Canadian Forces and Canadian diplomats and aid agencies were involved in this change from the outset. Thus, Canada's ISAF mission in Kandahar is not a deviation from Canada's recent peacekeeping experience, but the most complex and most sophisticated iteration of this evolving approach to "Human Security."

In Bosnia, Somalia, and Haiti, diplomatic and development organizations went to work at rebuilding governments and institutions, while peacekeepers provided a shield to protect both the external agencies and the locals they worked with. Often the first point of contact between the local population and the external agencies, soldiers served as the eyes and ears of these rebuilding efforts, doing needs assessments in communities to determine what they wanted and needed to survive and rebuild in the aftermath of war. With their ability to move through dangerous territory, soldiers could check on the progress of widely dispersed development projects and, where necessary, protect the population and those helping them. In fits and starts, a "new peacekeeping partnership" was emerging.[37]

The peace process in Bosnia was a case in point. Bosnia in the late 1990s suffered from many of the same problems that plagued Afghanistan, and Kandahar in particular. It was a fragile state, its population displaced and traumatized by war, and its economy and infrastructure in ruins. Political parties and leaders were beholden to strongmen with leftover militias, and the population—especially minorities—were victimized by criminal gangs who thrived on lawlessness, ethnic mistrust, corruption, and the illicit economy that had flourished during the war. So, the initiatives Canadian and other NATO troops carried out in Bosnia and elsewhere in the post-Cold

War conflicts are similar and relevant to what they are carrying out in Afghanistan. In many respects the peace-building mission in Kandahar is just one more example of the "new normal."

In January 1996, NATO stood up its Implementation Force (IFOR) peacekeeping mission in Bosnia–Herzegovina to support the political solution—the Dayton Peace Accords—imposed on the former warring parties. IFOR's task was to compel the rival factions to lay down their weapons, obey the rule of law, and implement the new peace accord. Having witnessed the UN's inability—and unwillingness—to enforce even its own resolutions and cease-fire agreements, owing in part to insufficient forces and resources, NATO left nothing to chance. It established a clear, single chain of command, with robust intelligence support, a force of 60,000 troops, and all of the tools of war.[38]

In short, IFOR deployed enough military power to outmatch all of the former warring parties. More important, NATO made it clear at the outset that, unlike the UN, it had a Chapter VII mandate to use the full scope of that power, and—most important—was prepared to do so if the armed factions violated the Dayton Accords.[39] Consequently, while open combat between warring parties and UN forces had been frequent between 1992 and 1995, IFOR hardly fired a shot. It did not have to; few dared to challenge the biggest dog on the street. So, where the UN Protection Force (UNPROFOR) mission had fluctuated between "traditional" peacekeeping and tentative, temporary peace-enforcement efforts, IFOR was peace-enforcement writ bold in indelible ink.

The advantages of using the NATO alliance for this kind of peace support operation were readily apparent. European and Canadian NATO forces had always been among the largest and most effective contributors to UN peacekeeping missions. NATO nations also had a 45-year history of working in concert as military allies. They shared common values, ethics, education, standards of professionalism, and understanding of international law. Their officers attended the same command and staff training courses, and served in each others' headquarters, formations, units, and training programs. They had similar doctrine and equipment and common radio procedures and frequencies. NATO's command structure included formation headquarters that could deploy to hot spots and direct stability operations 24/7. Such command-and-control capability always had been lacking on UN missions, most notably in Yugoslavia and Rwanda where Canadian UN commanders, Lewis Mackenzie and Romeo Dallaire, had struggled to get direction and to pass information to a UN office thousands of miles away.[40]

Even more important, IFOR was not a stand-alone operation. IFOR's security task was only one of several pillars of the comprehensive nation-building process that included political, social, and material reconstruction. So, coming in behind the IFOR shield was a small army of diplomats, development officials, police, and aid agencies whose job was to rebuild police forces, judicial systems, government, and public services. In 1997 IFOR evolved into the Stabilization Force (SFOR). With each passing year its mission emphasis shifted from military operations to rebuilding Bosnia.[41] Canadians soldiers were still peacekeeping. But it was a new type of peacekeeping that was laying the ground work for the Afghan mission that began even as NATO carried on its peace-building task in Bosnia.

In fact, for the purpose of this story, the most important link between the Afghan mission and the earlier post-Cold War operations is experience. Among the resumés of the older TF 1-07 officers and non-commissioned officers (NCOs) could be found the cumulative experience and wisdom gained from all of Canada's peacekeeping, peace-enforcement, and international assistance missions undertaken since the 1980s. That shaped how soldiers responded to the challenge of Afghanistan that involved war-fighting, peace-building, and aid delivery at the same time. Among the sergeants commanding sections, the captains and majors directing companies, and among the contingent commander and his headquarters staff were the experience and expertise that enabled Canadian troops to understand the difference between the Afghan people they were sent to help and the Taliban and criminal elements that were operating among and trying to exploit their country men. Just as in the Medak Pocket battle, experience enabled soldiers to turn on their war-fighting skills when they came under attack, to return fire with discrimination, and then to resume the peace-builder role when the firing stopped.

LCol Christopher Hand, veteran of multiple tours with 2RCR and most recently Commandant of the Tactics School at the Combat Training Centre, explained that, "the command team of 2RCR, including nearly all sergeants and above, [had] at least one tour in Bosnia and then another in Haiti, or Ethiopia, or Kabul, or more than one of those." Collectively, those missions provided a body of knowledge that informed the way TF 1-07 prepared for its Afghan mission. LCol Hand, who commanded a company of 2RCR in Bosnia under SFOR, says, "for those who don't think that the Balkans are relevant, because Afghanistan is not peacekeeping, think again."[42]

Wayne O'Toole's career is a case in point. While serving with 2RCR in UNPROFOR, then Sergeant O'Toole escorted aid convoys to Sarajevo at a time when the UN had neither the means nor the will to enforce its mandate. A few years later he saw the new order of things while serving as Warrant Officer (WO) in SFOR. Then, in 2006, as 2RCR readied for Kandahar, Master Warrant Officer (MWO) O'Toole was appointed company sergeant-major (CSM) for Hotel Company, one of only six CSMs in the battlegroup. All brought a similar package of experience and wisdom to their jobs.

The main task performed by all Canadian units in SFOR was "framework patrolling," another term for presence and security patrols—the very same as those done in traditional UN missions, including Cyprus. Hand's patrolling aims were "to let people know that Canadians are there and there to help and that there will be a response for those who use violence to achieve their aims." These patrols included conducting routine meetings and visits within company and platoon areas with lower-level community leaders, school teachers, police chiefs, mayors, and village leaders. They also provided security for "Key Leader Engagements" with major leaders of warring factions and other more senior leaders. Thus, framework patrolling combined area security, situational awareness, intelligence-gathering, community relations, tactical diplomacy, and force protection, all in one.

During their SFOR tour, 2RCR provided security cordons for Special Operations Forces that swooped in to arrest war criminals and for International Police Task Force seizures of weapons banned by the Dayton Accord. They did spot checks at weapons cantonment sites, random vehicle searches for weapons, and cordon and search operations for illicit weapons hidden in towns and homes.

A further major task for 2RCR was assisting the UN High Commission for Refugees (UNHCR) with the repatriation of families displaced by war. They also supported community reconstruction work or provided security for reconstruction. Observes Chris Hardy, "This is especially the case in 1999 when the battalion was moved to support Kosovar refugees. We were really doing what a Provincial Reconstruction Team does in Afghanistan; we just didn't call it that then."[43]

The troops monitored and mediated between local disputes, especially when these became violent. "We used a business plan approach to operational planning to manage all of the peace-building effects we aimed to achieve." And they did all of these jobs with an ever-present mine threat necessitating careful route planning and route clearance before setting off to drive down any road. Hand's main message about Kandahar is that "people in 2RCR and in the army in general had seen all this before at all rank levels." Daily tasks and aims were very similar. What was different in Bosnia was that since NATO brought in overwhelming force, "we never had to shoot to achieve the aim."[44]

In 2004, only three years before deploying to Kandahar, 2RCR carried out similar activities in Haiti. That difficult UN peace-building mission left deep impressions, on officers and soldiers alike, about how to provide stability in the midst of chaos. Maj Russell King, 2RCR's deputy commanding officer (DCO), was a company commander in Haiti. "We made Haiti work," he recalled, "with presence and stability patrols, vehicle checkpoints to control the flow of arms, gradual disarmament of the people, and taking power away from armed gangs, while the diplomats, police, and aid workers tried to make the government work. We did exactly the same thing in Afghanistan in 2007, except that the folks with the guns would risk more and use their weapons more often to try to stop us."[45]

Maj Shawn Courty was a Civil-Military Co-operation (CIMIC) team leader in the Provincial Reconstruction Team (PRT) in 2007. He also had learned his job in Haiti, where he observed RCMP efforts to train and mentor the Haitian police. The challenge there,

Courty saw, "was to create more than just a group with uniforms and weapons—but to turn them into a professional organization with a sense of duty and service to their people. We needed Haitian police that wouldn't steal from their own people."[46] That was the toughest job in Haiti, and it remains among the toughest in Kandahar.

Co-ordination of these military, political, and development efforts was rudimentary in Bosnia and Haiti. The various military, governance, policing, and aid and development organizations (both official and NGO) had a lot to learn about working with each other. But this experience laid the foundation for the Canadian "3D" approach—defence, diplomacy and development (now called "Whole of Government")—championed by then-Defence Minister Bill Graham and applied in Kandahar. At its heart is the PRT, which brings together a civil-military Human Security team and applies their combined skills to the nation-building task.[47]

The key to all nation-building missions is persuading people to take a non-violent approach to their future. So, reconstruction and Information Operations (IO) combine to wean leaders and members of warring groups away from violence and into a new political process. In Bosnia, most members of armed groups agreed that their future was better served by employment than by armed conflict. In Kandahar this kind of diplomacy is used regularly to encourage low level, part-time Taliban fighters lay down their arms. Likewise, restoring education systems is seen as central to rebuilding stable states in which children can live to adulthood and develop a desire for non-violent career options. This is as true in Afghanistan as it was in Bosnia. The most important lesson of the post-Cold War peace support operations is that the military/security side of the mission only works as part of a much larger rebuilding effort. The Canadian, UN, and NATO approach, learned in the mean streets of Sarajevo and Port-au-Prince, is to use military force to prevent armed groups from interfering with what is primarily a humanitarian effort.

To sum up, the Canadian Army—and, in this case, TF 1-07—did not arrive in Afghanistan as a blank slate. It was an army of long service professionals among officer and NCOs with an institutional memory full of relevant experience. Canada's 3D policy toward Afghanistan was shaped not just by the immediate requirements of the War on Terrorism, but by decades of military, diplomatic, and development efforts in many peace support operations around the world. The army that executed policy in Kandahar in 2007 was shaped by those same missions.

ISAF and PRTs

The role of the International Assistance Security Force was no different than that of most post-Cold War peace support operations: to create a climate of stability so that political and social reconstruction could proceed. ISAF's efforts provided enough security in Kabul that civilian agencies could start setting up government ministries and readying the country for national elections. Both tasks were vital to building legitimacy for the office of the interim president and to allow the new government to begin delivering services.

Unfortunately, outside of Kabul early rebuilding efforts were modest. In the immediate aftermath of liberation in 2001, neither the international community nor the interim government had the means to extend "peace, order, and good government"—let alone economic development—to all parts of Afghanistan. And at first, those efforts were heavily dependant on co-operation from the very people many Afghans most feared: the former mujahideen warlords. In fact, it took several years of skillful political manoeuvring before President Karzai could exert his authority inside Kabul and latterly outside it. The presidential elections in October 2004 and the parliamentary and council elections in September 2005 greatly strengthened the legitimacy of the government; both were votes of confidence in plans for a better future. But, it would take years to deliver on them.

In the meantime, the situation in Kandahar province, and the south generally, remained chaotic. The physical infrastructure had been destroyed during the Soviet occupation. The educational system had collapsed under the Taliban regime. The new national government and police presence was sporadic and was more a law unto itself than a welcome representative of a legitimate authority. The normal agrarian economy—devastated first by war and then by drought—had long since ceased functioning. The only viable cash crop was the opium poppy, whose yield fuelled the rising Taliban insurgency as well as corruption among the police and the government. Linked to the area by kinship ties and funded in part by the opium trade, the Taliban operated with impunity. Little development could occur in such a lawless environment.

The international security effort there initially was limited to sporadic forays by the remnants of *Operation Enduring Freedom* (*OEF*). American and coalition forces had continued to hunt al-Qaeda and Taliban fighters in what amounted to a "free-fire zone" in the southeast borderlands. The forces were extremely light on the ground, made up mostly of small Special Forces teams, supported by a small number of coalition partners, a heavy reliance on airpower, and a handful of Afghan National Army (ANA) troops. Their task was to disrupt and interdict Taliban insurgents. They had few troops to spare to provide security outside of Kandahar or around Qalat in Zabul Province. Their reconstruction efforts were limited to so-called "quick-impact" projects intended mainly to enhance protection and elicit information for the Taliban hunt. Most US reconstruction dollars directed at southern Afghanistan were spent trying to rush Afghan police into service, to make up for the lack of a permanent military presence on the ground. This was due partly to Germany's failure to deliver on its Bonn Agreement promise to build an effective Afghan police force. But it was also a result of a counter-insurgency strategy of fighting the Taliban with police, but without a military security framework to protect them. The hastily trained Afghan National Police (ANP), as often as not, became part of the problem rather than part of the solution.[48]

As the Taliban regenerated and security outside the capital deteriorated, UN and other aid workers became targets. It was obvious to the UN and NATO that Afghanistan's restoration would never succeed if the international community stayed locked up in Kabul. In 2004, NATO began to expand the ISAF presence throughout the country. Backed by new ANA units, ISAF deployment into the north and west in 2004 continued to build public confidence in those areas.

ISAF followed the US model of creating Provincial Reconstruction Teams made up of diplomats, government development officials, civilian police trainers, and soldiers for engineering and protection tasks. The PRTs quickly spread across the country, but their initiatives varied widely to meet the needs and security situation in the host province. NATO nations provided the personnel and aid dollars in the relatively stable northern and western regions, while American *OEF* forces set up PRTs in the more dangerous south and east, including one in Kandahar City. The separate missions of ISAF and *OEF*, and the duplication of headquarters, caused disunity between the two efforts, both in co-ordinating development work and in handling the Taliban threat. It quickly became clear that the two programs could not remain separate. NATO would have to expand south and east, but that meant absorbing OEF's counter-terrorism mission. NATO understood that expansion into the south would be difficult; the Taliban threat was higher there than anywhere else in Afghanistan. The comparatively small Canadian and NATO struggle to prevent the Taliban from interfering with reconstruction was about to dramatically increase and become bigger and far more bloody.

THE RETURN OF THE TALIBAN

Canadian and other media refer to all armed Afghan groups collectively as the Taliban. We use the same term here as a convenient shorthand. But this does not mean that they are the same group that had ruled Afghanistan from 1996 until 2001. That original movement had been effectively dismantled, although not completely destroyed, during the post-9/11 war. Some simply melted back into the local population, while many others fled to Pakistan.[49]

The Taliban that rose up to attack the Afghan government and ISAF security and reconstruction efforts was a quite different phenomenon. After 2001, a more diverse, complex movement emerged. Across Afghanistan the insurgency encompassed a range of groups, including the Taliban, the Haqqani network, the Hizb-i-Islami Gulbuddin (HIG), and al-Qaeda, along with other improvised, unnamed, militias. In the Taliban heartland in the southern provinces, however, these latter groups were not present in any significant numbers.[50]

Still, the Taliban insurgency in the south never was a single, monolithic movement, motivated solely by religious-political fervour. Rather, it was a dynamic collection of groups and individuals with a wide range of motives for attacking civilians, the police force, government officials, Canadian and other ISAF troops, NGOs, and their activities. It included a mixture of old Taliban (remnants of the

previous regime) and zealous new converts, along with former insurgents, armed gangs, criminals, smugglers, drug lords, and tribal
leaders. Tragically, some were simply locals frustrated by the lack
of security and services, by government and police corruption, or
by the slow pace of development; others—including young, unemployed men—were recruited with the promise of money. Kinship
ties and cultural traditions among the Pashtun tribes may also have
influenced decisions about which side the locals support. In short,
the post-2001 Taliban was not a classic unified national liberation
movement along the lines of the Viet Cong.[51]

But the Taliban's strategic aim was clear: to drive out the foreign
forces, topple the democratic government, and seize power. Their
ultimate goal was to restore the Islamic regime they ran before
9/11.[52] So, how did this new movement emerge from the ashes of
the old?

Journalist turned relief worker Sarah Chayes chronicled the
return of the Taliban in her book *The Punishment of Virtue*. She writes
that in the immediate aftermath of the 2001 war, there was a period
of about six months of relative calm inside Afghanistan. While that
may have been true for much of the interior, it did not apply along the
mountainous Afghan–Pakistani border, where coalition forces battled
al-Qaeda and Taliban remnants well into 2002. In the meantime, the
Taliban leadership, including Mullah Omar, went to ground inside
Pakistan and began to regroup, with only the occasional foray into
Afghanistan. They appeared openly in cities such as Peshawar and
Quetta, unmolested by Pakistani security forces and untouchable by
the Americans or by the new Afghan government.[53]

The first hints of resurgence were the *shabnamah* (night letters)
that began to appear later in 2002. Drawing upon the story-telling tradition that pervades Afghan tribal culture and the experience of using
them during the anti-Soviet war, the Taliban began to leave threatening messages at mosques and in villages, sometimes posting them in
public places. These would be read out loud by educated members of
the community and the themes found their way into mosque sermons.
The messages were simple and direct: the Americans and their allies
are infidels, Karzai is their puppet, and those who co-operate with
either are equally guilty and will be punished when the Taliban defeats

the enemy. But to enhance their appeal, the night letters were laced with allusions to Afghan history, traditions, Islamic laws, and to the sacrifices of the Afghan resistance against the Soviets—themes that would resonate with many Afghans. This skillful Information Operation was intended to prepare the "hearts and minds" of the population for the Taliban's return and victory. Chayes argues that given the devastating psychological impact of the brutal Soviet war, "the impact of an intimidation campaign cannot be underestimated."[54]

The threats implicit in the *shabnamah* were driven home in fall 2002 with nightly shelling of Kandahar City. Initially random, it caused few casualties and little damage. But by 2003, the attacks clearly began to target the foreign presence, such as humanitarian groups. Again, the message was clear: get out or we'll kill you. And as the violence increased some groups, like the Red Cross, did leave.[55]

In spite of a series of *OEF* operations, by the spring of 2003 Taliban were returning to Afghanistan from Pakistan in groups of 25 to 30 at a time. They came first to Kandahar province and then extended their presence into Helmand. According to informants, the insurgents' plan was to operate in the outlying areas first, then gradually advance on and encircle Kandahar city. They were particularly active in and around Spin Boldak. Across the border, in Quetta, Pakistan, the Taliban continued to gather openly, allegedly protected and aided by Pakistani security forces. With local governance and policing in Kandahar province either non-existent or incompetent and corrupt, it is not surprising that the population exhibited some nostalgia for the return of the Taliban, who at least had brought order and certainty to their lives. Chayes reports that by summer that year, fear was pervasive and the mood was shifting against the US.[56]

Dr. Larry Goodson, long-time scholar of Afghanistan, spent time in the border areas during this period interviewing Taliban leaders about their goals. Among other things he learned that one of the main drivers of Taliban rebirth was a perception that the Americans would leave, that reconstruction would not succeed, and that Afghanistan would return to chaos. Taliban leaders were keen to exploit popular dissatisfaction in the south over the gap between the expectations of western assistance and the reality that virtually none had arrived by 2003.[57]

The conflict took an ominous turn in June 2003 when—apparently in direct response to Bin Laden's call for such attacks—a suicide bomber killed four German ISAF soldiers and an Afghan national in Kabul: the first attack of its kind in the country. After that, the number of suicide attacks and the casualties they inflicted would climb steadily.[58]

Later that month, the Taliban announced the creation of a 10-member *rahbari shura* (leadership council) to lead a jihad under a new military strategy. Clearly, suicide bombing was one element of that new strategy. *Shabnamah* were also part of it. One, addressed at this time to the residents of two towns in Kandahar, reminded them that the Americans would not always be there to protect them, and once they left the Taliban would come and kill everyone who had collaborated. Asserting that "the Americans have the wristwatches, but we have the time,"[59] the Taliban were committing themselves to a protracted war. The third element was a spreading, asymmetric, guerrilla war. Over the summer of 2003, Taliban raiding parties, sometimes numbering in the hundreds, attacked Afghan government outposts, ambushed American, Afghan, and coalition troops, burned schools, launched rocket attacks on coalition bases, attacked Afghan police, and assassinated pro-government clerics. In the aftermath of clashes they would withdraw across the border to their sanctuary in Pakistan, secure in the knowledge that coalition forces would not follow them there.[60]

The Taliban kept up the pressure in 2004, attacking NGOs and foreign workers, as well as Afghan security forces and coalition troops and bases. They claimed responsibility as well for bombings and rocket attacks inside Kabul and other major cities. As a result, the renowned medical aid NGO Médecins Sans Frontières withdrew from Afghanistan, citing the lack of security, especially in the south and east. The UN High Commission for Refugees also scaled back its activities in those areas during the summer. The *OEF* forces that bore the brunt of open combat against the Taliban were simply too few in number to provide a secure environment in that region. Moreover, Taliban pressure on the American *OEF* units was growing at the very time when their numbers were shrinking. The US invasion of Iraq had turned into a complicated counter-insurgency war that drew away American attention—and resources.

In Kandahar, Helmand, Uruzgan, and Zabul provinces, the Taliban took advantage of the fact that the writ of the central government and the international security footprint were weak. In Zabul, for example, they killed Afghan citizens who had registered to vote. That said, the insurgents did not have things all their way. Not only did Afghan and coalition forces inflict serious casualties on them, they suffered a stunning blow to their claim to political legitimacy. In October, Afghan citizens defied Taliban threats and pre-election violence and voted in massive numbers to elect Hamid Karzai as president.[61]

Still, optimistic predictions of the Taliban's defeat proved seriously premature. Although the UN claimed in February that most of Afghanistan was safe enough for refugees to return and settle, and nearly a million had done so in 2004,[62] the violence continued unabated through 2005. Sometimes aided by foreign fighters, the Taliban abducted or killed women, government and security officials, and NGO personnel, and ambushed ISAF and Afghan troops. Captured police were often killed execution-style or beheaded. Kandahar city itself was plagued by a lethal mixture of Taliban activity and tribal and criminal violence, such as the bombing of a mosque that killed the visiting chief of Kabul police[63]—all symptomatic of the power vacuum in the south, which allowed the insurgency to flourish. But the Taliban suffered many casualties at the hands of coalition and Afghan troops. And again, in spite of the violence and intimidation of both voters and candidates, nearly half of all Afghanis voted in parliamentary elections in September,[64] repudiating once more the Taliban's political ambitions and its insurgent strategy. The Afghan government's newfound political credibility, and its increasing capacity—helped greatly by the international community—to offer its people real services, was an increasing threat to the Taliban's resurgence.

The original Taliban's seizure of power in the late 1990s had been the result of a mixture of coercion and persuasion—a time-honoured Afghan way of war. Its successors employed a similar approach, while adding some new tactics, such as suicide bombers, assassinations and executions, and IEDs, largely borrowed from the insurgency in Iraq and encouraged by al-Qaeda. Thus, while using traditional guerrilla warfare against ISAF and the Afghan security forces, the Taliban ratcheted up their terrorism and information operations to erode the government's authority and control, and to reassert their own hold over the population. It was a classic "two-front insurgency": a strategic political battle for legitimacy and a tactical para-military battle for control. Their job was made much easier by the fact that in much of southern and eastern Afghanistan the government presence was negligible and, where it existed at all, often unwelcome. They recognized that there was a vacuum in the Afghan political space and they were determined to fill it.[65] But that was just a means to their ultimate end: defeating the foreign forces and the government, and seizing power.

They brought a number of strengths to this struggle: several thousand full-time and part-time fighters; a sanctuary inside Pakistan, which allowed them to regroup, recruit, re-arm, and re-train in relative security; support from the Pakistani ISID; funding from the narcotics trade and from external donors; assistance from al-Qaeda and other foreign fighters; a flourishing regional black market in arms; and skillful use of various media, from *shabnamah* to the Internet, to spread their propaganda. Local ties and local knowledge facilitated infiltration among the population and an ability to choose targets of opportunity. With experience and training, their tactics had improved and they were able to operate in larger groups. Thus, they were able to inflict significant casualties on Afghan and ISAF forces, intimidate the civilian population, drive out NGOs, disrupt development, and were even able to capture small areas and hold them temporarily.[66] These factors conferred significant advantages on the insurgency, especially in the chaotic milieu of Kandahar province. The head of the US Defense Intelligence Agency told Congress in February 2006 that "the renewed Taliban insurgency presented a threat to the authority of the Karzai government more severe than any since 2001."[67] In short, the Taliban were a force to be reckoned with and ISAF commanders were disinclined to underestimate them.

That said, they were hardly "supermen." Their long string of failed attacks earned the Taliban the reputation as "the world's worst suicide bombers."[68] And while they coerced and persuaded some Afghans into tolerating their presence, they had not translated that tolerance into a mandate to rule.[69]

Afghans came out to vote in the 2004 presidential elections in vast numbers, a telling sign of faith and hope in their new government. For that faith to be maintained, UN and NATO leaders recognized they could no longer wait to make southern Afghanistan a priority. They had to give the people of the south the same access to the aid and development assistance—and the same evidence of effective governance—emerging in the north, or the entire national effort would be undone.

At the same time, American commanders and policy-makers recognized that they could not manage the south on their own, and that rising Taliban influence would not be defeated by military power alone but with the spread of aid, security, and good government. It was time to roll *OEF* and ISAF together, get the Taliban insurgency under control, and accelerate the pace of reconstruction.

The struggle in the south, therefore, was a vital theatre within the larger competition for legitimacy and control between the new Afghan government and the Taliban. Each side was trying to establish its preferred state system. The former, backed by the world in the form of the UN and NATO, aimed to rebuild and modernize the Afghan nation. The latter sought to restore the militant Islamist state of the late 1990s. The objective both sides sought to "capture" was not key strategic terrain or lines of communication, but the confidence and allegiance of the Afghan people. The winner in this struggle would be the side with the patience to prevail and the one which the Afghan people saw as the most able to provide them with security and the means to survive. The most decisive location for this struggle, the place where it will finally be won or lost, is the birthplace of the Taliban, the area where in 2005 it still operated freely and commanded loyalty: Kandahar.

YOU'RE IN KANDAHAR

The first thing that hits you as you step off the plane is the dust. As fine as talcum, it quickly settles onto every part of your body, onto every piece of clothing, and onto the food that you eat. You walk in dust, drive in dust, sleep in dust, and breathe in dust. A cloud of dust follows you wherever you go. It is the single common feature of this desolate province: 50,000 square kilometres—of dust.

Kandahar City is a ruined but reviving sand-coloured community teeming with more than a half-million people, half of them refugee squatters. It is a city struggling to reclaim its place as the food production and distribution hub of southern Afghanistan, rather than as the locus of a booming opium trade. Reducing the influence of the drug trade is crucial for the future of Afghanistan.

The city—an ancient commercial, political, and cultural centre—lies in the middle of the province, on the edge of the fertile valley carved by the Arghandab River, one of the few major sources of water in this drought-stricken land. Kandahar's narrow streets are jammed with people, animals, "jingle trucks," taxis, minivans, and pickups, all jostling for position in the tight spaces between the slap-dash stalls of the street vendors. The noise is constant. And from the streets, alleys, stores, and stalls waft the mingled aromas of overcrowded humanity, sewage, animals, commerce, cooking, and transport. It takes some getting used to. And it lingers in the senses long after you break free of the city and venture cautiously into the hinterland.

Flanking the river just west of the city are the lush fields and populous villages of Zharey and Panjwayi Districts. Here beats the economic heart of the province. An irrigation system of indeterminable age captures the winter rains (when they fall) and turns the desert into an oasis yielding a bounty of fruits, vegetables, and grain. By 2006, after 20 years of war and drought those crops had been displaced by the much more lucrative opium poppy. Since this area can produce either enough food to free Afghanistan from outside aid or enough poppy to cement Taliban and drug lord control over poor tenant farm families, it is the decisive ground of southern Afghanistan. Once home to Taliban leader Mullah Omar, with its plethora of hiding places and firing positions amid the maze of mud-walled houses, grape-drying huts, water-filled ditches, and lush greenery, this is a natural insurgent base area. So, it is here that the battle for Kandahar's soul will be lost or won.

To the northeast a chain of hills acts as a natural barrier. It can be crossed in a myriad of places, but not easily. The south-west, stretching to Pakistan's Baluchistan province, is mostly desert, lightly populated by nomads, and traversed by few roads. But one hundred kilometres down Highway 4 to the south-east, across the low, barren foothills of the Hindu Kush mountains, lies the border town of Spin Boldak. In 2006, it was home to a quarter-million refugees and is a major gateway to Pakistan. From there the road runs to the bustling Pakistani city of Quetta, sanctuary of the Taliban senior council. This makes Spin Boldak the most important crossing point for legitimate trade, for smuggling, and for insurgents. Imposing control over it is the key to restoring healthy regional trade and reducing the flow of weapons, drugs, and militants in both directions.

To the north of Kandahar City lies the Shah Wali-Khot, a forbidding, inhospitable region of ragged ridges and deep valleys that Canadian soldiers called "Middle Earth," after the land of Tolkien's novels. With hard work and some simple engineering the bleak, but strangely beautiful, rocky bowls serve as giant catch-basins for winter rains, feeding the Arghandab River that waters the green-belt of Zharey–Panjwayi. Soviet generals recognized its significance and tried to destroy the catchment system. Rebuilding it is yet another key to rescuing southern Afghanistan.

Freezing with a raw desert cold in winter, unbearably hot, overrun by sand fleas, and swept by dust storms for most of the year, Kandahar is an awful place to send soldiers from Canada. But to this unforgiving clime and locale they came to rebuild a country. Critics of the deployment there have argued that Canada should have committed its soldiers and resources to a safer and easier section of Afghanistan. Even Col (Ret'd) Mike Capstick, former commander of the Canadian Strategic Advisory Team in Kabul, has said that "looking at Afghanistan through the window of Kandahar is like looking at it through a straw!" But if help did not come to Kandahar, hope for a stable country would end. Afghanistan's restoration could not work without tackling the south's problems. And its problems were legion.

A LAWLESS LAND

Prior to 2006, the southern provinces were run by an array of armed groups that profited and thrived on the anarchy that prevailed there, and were unwilling to allow the restoration of an effective central government that would deny them profit and power. The UN Secretary General warned that drug gangs had a "symbiotic relationship" with the Taliban and shared with them a "common interest in preventing the imposition of state authority." [1]

In fact, most people outside the large provincial capitals in the south were trapped in a spiralling cycle of feudal slavery, poverty, debt, drought, and chaos. In an already remote region with few good roads and little infrastructure, drug lords and the Taliban offered the only real authority. The rule of central government and its delivery of services had never been strong in the south. But, if Afghanistan was to ever function normally with order restored and maintained, then control of the south, especially its rural agricultural areas, had to be wrestled away from insurgents and criminals.

Corruption, the survival mechanism for people living in a shattered society, was also dangerously out of control there and by 2006 was feeding the Taliban's revival. Nowhere was this more evident than in the Afghan National Police (ANP), the only functional national institution in the province and the only measure Kandaharis had of their new government. That measure was poor. Undisciplined, underpaid, or unpaid, Afghan police officers fed their families or their drug addictions by taking bribes and by pillaging already poor Afghan homes. Corrupt police commanders siphoned off pay, driving their charges to desperation. ANP thievery badly shook Kandaharis' limited faith in their government's ability to "serve and protect" them.

They assumed—quite rightly—that many policemen were in the financial pockets of the Taliban and the drug lords.

When the police did do their jobs, they behaved more as counter-insurgency war-fighters than police officers. But in a land where the people were fed up with corruption and hungry for reliable government, cops who fought the Taliban one day then took bribes the next were the worst possible combination. The policing problem was so massive and disjointed, with so many donor nations and agencies competing and overlapping, that before 2006 little serious training and mentoring could be done. Ali A. Jalali, former Afghan Minister of the Interior, complained that in the aftermath of the defeat of the Taliban rebuilding the police force was too low a priority on the international community's task list. At that time, Jalali stated, the Americans were more focused on protecting their national security by hunting down the Taliban and al-Qaeda than on rebuilding the Afghan state. So, the initial American commitment to Afghanistan was predominantly military. The critically important task of creating responsible police services was deprived of attention and resources. Nor, Capstick noted, "could the Canadians in 2006 do much about the police problem that was being run by too many different nations and agencies and with little real presence on the ground."[2] It would take a full-blown police corruption crisis in 2006 to finally persuade the west to take real action.[3]

CHOOSING KANDAHAR

Thus, Kandahar and the south was the part of Afghanistan that was at once the most dangerous and the most in need of the help. Janice Stein and Eugene Lang's, *The Unexpected War: Canada in Kandahar*, about the Canadian decision to deploy there, has helped to dispel the myth that Prime Minister Paul Martin took too long to choose a location for a Provincial Reconstruction Team (PRT), leaving that province as the only option. Although they glibly describe the interdepartmental policy review as "bureaucratic dithering and bickering," they emphasize that Kandahar was always a front-runner among Canadian officials, who understood that Afghan rebuilding efforts were useless if not extended south. But, Stein and Lang caused a small uproar by claiming that the Chief of the Defence Staff, Gen

Rick Hillier, wanted Canada to take on the toughest job in Afghanistan in order to prove something to the United States and that he was responsible for adding a large combat element to Canada's PRT.[4]

Richard Arbeiter, Deputy Director of Policy on the Afghanistan Task Force at the Department of Foreign Affairs, balks at the idea that Gen Hillier drove the Kandahar commitment. He watched as specialists in his department vetted and approved cabinet recommendations about Kandahar and about the addition of combat forces to the proposed PRT. According to Arbeiter, what mattered most was figuring out the best possible impact Canada's troops and aid could make so that the re-building strategy in Afghanistan worked. That meant time-consuming but necessary diplomacy with other UN and NATO nations to agree on who would go to the south.[5]

Like Arbeiter, Gavin Buchan also dismisses the claim that "Hillier wanted a deployment that would get Canada deeper and deeper into the most troubled part of Afghanistan" in order to "impress the Pentagon."[6] A Foreign Service Officer who has spent much time on the ground in Kandahar and now directs NATO policy in National Defence Headquarters, Buchan says that he and other NATO planners understood that Kandahar, Helmand, and Uruzgan were provinces where PRTs needed at least a battalion of combat troops to defend them. Therefore, as soon as Kandahar was on the table, Canadian policy makers had to choose between letting a US Army battalion defend their PRT, or adding a Canadian battlegroup to the mission. The British planned to commit two infantry battalions, and the Dutch, one. Buchan asserts that a Canadian PRT would not have had the diplomatic clout it needed with Kandahar community leaders without Canadian troops providing security for the province and for themselves.[7]

Canadian cabinet ministers, senior public servants, and military officers agreed. They all knew that Kandahar would be dangerous. Both Minister of National Defence Bill Graham and Gen Hillier cautioned Canadians to expect that their soldiers would fight and that they would suffer casualties. When NATO made the collective decision to expand into southern Afghanistan, it was clear that the threat level would be higher than in northern and western parts of the nation. The Taliban had deeply penetrated Kandahar, Helmand,

Zabul, and Uruzgan provinces, where much of the countryside had become "no-go" areas for government and foreign forces. Violence compelled villagers to co-operate with the insurgents and likewise avoid attempts by PRT detachments and aid agency representatives to set up new Community Development Councils (CDCs).[8] But nobody making decisions in 2005 anticipated the 2006 spike in Taliban attacks. It came as a surprise and forced an adjustment from all member nations that committed to the south.[9]

Buchan also remembers that the 2004-05 PRT selection process took time because NATO as a whole needed agreement on which member nations were willing to commit and which had the right type of forces to apply to the various portions of Afghanistan. And they had to reach an agreement while the alliance still had thousands of troops maintaining stability in the Balkans.

The fact is NATO recognized that southern expansion was critical. Someone had to go. Pieces started falling into place when Britain picked Helmand Province.[10] Around that time the Canadian policy review process was completed and Kandahar was indeed the only choice left. But since it always had been one of the main options, it was not a case of being stuck with the "leftovers." It also looked feasible because the British and the Dutch were going to be in neighbouring provinces Helmand and Uruzgan. The British, Dutch, and Canadian armies worked well together. They shared a familiar professional culture and ethos that exceeded the NATO standard. Between them they possessed the necessary helicopters, wheeled armoured vehicles, and other compatible equipment, and used common language. They had a long experience working together on complex stability-building missions, demonstrated by their very effective partnership in the NATO Multi-National Division Southwest in Bosnia. Nor were they deploying alone. They would be joined by large contingents from Rumania, Poland, Estonia, and Denmark, and by smaller but essential headquarters and support units from almost all NATO nations, including France and Germany.

Kandahar was also the physical centre of what was to become the International Assistance Security Force's (ISAF) Regional Command South (RC South). Regional command would then rotate between the three NATO partners. Given Canada's long-established interoperability with American forces, it made sense for a Canadian brigade head-quarters to take on that command and control task first and manage the handover from US *Operation Enduring Freedom (OEF)* headquarters when the time came.

Even so, southern expansion was gradual. ISAF and the United Nations Assistance Mission to Afghanistan (UNAMA) could not operate effectively there without first establishing stable develop-ment and reconstruction regions in the north and west. Securing those areas would allow the government to recruit and train the new army, police forces, and public service; to hire Afghan contrac-tors and purchase Afghan goods to stimulate reconstruction; and to rebuild food production facilities. The move south also had to wait until NATO nations offered enough military forces and aid resources. That decision was closely tied to winding down the NATO mission in the former Yugoslavia in 2003-04. However, Jalali argued that most importantly the move had to wait until US Defence Secretary Donald Rumsfeld was willing to transfer control of the area from the primarily counter-terrorist *Operation Enduring Freedom* to ISAF and UNAMA.

In many ways what happened next was a traditional Canadian stability-building mission story. A well-intentioned strategic policy decision taken in Ottawa was followed by people and dollars being committed to solve a problem. Missing was a clear sense of how best to fix that problem. That could develop only after Canadians had spent time on the ground, meeting people, seeing the terrain, and studying the scope of the problem first hand. But once committed, they rode a steep and bloody learning curve.

CANADA MOVES SOUTH

Canadian soldiers, diplomats, and aid workers began moving from Kabul to Kandahar Province in the summer of 2005. An American PRT had been operating there for only a year but had started a number of road- and school-building projects, as well as taking the first small steps toward justice reform. Canada's PRT took over the province from the US Army in August. A battlegroup followed in early 2006. The Canadian and British PRTs and their associated combat forces temporarily came under *OEF* command through the winter of 2005-06.

NATO officially took command of RC South in the summer of 2006.
By that time, the influx of troops and aid workers, including the Dutch
PRT and security force, doubled what OEF had in the area one year
earlier. Numbers more than doubled again by year's end.

Foreign Affairs Political Director Glyn Berry, and Michael Callan
from the Canadian International Development Agency (CIDA), headed
the civilian PRT elements. Col Stephen Bowes led the military component and held nominal command over the mission; in practice he
shared responsibility with his civilian counterparts. Their job was to
put into practice Canada's "Whole of Government" (previously "3D")
approach to stability-building missions.

In Kandahar province, reform had to start at the top: in the office
of the provincial governor. Kandahar's first post-Taliban governor, Gul
Agha Shirzai, was a local warlord who had played a role in the Taliban
defeat. This hardly qualified him as an effective political leader. His ties
to old disputes and ongoing clashes between rival warlords called into
question President Karzai's commitment to establishing responsible
government.[11] Fortunately, just as the Canadian PRT arrived Karzai
launched a major shuffle of governors. While some were fired, most
were transferred between provinces on opposite sides of the country to separate them from their power bases. The new governor of
Kandahar was Asadullah Khalid, a young, modern Pashtun from the
north. The simultaneous arrival of the new governor, ISAF, and more
UN aid, sent a strong message of change to the south.

Mentoring and advising Khalid was Berry's job. He was also expected to help reform the provincial government and especially to
co-ordinate Kandahar's reconstruction with President Karzai's vision
of the larger national Afghan effort. As lead diplomat, Berry spread
word among Kandahar's power brokers about how the international
community and the Kabul government wanted to help.

The most important task facing Berry and members of the Royal
Canadian Mounted Police (RCMP) seconded to the PRT was security sector reform (SSR). That meant taking the first steps toward
addressing the Afghan National Police problem. The PRT started map-
ping out the scope of the challenge with visits to every substation,
assessing quality, quantity, and accountability. Berry and the RCMP
spent a lot of time meeting and co-ordinating with the Kandahar ANP

leaders. They found some officers who took their duty quite seriously, but standards of professionalism and capability varied wildly, and some detachments were plagued by corruption, drugs, and worse. Police in the rural districts were a massive problem. Unfortunately, the Canadian PRT was unable to change the situation much outside Kandahar City. About all they could do was gather information about the sorry state of the ANP and push it up the Canadian and ISAF chain of command. Their complaints did not fall on deaf ears, however. All NATO nations running PRTs in the south discovered the same problem. The Americans were aware, too. But it would take time and money to tackle the problem and some strenuous searching for people to staff it.

Michael Callan's CIDA team, working with UN agencies, the World Bank, the International Monetary Fund, and NGO aid agencies in the area, mapped out long-term development projects. CIDA's main task was to "build capacity"—to shore up the Kandahar provincial government's ability to deliver services and rebuild the infrastructure that would make the province self-sufficient. But Callan's flagship was the National Solidarity Program (NSP). The NSP was the Canadian-UN-Afghan "secret weapon" in the struggle to undermine warlords, drug-traffickers, and Taliban. CIDA did not deliver the program itself. Instead, community councils, supervised by Afghan UN workers and Afghan government officials, were set up to make decisions about local needs and projects. Callan and his tiny staff only looked after planning and co-ordinating. The NSP thus served a dual purpose: as a training and development opportunity for new Afghan officials, and as a showcase, giving Kandaharis a chance to see their own government and their own citizens taking positive action.[12] The fact that CIDA pays for and co-ordinates the NSP but delivers it through Afghans is a point of honour for development officials. Unfortunately, its very success in this regard probably contributed to the impression in Canada that CIDA was doing little in Kandahar. The record suggests, however, that the NSP has delivered a disproportionate—and positive—return on its modest investment.

The strength of the NSP was not that it built wells or bridges, but that it forced village elders to put their personal and family needs aside and consider the greater good of their community. CIDA efforts depended on long-term planning, identifying Afghans who could do the work, and persuading them to work together. That was a tall order for a people suffering from collective trauma of war and who in recent memory had no one to look after their interests but themselves. But in all of the parts of Afghanistan where the NSP became operational, Taliban influence waned and opium production slowed or stopped. Even so, a program that worked well in the north and west would be a much harder sell in the Taliban and drug production heartland of the south.

The CIDA approach of working only with full Afghan participation represented a shift from the American PRT model. That effort had been loosely tied to the goal of rebuilding Afghanistan, but its primary purpose remained to support the counter-terrorism campaign. Nation-building was a secondary task. American aid dollars often had been spent in the south to provide protection for military forces by pacifying local communities or leaders with projects they wanted. While many of these projects provided enduring value, others—like schools built without local consultation—yielded no benefits. Often they were undertaken by foreign contractors or those with ties to former Governor Shirzai. Whatever the intentions of some American military and civilian officials in Kandahar, *Operation Enduring Freedom* was a security operation. It had few of the assets most needed to stabilize the region and win it away from Taliban and drug gang control. This approach also failed to tackle Kandahar's huge unemployment problem, to ensure local input on projects, or to connect them to the larger vision of national rebuilding.

The American PRT was not the only organization launching projects in Kandahar Province without consulting local Afghans. By 2006 several foreign NGOs also had done so. The most notable examples included a number of large schools that had been built in open ground five to six kilometres between villages. This was not the traditional Kandahari way, and many lay at the end of roads considered far too dangerous to use. These schools and some medical clinics were also built without checking with the Afghan Ministries of Education and Health to ensure that they could be staffed with teachers or doctors and be properly supplied. Thus some modern buildings lay empty for lack of staff and clients, and became strong-points that were fought over between the Taliban and the ANP. But it is too simple to suggest that quick-impact projects should have be passed over in favour only of long-term development work. Kandahar was so badly broken and its basic needs so high that some rebuilding could not wait. Thus it fell largely to Col Bowes and his soldiers in 2006 to reverse the effects of these well-intentioned, if misdirected, efforts.

The international community as a whole understood that Afghan reconstruction needed better co-ordination. In January 2006 the major donor nations to Afghanistan convened the London Conference. It was here that 60 countries entered into the Afghan Compact, pledging to dramatically increase assistance to the Islamic Republic of Afghanistan. Signatories also agreed to better organize their rebuilding efforts, a decision which produced the Afghan National Development Strategy (ANDS). This new strategy, endorsed by a UN Security Council Resolution in February 2006, finally provided clear strategic guidance to all 26 PRTs in Afghanistan. However, each of them would have to figure out how to execute that strategy in the unique conditions of their assigned province.

The task for Col Bowes's PRT in 2006 included using his infantry company to protect civilian members of the team. He also became the eyes and ears for Foreign Affairs and CIDA in the far reaches of Kandahar Province. Bowes conducted *shuras* (council meetings) with village elders from one end of Kandahar to the other, hearing their grievances, especially about the police, and their views on what development projects were most needed in their communities. Bowes and Berry concluded that certain immediate needs could not wait for the political process and the consensus needed for the deeper-reaching CIDA development work.

This meant that the American practice of quick-impact projects had to continue, but with some modifications. Bowes and his Civil-Military Co-operation (CIMIC) detachments developed a simple solution: they connected with officials from Afghan government ministries, the CIDA-supported CDCs and, through Glyn Berry, to the new governor, who was developing a plan for the province. They attended *shuras* with CDCs and the larger district-level Development Assemblies to determine the Kandaharis' most urgent needs. They took the information, cleared the requests with the national ministries, and checked them against the governor's plan to make sure they did not work at cross purposes. The CIMIC teams then contracted out quick projects that fit larger provincial and national rebuilding goals. These rarely involved building something new, focusing instead on fixing schools, bridges, and irrigation canals.[13]

The solution worked, but because it was a typical Canadian ground-up innovation the money did not exist to support it. CIDA funds were already earmarked for the NSP and large-scale sustainable development projects. Foreign Affairs dollars were targeted at police and government reform. Bowes had nothing like his American predecessor—a large commander's contingency fund. His solution was to adopt the age-old Canadian Army tradition of scrounging. While he had no Canadian dollars, Bowes did have a US Agency for International Development (USAID) officer and a British Department of Foreign Aid and Development officer in his camp. Not long after sizing up the problem, Bowes was using American and British money to get things done.[14]

The Canadian PRT was not operating in a vacuum. The UN High Commission for Refugees operated a number of camps in the province, the UN World Food Program delivered food aid for the vast number of hungry families, and the UN Children's Emergency Fund helped with school supply and staffing. A small number of Afghan and international NGOs also worked in the area, providing everything from education to agricultural rebuilding and direct employment. Two small development agencies were operated by dedicated individuals: Sarah Chayes's Arghand fair trade soap company, and Drew Gilmour's Development Works, which started fixing the ruined road network so farmers could get crops to the city.

Working the bugs out of this new Whole of Government approach and liaising with the Afghan national government, the UN, and the NGOs proved challenging. Each Canadian department deployed experienced professionals but they worked according to vastly different practices and professional philosophies. Col Bowes recalled that it took some time for civilian officials to get used to working in a high-threat war zone. Each department also had very different expectations when it came to planning timelines. Berry's successor,

Gavin Buchan, observed that Bowes and his soldiers planned over weeks to deliver their effects before the end of their six-month tour. The Foreign Affairs team gathered information and planned over 12 months to deliver effects out to two years. Callan and CIDA worked toward building consensus, infrastructure, and institutions that could make the country work in the next generation. They all had some preconceived ideas of each other that had to be overcome quickly. But they were united in their will to help Afghans and from that common ground they forged ways to get their work done. The three men looked beyond their institutional and philosophical differences and, as Bowes recalled, "We made it work on the ground because we had no other choice." Without a doubt, the personalities of these men and their willingness to co-operate were critical to forging a new PRT doctrine.

As challenging as this process was, their collaboration had enormous potential. It laid the foundation for these three departments to blend their methods and resources. Subsequent rotations picked up where this first Canadian PRT left off. The main accomplishment of this experiment was to map out the sheer scale of the reconstruction task. It was not only about "bricks and mortar" but about creating a new provincial government as well as local councils so that the voice of the people could be heard.

THE TALIBAN STRIKES BACK

Meanwhile, the Taliban and the drug-traffickers heard about how the Canadian PRT and the new provincial government planned to spread public services, to reform crooked police, and to fix broken infrastructure. They observed whom the Canadians talked to. They watched them move all over the province and start the CDCs. This PRT constituted a kind of threat that the American PRT had not. The Taliban had believed that the *OEF* forces eventually would leave and that—at least until the first US PRT was set up in 2004—their reconstruction projects would not be enough to win the confidence of locals. Indeed, the patience of many Kandaharis, especially farmers, had run out by the time the Canadians arrived. The Taliban had thrived on that frustration. But when Canada finally started to deliver what people were looking for, the insurgents and drug lords recognized that the window to exploit local disenchantment was closing. A new governor, new police chiefs, a more effective PRT, and programs that delivered real results constituted real threats. They had to be stopped.

January 2006 saw Canada's world in Kandahar turned upside down. On the 15th, after finishing one of their regular meetings with local police commanders, Glyn Berry and RCMP Superintendent Wayne Martin headed back to Camp Nathan Smith along with their security detail from the Force Protection Company. Only a kilometre away from the camp, the enemy struck. A Toyota taxi laden with seven rockets slammed into the lightly armoured Mercedes "G-Wagon" carrying Berry and MCpl Paul Franklin. The explosion threw the vehicle in the air, killed Berry instantly, and badly smashed Franklin's legs. The other two soldiers in the vehicle, Cpl Jeffery Bailey and Pte William Salikin, were also seriously injured. The attack was not just the first successful suicide car bombing, causing the first Canadian death, in Kandahar. It was a message from the Taliban: they were not going to let Canada rebuild anything without a fight.

The strike was the first of a wave of insurgent attacks on the international community and Afghan Police in 2006. It was an earth-shattering moment for Canada. And it was temporarily effective. Berry's death shut down the work of all civilian officials at the Kandahar PRT as Ottawa scrambled to reassess the security situation. CIDA and Foreign Affairs staff were pulled out of Camp Nathan Smith for a time and had to try to carry out their work from Kandahar Airfield. Unfortunately, this occurred just as the PRT effort was making headway in its relationship-building and information-gathering stages. The violence slowed the pace of development, but did not stop it. The civilians continued identifying the most needed reconstruction projects and finding Afghan workers and leaders to get them started. Nevertheless, Canada's first efforts had encountered a major obstacle.

THE BATTLEGROUP ARRIVES

Fortuitously, the strike came just as the balance of Canada's military commitment was arriving on the ground. On the day of Glyn Berry's death, LCol Ian Hope's Task Force Orion, based on 1st Battalion, Princess Patricia's Canadian Light Infantry (1PPCLI), was staging into Kandahar Airfield and beginning to take up residence in Camp Nathan Smith. They were the vanguard for the multi-national brigade about to establish RC South under Canadian BGen David Fraser. Their first job was to take over from the US Army's 173rd Airborne Brigade and spread out across Kandahar, Helmand, and Uruzgan Provinces to prepare the ground for the British and Dutch PRTs and their battle-groups. Hope's infantry companies and combat engineers were soon roaming the south, reaching out to Afghan communities west and north of Kandahar City, and Qalat in Zabul Province. For many, these foreign troops were the first who had come to help them.

In that first half of 2006, LCol Hope's main effort was to secure Forward Operating Bases (FOBs) like Martello in northern Kandahar on the Uruzgan border and FOB Robinson near the Helmand provincial capital of Lashkar Gah. The Patricias also had to secure the towns and their environs, as well as the key roads that Allied formations needed to spread their presence into the southern countryside. Their other role was to extend the reach of the Canadian PRT and the new governor's authority. Both tasks meant pushing the battlegroup to be everywhere in a vast space to show the people of southern Afghanistan that help had finally arrived. It was the start of a long uphill struggle to win people over to the new Afghan government.

Hope's battlegroup added to PRT efforts to spread assistance farther into the south than ever before. They brought "reconstruction bombs," the soldiers' name for village aid kits: sea-containers full of medicine, soap, food, and tools. Company commanders met with village elders in *shuras* all over the province to listen to their wor-ries and complaints about the Taliban, drug-traffickers, and corrupt police. They also spread the NSP concept of community rebuilding project planning. The soldiers walked and drove security and pres-ence patrols in Kandahar City and on key roads near the new FOBs to establish a sense of safety and order that would allow the PRT to carry on with aid projects. The evacuation of civilian personnel fol-lowing Berry's death had shrunk the PRT to fewer than 50 soldiers and police, under the command of Bowes's successor, LCol Simon Hetherington. So, with such a vast area to influence and the risk so high, for this rotation the PRT and the battlegroup became, for all intents and purposes, one unit.

Thus, the soldiers ranged outwards through early 2006, funding projects to repair existing schools, roads, and bridges. Even these quick-impact projects adhered to the principle that Afghans' labour should be hired and Afghan construction materials purchased to kick-start the southern economy. Wells were dug to supply clean drinking water and irrigation systems were repaired. The battlegroup's Field Ambulance Platoon also ran village Medical Outreach Clinics to assist with the UN country-wide polio vaccination program intended to reduce infant mortality rates. The PRT's RCMP and Military Police (MP) carried on with the onerous task of Afghan police reform. The Mounties and MPs ran courses and supervised improvements to ANP stations and check-points. The huge challenge of police corruption, the small number of Canadian police then available, and the more dangerous security situation limited this effort to Kandahar City, but it was a start.

As was the case in the early days of the post-Dayton mission in Bosnia, it was only after work began in earnest that it became clear which roads and waterways were most badly needed and which relationships with local leaders had to be forged before stability could take hold. In Kandahar, one of the chief goals for Task Force Orion was to impose some structure on the haphazard provincial government system of police command and development work. LCol Hope's most important accomplishment during TF 1-06 was to establish the Joint Provincial Co-ordination Centre "JPCC" to improve and in some cases open connections between the various police and international military forces in Kandahar.

In the same vein, Foreign Affairs set up the Provincial Development Council, chaired by Governor Khalid, to co-ordinate aid and development work. With so many new international development organizations, UN agencies, and NGOs starting to operate in Kandahar, the governor and LCol Hetherington were run ragged trying to meet with them and track their work. In this part of Afghanistan co-ordinating what to build, where to build it, and who would do the work, were among the most important and painful first steps, even if they went largely unnoticed or under-reported.

Thus, in this first full rotation to Kandahar, in spite of a growing insurgency and the daunting task of trying to secure the whole southern region, the 1PPCLI Battlegroup did its level best to deliver the mission the way it had been conceived. Reconstruction, or at least paving the way for it, was the main effort, with the battlegroup providing security and stability. Unfortunately, the Taliban would not allow the battlegroup to devote all its time to protecting PRT activities. As 2006 wore on, insurgent attacks increased and the Patricias found themselves frequently fighting small battles against guerrilla forces or dodging a rising number of improvised explosive devices (IEDs) and suicide bombers. Taliban attacks were intended to deny the international community the ability to move freely around the south.

But Task Force Orion had at its disposal the means to keep the roads open. The battlegroup's three companies each deployed 16 LAVs: eight-wheeled, lightly armoured, infantry fighting vehicles. They were armed with a small auto-cannon and a machine gun that delivered accurate fire from under armour protection. They gave the troops good off-road mobility and a fair degree of protection from blasts, bullets, mines, and fragments. Hope also had brought 11 Field Engineer Squadron, with its capability for sniffing out explosives, building fortifications, and repairing roads. As much as possible, the Engineers kept the Patricias protected when camped and safe when on the move.

In those early days, before the rest of the NATO team was in place, the Patricias were spread thin and over-committed. One company group worked in the mountainous northern districts around FOB Martello. When spring arrived they were joined in large numbers by Dutch troops and Australian Task Force Uruzgan. With Canadians securing the main road to the provincial capital at Tarin Kowt, the Dutch PRT and an Australian Reconstruction Team were ready to work by summer 2006.

One of the toughest jobs for the Patricias was holding open the door to Helmand Province in the western districts of Kandahar so the British Task Force could move into their area of responsibility (AOR). This task was especially dangerous. Each passing month saw more IED attacks and ambushes on the east-west Highway 1 between Kandahar City and Helmand. Among the more troubling areas where the Taliban lashed out with increasing violence were the villages of Pashmul and Bazaar-e-Panjwayi. In an effort to stop insurgent attacks, a Patricia company started patrolling into the villages of Zharey and Panjwayi Districts along the road and the Arghandab River.

The one area in Kandahar province where the Canadians did not deploy in early 2006 was the border country around Spin Boldak. There, American and French Special Forces under *OEF* were still running counter-terrorist operations. It would be another year before Canadian troops under ISAF would take over that region.

By the summer of 2006, with the British and the Dutch in position, much of the 1PPCLI Battlegroup returned to the outskirts of Kandahar City, where Taliban activity was rising alarmingly. The Canadians received an increasing flow of intelligence about power struggles between drug lords over opium production and control of the peasants who farmed it. Reports also filtered in about Afghan Police shakedowns and extortion of farmers in the Arghandab River greenbelt. Trouble was gathering in the shadows of the mud-walled fields of Zharey–Panjwayi. But what the Taliban would do next and even how many of them were around was still uncertain.

The Battle of Pashmul's White School

Taliban ambushes and IED strikes on the main roads west of Kandahar City rose sharply at the end of July. BGen Fraser recalled that they were probably aimed at Patricia patrols supporting Governor Khalid's encouragement of the grape harvest and efforts to move produce out of the agricultural areas to the city for processing. Attacks spiked on the Highway 1 choke-point west of the city. It was clear they were coming from areas around the village of Pashmul. Hope's battlegroup had to shut this down. In the early morning darkness of 3 August, the LAV-mounted 3 Platoon from Charles Company patrolled toward Pashmul with an ANP platoon in an effort to flush the Taliban into the open. The leading LAV struck a large IED killing one man and wounding another. The small force was 500 metres from an empty quick-impact project site soon to become infamous as the Pashmul "White School." The Platoon Leader dismounted his three rifle sections from their carriers to provide cover as the casualties were treated and preparations made to pull out the damaged LAV.

Not long after the sun rose a second LAV hit a large IED, wounding three more Canadians. Rifle and machine-gun fire from a Taliban unit in the White School made it difficult to do rescue and recovery at the blast site. So, the dismounted members of the platoon set off on foot for the school to finish the job of taking down the Taliban cell. They reached the objective only to find that the cell was part of a much larger, heavily armed group, some 40 or 50 in number, dug into fire positions surrounding the school on three sides. A volley of automatic weapons fire and rocket-propelled grenades (RPGs) slammed into the Canadians. Soon dead were Cpl Christopher Reid, Cpl Bryce Keller, Pte Kevin Dallaire, and an experienced Patricia warhorse and veteran of multiple peace-building tours, Sgt Vaughn Ingram. Six more members of 3 Platoon were wounded. LCol Hope, located nearby, ordered the two remaining LAVs to damn the IEDs and mines, punch through to the survivors at the school, and get them out. By then virtually every man in the platoon was wounded or injured. As the platoon fought for its very life and LCol Hope moved in "A" Company to reinforce it, a suicide car bomb struck a Canadian convoy south of the Arghandab River near Bazaar-e-Panjwayi, wounding two more soldiers. The Taliban clearly had much more force in the Pashmul area than a few terrorist cells. It took Canadian artillery fire and an airstrike called in at very close range to get the withdrawing Patricias to safety.

The engagement on 3 August was the First Battle for the Pashmul White School. Along with other actions fought in Zharey–Panjwayi before that day and in the two weeks after, and with intelligence reports and information from terrified locals, it was obvious that the Taliban had deployed a large force in Pashmul and had thrown down the gauntlet to ISAF.[15] The flow of aid and assistance and the potential for real Afghan government reform offered new hope in the south. But this also challenged Taliban and drug-trafficker control there. They were prepared to fight ISAF for that control. As Col Capstick put it, the "Canadian arrival stirred a hornet's nest."[16]

Preparing for a Showdown

The size of the insurgent force gathered at the gates of Kandahar City took everyone by surprise. In the spring of 2006 the Taliban leadership had concentrated hardcore fighters from all over southern Afghanistan and from training camps in Pakistan in the green-belt of Zharey–Panjwayi districts. This growth of the Taliban was fed not just by unemployment, corruption, and incompetence within the police

force, but also by the booming narco-economy.[17] ISAF's arrival in the
south had coincided with a US-backed drive from President Karzai
to eradicate opium production. This helped trigger the defensive
reaction by the drug-traffickers and the Taliban who depended on
that production for their operations budgets.[18]

Other observers added that Taliban resurgence in general, and
the massing in the summer of 2006 in particular, reflected a perception among southern Afghans, fed by Taliban Information Operations,
that *OEF* was headed for failure and that the UN and ISAF had no
stomach for a fight. This only magnified the widespread dissatisfaction
with the massive gap between people's expectations for reconstruction and the paltry delivery in southern Afghanistan thus far. Again,
the Taliban spun this as a failure of the international community to
protect Afghans. Ironically and tragically, they made this claim just
as the world finally arrived in the south in strength, ready to do what
the people there needed and most wanted.[19]

So, ISAF and UNAMA had expanded their presence in the south
at a crucial moment for the insurgency. Some in UNAMA, among
them Chris Alexander, then the UN Deputy Special Representative
for Afghanistan, knew that the Taliban leadership had an ambitious
goal. Using Panjwayi District as their base, they aimed to re-capture
Kandahar City and then to march on Kabul. They hoped to crush
the government and drive off ISAF before reform rallied the people
against the insurgents.[20]

All parties concerned, from the UN, to President Karzai, to ISAF
commanders in southern Afghanistan, recognized that they could not
back away from this showdown. If the Taliban captured Kandahar,
all UN efforts to assist Afghans and build a functional government
would end. They had to be stopped. As it had at only a few times in
history, the UN decided that resolute military action was necessary.[21]
Likewise, the international community had to prove to the sceptical
people of the south that they would not cut and run at the first sign
of danger. To win respect in Kandahar, ISAF would have to fight. In
fact, Pashtun culture expected nothing less. Neither side could afford
to back down. The stage was set for a pitched battle.

Unfortunately, although ISAF had doubled the number of troops
in the south over what the Americans had deployed there a year

before, it still was not enough. Nor were Afghan National Army units available. Ian Hope, like the other ISAF battlegroup commanders in the south, could not yet "hold any ground that he cleared." The Taliban always came back into villages following ISAF patrols and instilled fear among the residents. Nor—for reasons discussed earlier—were the police an effective bulwark against the Taliban. But help was on the way.

In fact, the looming crisis developed just as Canada's Joint Task Force Afghanistan was in the midst of a rotation. Based on Task Force Orion's or TF 2-06's experience in Kandahar, Roto 2 or Task Force 3-06, as it was known by the new Canadian-NATO mission rotation title, brought with them more of everything. The battlegroup was built around LCol Omer Lavoie's 1st Battalion of the Royal Canadian Regiment (1RCR), 23 Field Squadron Royal Canadian Engineers, "E" Battery of the 2nd Regiment Royal Canadian Horse Artillery, and the Coyote reconnaissance vehicles of the Royal Canadian Dragoons. Another new part of the Task Force was an Operational Mentoring and Liaison Team (OMLT) that would take over assisting an Afghan National Army Kandak (Battalion) from an American Embedded Training Team (ETT). The PRT was rebuilt and its civilian members returned. It was poised to expand reconstruction operations, complete with its own infantry company for force protection.

With British and Dutch forces now in place and ISAF formally in command of RC South, TF 3-06 was supposed to carry on with the original mission concept of rebuilding Kandahar behind the shield of the battlegroup. According to that plan, security and assistance would be expanded outwards to the very edges of Kandahar Province: north to Shah Wali-Khot, south to Spin Boldak, and west to Maywand District on the Helmand border. That is what TF 3-06 had planned and trained for. No one had anticipated what was about to happen. As soon as they were complete on the ground, BGen Fraser warned the battlegroup, as well as Danish, Dutch, and American troops under his command, to prepare for a conventional offensive into the Pashmul area to take it away from the Taliban. The attack would include a preparatory artillery barrage and something no Canadian soldiers had done since the final weeks of the Second World War: an assault river crossing.[22] Suffice to say, most were stunned when the orders came.

Operation Medusa

Operation Medusa was the defining event of TF 3-06. It shaped all things that came after it. Thus, it is important to understand its impact on the situation that TF 1-07 inherited from their predecessors.

In light of the debate over negotiating with the Taliban, it is significant that the first shots fired in *Medusa* were diplomatic. Through the medium of three local district *shuras* in late August, BGen Fraser asked the Taliban leaders if they would leave peacefully and allow reconstruction to carry on. The tactic had worked in previous showdowns with disgruntled local warlords in Zabul. But this time the message from the insurgents came through loud and clear: they intended to evict ISAF from Kandahar by force. Around that time Fraser received a visit from the NATO Secretary-General and the Supreme Allied Commander Europe (SACEUR); both made it equally clear to Fraser that NATO could not allow this threat to continue.

Before the fighting began, ISAF warned local residents to move out of the area for their own safety. That proved unnecessary; most had already done so. Thus, the battlefield seemed like a wasteland. Pashmul was about to become a free-fire zone.

The 1RCR Battlegroup concentrated for a two-pronged assault on both sides of the Arghandab River, north and south of Pashmul. The size of the task before them meant stripping away the PRT's force protection company to reinforce the assault. In fact, the whole of the PRT would be diverted from reconstruction tasks for this operation. 1RCR was also backed by a Dutch parachute company and a Danish recce company that cordoned off access to Zharey–Panjwayi from the Taliban base in Helmand Province. American and Canadian Special Operations Forces were also on hand, and a light infantry company from US 10th Mountain Division stood in reserve.[23]

The battle opened on 3 September with a combined aerial and artillery bombardment of known and suspected Taliban positions around the White School. Nonetheless, when Maj Matthew Sprague's Charles Company and 2 Troop of 23 Engineer Squadron launched their assault over the Arghandab River, they met a wall of fire from well-armed

Taliban infantry fighting from dug-in defences. Any hope that Pashmul could be cleared quickly with minimal damage evaporated with the smoke of battle. The tally of five men dead and eight wounded worsened the next day when a US Air Force A-10 Thunderbolt ground-attack aircraft mistakenly strafed Charles Company as it formed up for a second assault. Virtually an entire platoon was struck down with blast fragments and rock shards at the bottom of the imposing mountain at Ma'Sum Ghar. Former Canadian Olympic Team member Pte Mark Anthony Graham was killed and 30 wounded, including Maj Sprague himself. The "friendly fire" accident stalled the attack and prompted the largest casualty evacuation NATO has had to perform.

For the next few days, anything that moved in Pashmul was pummelled with fire from all directions. On 10 September, 1RCR's Bravo Company, the Patricia PRT company, and the 10th Mountain Division company closed in on Pashmul from the north, while survivors of the first assault made a feint from the south side of the river. This time the Canadians and their attached US troops were supported by "armour" in the form of three armoured bulldozers that 23 Field Engineer Squadron's commander, Maj Mark Gasparatto, had "borrowed" from contractors at Kandahar Airfield. Gasparatto used the dozers to breach crop walls and a series of deep wadis or creeks barring their approach and forming part of the Taliban defensive system. This time movement was slow and deliberate, with plenty of fire support and engineer work on route clearance and building fire positions for the LAVs. LCol Lavoie mounted a set-piece conventional attack, while integrating the new "Three Block War" approach to stability operations. LCol Hetherington's PRT detachments followed behind the combat elements, conducting immediate battle damage assessments to hasten repairs and to mitigate the destruction raining down on surrounding communities.

As 1RCR and Gasparatto's sappers worked their way southward through a series of defended compounds they found an elaborate defensive position obviously prepared with heavy excavation equipment. It included fire trenches and bunkers to protect the Taliban fighters from bombardment. All were connected to earthen grape huts, which served as fighting bunkers complete with firing ports in the form of the air vents normally used for turning lush Kandahar grapes into sweet raisins. The area had been liberally sown with mines and IEDs, especially on the north-south roads leading from Pashmul to the Zharey District Centre at Patrol Base Wilson (PBW) on Highway 1.

By the time that the north-south line was cleared of an immediate threat, an ANA Kandak arrived with its American ETT. This force took the lead clearing compounds eastward back toward Kandahar City. This Afghan contribution was particularly important because it was the first exposure of Canadian troops and local Kandaharis to professional and capable Afghan security forces. Given that the public servants most southern Afghans had encountered up to that time were corrupt police, the arrival of competent, disciplined Afghan soldiers acting to protect rather than to rob them sent a powerful message to the people of the area. It demonstrated that ISAF and their own forces would protect them from the Taliban. That, in turn, marked the start of the process of rebuilding public confidence in government.

As the ISAF/Afghan team continued to sweep villages in eastern Zharey District of Taliban, they seized large amounts of weapons and bomb-making supplies. A number of powerful IEDs ate into the Canadian vehicle fleet and wrecked an American Husky mine-clearing vehicle. Fortunately, the armoured vehicles performed as designed and saved the lives of their crews. But the sheer number of mines and IEDs in the area, coupled with continuing Taliban raids and sniping, meant that the Canadians were going to have to hold this ground after they cleared it. That was unavoidable if they were going to rebuild the devastated battlefield and enable families to return. But to do that, they needed safe roads to navigate the maze of walled fields, grape huts, and houses. Thus was born the concept for FOB Ma'Sum Ghar and Route Summit.[24]

The Taliban had suffered a major defeat at Pashmul. To this day it is still uncertain how many were killed then and in the battles that followed. Estimates run from as few as 300 to as many as 2000. But they did not give up the fight. Attacks on Canadian and ISAF troops in the area continued throughout October and November. When Strong-Points North, Centre, and West were built to defend the new road being built between Pashmul and the Zharey District Centre at PBW, they became focal points for Taliban counter-attacks. Those attacks were smashed with a mixture of observed artillery and mortar fire and 25mm gun and small arms fire from the strong-points. Normally, in counter-insurgency operations finding the insurgents is among the most challenging tasks. In the aftermath of *Medusa* that was not a problem; the Taliban continued to come to 1RCR. [25]

Route Summit was built as a combat road so that the battlegroup could sustain operations against insurgents launching raids on the strong-points. However, like other quick-impact projects, it was tied to the long-term vision for provincial reconstruction. USAID had plans to build a permanent road bridge to connect Bazaar-e-Panjwayi to Zharey District. The road and bridge would also tie into a Highway 1 bypass around the south end of Kandahar City that would divert trac-tor-trailer and military traffic around the congested and dangerous downtown core.

Operation Medusa prevented the Taliban from retaking Kandahar City in 2006. But the losses they inflicted on Canadian Forces, however small compared to their own, caused ripples of concern in Canada. The trickle of Canadian casualties from IEDs and suicide bombs dur-ing the summer spiked in September with well over 100 killed and wounded in open combat. That shock to the Canadian public may have been the only gain the Taliban achieved in return for their defeat, but it was important. What they could not win on the battlefield in Afghanistan they might achieve by eroding support for the war on the home front. [26] Keeping up the pressure in the information war, they warned of a major spring offensive while al-Qaeda threatened to carry out a major attack in Canada. [27] So, *Medusa* was a significant event that allowed both sides to influence Canadian debates over the mission.

Aftermath

After *Operation Medusa* the balance of TF 3-06's tour was dominated by consolidating the key terrain and post-battle clean up to make way for the return of refugees from Pashmul. The problem for Canada and NATO was that this task consumed most of the PRT's resources and time. Thus, it continued to divert attention from their main job: getting the provincial government and the city functioning normally. Still, Hetherington's PRT, especially the Foreign Affairs and CIDA staff, never stopped their behind-the-scenes work, following up ear-lier efforts to decide what infrastructure was most vital to repair, who the power brokers were, and which Afghans could be trusted to get work done.

Battle damage repair and re-opening relationships with local village leaders in eastern Zharey–Panjwayi was the focus of *Operation Baaz Tzuka (Falcon Summit)* from the late fall into the winter and end of TF 3-06's tour. Sometimes erroneously described as another anti-Taliban offensive, it was more of a classic counter-insurgency operation. It involved clearing areas of insurgents and weapons, establishing a security presence with new Afghan police and army units, and then launching long-term rebuilding projects.

According to LCol Lavoie, *Medusa* was a conventional battle, forced on him by Taliban action, while *Baaz Tzuka* looked more like the kind of operation for which he had trained his battlegroup. It was critical for creating the environment TF 1-07 would inherit. Among other things it included *shuras* to establish cease-fire agreements with locals who had supported the Taliban's summer wave of attacks. It also included setting up Afghan National Police checkpoints to hold ground, including along major roadways. This work continued until the time came to hand over to TF 1-07 in February 2007.

Taliban actions in the summer and fall of 2006 made it clear that securing Zharey–Panjwayi was the key to controlling Kandahar Province. So, a permanent and sizeable military presence had to be established there. Consequently, after completing Route Summit, 23 Field Engineer Squadron improved existing defense and observation positions and built new ones on key hills from which ISAF soldiers could see critical towns, roads, and river crossing sites. From the commanding heights of Ma' Sum Ghar and Sperwan Ghar, they could control the most decisive ground in the province. These new FOBs became home to follow-on Canadian contingents and eventually to Afghan National Army units mentored by Canadian soldiers. The PRT also used them as forward offices. So, TF 3-06 did not just clear and leave. They cleared and stayed—a significant step in the counter-insurgency and peace-building campaigns.

Ramping Up 3

WARNING ORDER 001

Modern, professional NATO armies do not send soldiers to war on short notice. While LCol Steve Bowes and Glyn Berry roved through Kandahar creating a uniquely Canadian presence, Land Forces Atlantic Area (LFAA) issued Warning Order 001. The order, dated October 2005, detailed instructions to commence with "force generation, training and preparation of personnel" in TF 1-07 for deployment to Joint Task Force Afghanistan commencing on or about January 2007. LCol Rob Walker, already aware his 2RCR was in the hopper for Kandahar, now had his official orders.

Training for War and Peace

It is conventional wisdom that senior officers—especially generals—make the crucial decisions that determine the outcome of military operations. But it says a great deal about the nature of the Canadian mission in Afghanistan that the critical decisions affecting the success of the mission are taken by individual junior soldiers. Every aspect of their behaviour, from full-scale combat to casual contact with the locals, demands a high degree of professionalism, judgement, and fortitude. It used to be fashionable to talk about the "strategic corporal," the section leader who had to decide when and how to act, and to remember that whatever he did could directly impact the success of the operation. Training for TF 1-07 pushed that thinking threshold even further, to the point where the actions of individual riflemen or gunners became critical. As a result, ramping up for TF 1-07 was a year-long, complex, comprehensive, and highly realistic process of training and preparation.

In 2006 few Canadians probably realized how good their soldiers really are, and how well prepared they were for the tasks that lay ahead. When LCol Omer Lavoie's 1RCR arrived in Kandahar in the summer of 2006, one Canadian newspaper carried a story of "a fresh batch of green Canadian recruits" making its way to Afghanistan. This well-intentioned but misleading attempt to capture the moment of the arrival of TF 3-06 belied the state of 1RCR's readiness for its mission. For once the decision was made to commit a series of Canadian battlegroups to the most difficult theatre in Afghanistan, pre-deployment training reached the highest level of sophistication in the army's history. That training, education in local cultural norms and behaviour, a high degree of good common sense, and the extensive experience of officers and non-commissioned officers earned on missions to other tough places served 1RCR very well, allowing them to adapt to a changing environment. All of that package and more was available to TF 1-07 as it prepared for the rapidly evolving world of Kandahar Province.

The Canadian Army did not expect to fight a conventional battle around Pashmul in 2006, but that does not mean it was untrained for one. During their first month in Kandahar, LCol Omer Lavoie's men stepped out of the stability-building and counter-insurgency role they had prepared for into a conventional, high intensity, war-fighting role. They made the switch easily and well because they were trained as combat soldiers first, and then as stability-building peacekeepers and culturally aware negotiators. Such flexibility is only found in the finest and most professional modern armies. Since the 1956 Suez Crisis and the subsequent United Nations Emergency Force peacekeeping mission there, Canada has developed a strong reputation around the world for sending only the best trained, disciplined, and professional soldiers on peace and stability missions.

One mark of a modern professional army is that it spends more time training than in action. This was true even for the most junior private soldiers in TF 1-07. Through early 2006 they all worked to bring their own individual professional qualifications up to speed, ensuring that their skills on weapons, vehicles, communications equipment, and other tasks within individual units were honed to perfection. Collective team training prepared sections of infantry, troops of tanks and reconnaissance vehicles, and their junior leaders. All of this purposeful activity was directed at getting the elements of the battlegroup ready for its six months of mission-specific training prior to deployment to Kandahar in February 2007.

Mission-Specific Training

Mission-specific training has been part of a Canadian soldier's preparation for service on peacekeeping and stability operations since the 1960s. In the last ten years the process has intensified. By 2006, it had reached a peak of complexity and sophistication shaped by a decade of deployments to the former Yugoslavia and especially by the first rotations to Afghanistan. Soldiers needed to know as much as possible about local customs, culture, and politics, and about the nature and motivation of groups that might oppose the establishment of peace and order. Armed with that information, commanders could tailor rules of engagement (ROE), and a more general policy on using force, based on assessments of the insurgency. At the same time, increased focus was placed on preparing the soldier and his or her family psychologically to ensure that the strain of separation and the impact of operational stress on the soldier were minimized when she or he returned. As a result, the process of readying TF 1-07 took more time than the actual mission itself. No Canadian military force had ever deployed overseas as well prepared.

In a sense, mission-specific training for the TF 1-07 battle-group began as early as 2005 when a group of young captains from across the country gathered at CFB Gagetown for the Combat Team Commanders Course run by LCol Chris Hand's Tactics School. The course runs top-rated armoured, artillery, infantry, and combat engineer captains through the paces of leading a combat team based on an infantry company and integrated tanks, artillery, and engineers, supported by air power. During the field portion, candidates led a real combat team in the attack and defence while mounted in the infantry fighting vehicle (LAV), and dismounted. The troops they led in their exercise combat teams, and that opposed them as the mock enemy force, came from the Gagetown-based units, the 2nd Battalion of the Royal Canadian Regiment (2RCR) and 4 Engineer Support Regiment (4ESR).

Among the candidates on the 2005 Combat Team Commanders course were Chris Henderson, Dave Quick, Alex Ruff, and Dave

"Boomer" Broomfield. Each completed the course successfully, was promoted to the rank of major and took command of what became key elements of TF 1-07. Quick and Ruff took over infantry companies from 2RCR; Henderson took over Charles Company (Parachute), 3rd Battalion of the Princess Patricia's Canadian Light Infantry (3PPCLI); and Broomfield got "A" Squadron of Lord Strathcona's Horse. These skilled and powerful personalities, alpha-males all, proved to be a gifted team of soldier-diplomats under the trying conditions of Kandahar province in 2007.

At the end of June 2006, the entire team of battlegroup officers and NCOs, as well as a good many from the designated TF 1-07 Provincial Reconstruction Team (PRT), gathered again in Gagetown for a full-day seminar on their mission. This leadership team was already experienced in stability-building in failed states and counter-insurgency operations, with a solid understanding of the complexity of the task which lay ahead. Most importantly, the day included briefings from and discussions with recent Canadian veterans of the Kandahar mission. LCol Steve Borland, second-in-command (2i/c) of the PRT during Roto 0 left the most lasting impressions. Borland drove home the message that no counter-insurgency operation and no effort to rebuild a nation ever worked when a foreign army imposed itself on a people. Peace and a civil society only came about when people felt safe under the protection of their own military and police. Making the Afghan National Army functional, professional, and responsible to the people of Afghanistan, Borland insisted, was the most important contribution TF 1-07 could make. His message rang in everyone's ears. It also became central to all field training the Task Force took on for the balance of 2006.

All present at this June 2006 seminar were told, in no uncertain terms, that the Afghan mission would only succeed when the Government of Afghanistan could provide for the needs of its people. This message was drilled deeply into the mind of every Canadian soldier, particularly those in leadership positions. It shaped every part of the mission. Moreover, the Canadian and NATO approach was to ensure that every military and reconstruction task was done alongside Afghan officials. This meant that every job outside the wire involved training, mentoring, and setting an example. It also meant that representatives of the Afghan state would be front and centre, doing things for the people of southern Afghanistan.

The session also impressed on the officers and NCOs of TF 1-07 that their war-fighting capability could prevent Afghanistan from slipping further into chaos, but it would never allow Afghanistan to stand on its own. Defeating the Taliban militarily was not the key to victory. That victory would be achieved by the PRT, Foreign Affairs, Canadian International Development Agency (CIDA), and Afghan security forces themselves. The battlegroup's job was to allow the others to get on with that crucial work. Officers and NCOs were also reminded that when they were compelled to use force it had to be applied with care and absolute precision. The message came home loud and clear that a hunt for insurgents that used military power without regard for the lives and property of innocent Afghan civilians was a recipe for mission failure.

At the end of the summer of 2006, news of the battles in Pashmul flowed to the army at home and training was adapted accordingly. It was clear that Taliban attacks could occur anywhere and in great strength, and that the Taliban were prepared to stand and fight. Everyone in TF 1-07, therefore, needed to sharpen their combat skills to a fine edge. With that in mind, practice for worst-case scenarios was essential. No matter how careful and measured their use of violence needed to be, TF 1-07 soldiers would more than likely need to count on their war-fighting skills to survive and succeed. The command team from TF 1-07 saw the value of this first hand when they all visited Kandahar in the fall of 2006, in the midst of 1RCR's difficult tour. Having the leadership of each follow-on Task Force visit the theatre in the middle of the preceding rotation, which they would replace, was a critical part of the mission's preparation. It ensured that the accomplishments and hard lessons learned by one rotation would be absorbed by the next one as seamlessly as possible. What the TF 1-07 leaders saw was a battlegroup fresh from *Operation Medusa*, the largest full-scale combat operation for Canadian troops since the Korean War. Not surprisingly, such operations in Afghanistan had their peculiarities, among them the nature of the local urban and agricultural landscape with its almost impenetrable mud walls and tight spaces. These lessons were woven into battlegroup exercise scenarios in Canada.

Royal Archer

A modern battlegroup is a complex entity, consisting of over a thousand soldiers from various branches of service performing a myriad of combat tasks all designed to blend in orchestral union. Like musicians in that orchestra, they must first master their own instrument before they can play in their appropriate section. By the fall of 2006, the basic units of the TF 1-07 battlegroup were ready to start bringing the orchestra together. This was done in two phases. The first, *Exercise Royal Archer* in October, brought together the infantry, engineer, and artillery sub-units at CFB Gagetown in New Brunswick. The second, *Exercise Maple Guardian*, brought all the elements of TF 1-07 together at CFB Wainright in Alberta for a final rehearsal.

The aim of *Royal Archer* was to cycle each of three rifle companies through a live-fire scenario that mirrored the recent battle of Pashmul. The scenarios, conducted on the rolling hills of Gagetown's manoeuvre area and in a newly constructed urban operations training site, involved isolating Taliban strong points with artillery smoke rounds, and then using tanks and armoured engineer vehicles to breach the walls of mud fortresses to allow the infantry to slip in and seek out the defenders. One of the key objectives of the exercise was to deliver the attack with near surgical precision, applying fire only on the compound selected as a fighting position, rather than the other homes and buildings nearby. Tanks were crucial to this new, highly focused assault method. At Pashmul and in other previous *Operation Enduring Freedom* and NATO battles, the task of wall breaching was performed by artillery. However, artillery is primarily an area suppression weapon; it could take out a Taliban fortified house or wall, but smash everything else around it in the process. The deployment of 40-ton Leopard tanks to Kandahar seemed to suggest that the Canadian Army was more interested in combat than in rebuilding. In fact, during *Royal Archer* tanks firing highly accurate High-Explosive Squash Head rounds demonstrated that they could blow breaches in walls and take out strong-points without destroying everything else nearby. With tanks in TF 1-07 there would be no more Pashmuls. If the Taliban used a village as a base, possibly with hostages or human shields inside, NATO now had a powerful, direct-fire, precision weapon that could hit the insurgents while sparing the civilians. No one, except maybe a few tankers themselves, appreciated how much the tanks could add to the delicate struggle for Kandahar until they arrived and were employed. In the meantime, the army had to scramble to assemble enough Leopards to deploy in Afghanistan—scrounging parts from around the world and driving previously discarded vehicles off of concrete display pads.

Counter-Insurgency Conference

Shortly after the *Royal Archer* live-fire exercise, Task Force officers and NCOs joined instructors from the Gagetown Combat Training Centre, academics from Canada and the US, and contemporary practitioners for a joint conference with the University of New Brunswick's Gregg Centre. The two-day symposium on counter-insurgency operations was planned as part of the intellectual preparation of TF 1-07. The aim was to further educate senior and junior leaders on the lessons of historical counter-insurgency experience, the most recent nation-building progress, and the large hurdles remaining. The scholars and their audience discussed a wide range of cases, including Malaya, Vietnam, Northern Ireland, Kashmir, Nepal, and Iraq. The consensus was that the successful counter-insurgency operations looked more like peace-building missions, such as in Bosnia. Rebuilding government and restoring basic services were more effective than destroying the opponent. These activities deliver hope to people who have none and it is only when hope is restored that a failed state recovers. Contemporary practitioners, including a German Provincial Reconstruction Team commander recently back from northern Afghanistan, assessed PRT models used by NATO allies. The commander and staff of a US Army brigade combat team shared their very different perspective from a year-long tour in Iraq.

Perhaps the most important session of all was a live video-teleconference with BGen David Fraser from his headquarters at Kandahar Airfield. At the time, TF 3-06 was fully occupied with rebuilding the Pashmul area in the aftermath of *Operation Medusa*. Fraser, clad in his

"Arid" Canadian disruptive pattern camouflage, packing a Browning pistol on his shoulder, and looking exhausted, brought the classroom seminar atmosphere of the conference crashing down to reality. Yet his theme was the same as that expressed in every session. The salvation of Afghanistan, or of any fragile or failed state, could only come from its people. The best TF 1-07 could do was to pick up where TF 3-06 left off: shielding the people of Kandahar from the Taliban and drug runners long enough for Afghans to re-generate their own government. However, he warned that, with well-armed insurgents and criminal gangs roaming the region trying to kill NATO and Afghan soldiers and to stop the Afghan government from delivering on its promises, that mission was far easier said than done.

Parts and People: The Task Force Assembles

The culmination of the collective training and education occurred in November 2006 during Exercise Maple Guardian. For the first time, all the pieces of TF 1-07 were assembled together in one location for a full dress rehearsal in the newly established Canadian Manoeuvre Training Centre (CMTC) at CFB Wainwright. The CMTC concept had been in the works for years but only became operational in 2006 when 1RCR readied for TF 3-06. The idea was that all formations on their way to an overseas mission would conduct their last major exercise before deployment at the CMTC. There, units and formations would use a complete stock of exercise vehicles and equipment, in the actual numbers they would deploy on the mission. They would confront an equipped "enemy" force and a real Afghan "civilian" population. Not only did CMTC allow TF 1-07 to do its final validation exercises without the need to move vehicles and equipment from all across Canada, it also allowed troops to leave their home station, go into an isolated exercise "box," and focus exclusively on the task that lay before them. The task force assembled for Maple Guardian was the largest and most complex battlegroup yet deployed by Canada. Based on the experience of the first two rotations through Kandahar in 2006, TF 1-07 included more of everything: more diplomats, more development officials, more aid dollars; more troops and more police officers to mentor Afghan soldiers, police and government officials; and a bigger battlegroup to protect them all.

The main change was a significant increase in the combat power of the Task Force battlegroup, virtually double in size and with much more punch than TF 3-06. In previous rotations the core of the battlegroup was a three-company mechanized infantry battalion, supported by a few artillery pieces, some combat engineers, and air support provided by NATO allies. With one company designed for PRT duty, the first two battlegroups were stretched very thin indeed trying to police and secure a vast area with only two manoeuvre companies (about 300 personnel). TF 1-07 would have another mechanized infantry company, a tank squadron, a designated reconnaissance unit, twice as much artillery, more engineers, and other support.

Equally important to the ultimate success of the battlegroup was its leadership, and this revolved around key individuals. Command rested in the sure and steady hands of LCol Rob Walker, commanding officer of 2RCR, which formed the heart of the battlegroup. A North Battleford, Saskatchewan native with an infectious grin and a sharp intellect, Walker was known as a charismatic and sensitive officer-diplomat. He had honed his skills during two tours in the former Yugoslavia, including one during the early and violent United Nations Protection Force (UNPROFOR) days in 1992–93. Like many Canadian army unit commanders he was also well-educated in modern conflict and operations, and international relations. A graduate of the Canadian Army and Canadian Forces command and staff courses, Walker had also completed a Master's degree in War Studies at the Royal Military College. An avid reader of military history, he made no secret of his intention to educate, as much as to train, his force to be masters of the best practices of counter-insurgency and stability operations.

Walker's leadership was enhanced by the two men who worked closely with him throughout the training program and later overseas. His deputy commanding officer (DCO), responsible for all aspects of the unit's training and planning, was Maj Russell "Rusty" King. A Cape Breton infantry sergeant commissioned from the ranks, King had been a part of 2RCR throughout his whole military career. He had served with the battalion on every one if its major stability missions, including Bosnia, Eritrea, and Haiti. He knew the capabilities of every one of its older hands, and he had handled more than his fair share of young soldiers. King's sense of humour was legendary in the Canadian Army, and so too were his rock steady nerves.

Walker's other key support was his Regimental Sgt-Maj (RSM), Chief Warrant Officer (CWO) Mark Baisley. Baisley was the furthest from a Hollywood sergeant-major that anyone could imagine. Like King, Baisley was a quiet, competent Maritimer, with roots in the heart of New Brunswick's Miramichi River valley. Tall, powerful, with fiery red hair and a commanding presence, the RSM was disarmingly soft spoken, personable, and a firm believer in leading by example rather than through fear. His career had taken him through some of the toughest units and the toughest jobs in the Canadian Army. His breadth of experience and gentle manner were vital to LCol Walker's instructions that there would "be no hat badges in this battlegroup." It was RSM Baisley's job to forge together soldiers from different stations, trades, and regiments with plenty of corresponding differences of approach. He gave Royals, Patricias, Strathconas, Dragoons, Horse Gunners, Sappers, and supporting arms no option but to be on the team. Baisley's method of leading through positive encouragement set the standard for the seven sergeants-major in the sub-units.

The core of Walker's force came from his own battalion, and here, too, he was blessed with bright, energetic, and gifted officers and NCOs. Maj Alex Ruff commanded Hotel Company, and Maj Dave Quick had India Company, 2RCR. The battalion's other sub-unit, Maj Joe Hartson's Golf Company, had served in Afghanistan in 2005 during the last stages of the Kabul deployment and would remain in Gagetown to form the Rear-Party. It was their job to handle the expanding system of support for soldiers deployed overseas and their families.

Other key elements and personnel at the heart of the TF 1-07 battlegroup came from all across Canada. The third infantry company came from the west: Maj Chris Henderson's Charles Company from 3PPCLI, based out of CFB Edmonton, was chosen to complete the roster. Edmonton also contributed the tanks of Maj Dave Broomfield's "A" Squadron of Lord Strathcona's Horse. A fourth mechanized infantry company, from the 3rd Battalion, the Royal 22e Regiment (3R22eR), was assigned to provide security for the PRT.

Each of these officers led a key unit of the Task Force and each had his own small but exceptional staff. At the core of their company or squadron command group was a 2i/c to provide a rear-link to the battlegroup headquarters, a LAV captain to run the Light Armoured Vehicle fleet in the infantry companies (or battle captains with the Tank and Recce Squadrons), and, most importantly of all, a company or squadron sergeant-major. The latter were the senior NCOs in the sub-units, responsible for "man-management" and discipline in camp and for combat resupply and casualty evacuation in action. All were experienced old hands and every one had an equally powerful personality to balance and supplement that of the sub-unit commanders. Between the lot of them, the battlegroup's seven company and squadron sergeants-major had around 200 tours in peacekeeping and stability building missions in every corner of the globe, most of them of the more dangerous, post-Cold War variety. To a man they were driven by extraordinary morale and physical courage.

Alex Ruff was from the Georgian Bay region of Ontario. Tall, shaven headed, athletic, and instantly likable, Ruff's toothy grin and jock-like presentation hid an agile mind that grasped modern stability operations and the task of Afghan reconstruction. Ruff was equally comfortable commanding a heavy mechanized combat team or sitting on a dirt floor cross-legged in the middle of a *shura* with village elders. His 2i/c, Mike Archibald, was an experienced senior captain with a deep voice and a presence that exudes traditional 2RCR quiet professionalism and reliability. Ruff's LAV captain, David Nixon, was unflappable and never without a smile and a laugh to bring tired men to life. This skill would come in handy under fire. Company Sgt-Maj (CSM), Master Warrant Officer (MWO) Wayne O'Toole was the lifeblood of the company. Outwardly tough, the Newfoundlander was a keen observer of the health and well-being of his soldiers, but a lousy singer!

David Quick, a Trenton, Ontario lad was known as something of an outspoken renegade from previous service and operations in Haiti. Fit, extremely confident, and a supreme motivator of soldiers, Quick's sharp mind held a wealth of knowledge of the latest counter-insurgency and stability-building methods, as well as tried and true infantry small-unit tactics. His 2i/c, Capt Mark Coté, was a bright, detail-oriented officer, well-suited to managing the complex plans they would soon have to execute. India Company's LAV captain, Neil Whitman, a short, quiet, and wickedly sardonic father of three (four at time of publication), possessed a keen eye for human behaviour that was to come in handy in *shuras* with village elders. The CSM MWO Stephen Jeans rounded out India Company's leadership cadre. Known for an "infectious" calmness, especially in high-stress situations, Jeans was another one of those long service senior NCOs with a mass of military experience and knowledge that comes from decades of service and tours in war zones. Quick and Jeans proved to be an excellent team.

Chris Henderson and his troops had a western-Canadian Patricia flare about them that made them unique from the more stoic, eastern Royals. Henderson himself was another intelligent, highly adept, and self-reliant renegade, a recurring quality among the sub-unit commanders. As events were about to prove, these characteristics of self-assured independence would become vital to changing the Kandahar dynamic after *Medusa*. Maj Andrew Vivian, Henderson's 2i/c, the odd Maritimer in this western Canadian company, was a planning and organizational workhorse. The company was light-infantry prior to their assignment to TF 1-07. In-theatre, they were to be equipped with the new RG-31 Nyala, a South African light armoured and mine-proof vehicle originally designed for South African police. And so they trained in a kind of motorized infantry role during pre-deployment work-ups. The CSM, MWO Green was short, wiry, and had the stereo-typical paratrooper NCO's low tolerance for BS or lapses of field discipline, thus ensuring Charles Company positions were always ready and defensible.

Tank squadron commander Dave Broomfield was every inch the flamboyant western cavalry officer, cut in the mould of Sir Sam Steele: thick-set and sporting a slightly wild nest of curly hair. Broomfield was a master of all things tank, both technical and especially tactical. He was well-versed in the importance of applying fire with caution, and if the situation warranted he could bring the hammer down on the nail head only. His 2i/c and right hand was Capt Craig Volstad, a native of Edmonton. Another typical cavalryman sporting an equally unruly tuft of blond hair, Volstad was the careful planner and rear link as well as a courageous tank commander in his own right. Boomer's secret weapon, however, was his squadron sgt-maj, MWO Bill Crabb. "A" Squadron of the Strathcona's was a heavy armoured unit that came with the old-style mechanized, manoeuvrable supply echelon that could move alone to find and replenish the squadron wherever it was and, if need be, fight to reach it. Crabb, an old Strathcona with hydraulic fluid for blood, made that system work.

These units—four infantry companies and a tank squadron—formed the heart of the battlegroup, but its supporting elements were extensive and well equipped. Among them was Maj Steve Graham's "A" Squadron of the Royal Canadian Dragoons from CFB Petawawa, which formed the core of a combined Intelligence, Surveillance, Targeting, and Reconnaissance (ISTAR) Squadron for TF 1-07. Armoured "recce," employing the Coyote Armoured Reconnaissance and Surveillance Vehicle, was now accepted as an integral part of any Canadian peace support mission. Their powerful suite of surveillance equipment, that allowed them to observe and gather intelligence over vast areas of real estate, made them the most sought-after piece of equipment deployed by any nation on recent stability operations. Consequently, Coyotes had served as the eyes and ears of commanders in Bosnia, Kosovo, and Kabul. For TF 1-07 the Coyote fleet was augmented by the infantry reconnaissance and sniper sections from 2RCR's Recce Platoon. Combining all the recce troops into a single sub-unit was new and innovative, giving LCol Walker and all the Task Force a powerful information-gathering tool.

Graham, a charismatic, intelligent, lean, and fit leader, was notable for his sensitivity, a characteristic not commonly associated with soldiering. But it was a quality essential for the kind of balance between fighting and negotiating needed on this tour. His squadron 2i/c, Capt Francis Conliffe, supplemented this skill, making the pair perhaps the most critical soldier-diplomat team in the battlegroup. The ISTAR squadron battle captain, Sean Piers, of Simcoe, Ontario, could shift in seconds between being the joker in the command post, to the measured voice over the radio managing enemy contact reports and co-ordinating squadron dispositions. Graham's "man manager" and squadron sgt-maj was MWO Bill Richards. Originally of St. Stephen, New Brunswick, Richards was the hard driver behind training the

Squadron. After having studied operations from previous tours, Richards knew that night operations and night recovery of damaged vehicles while under enemy observation and fire were the toughest challenges facing the force. He was right, and this training emphasis would pay off during the tour.

CFB Petawawa also provided the heavy guns and TF 1-07 had more of them than previous Rotos. The 2006 rotations to Kandahar deployed with two troops of guns, made up of the new M777 155mm howitzers and the old, tried and true 81mm mortars. Since TF 1-07's security zone was going to expand, the artillery protective screen had to increase as well, so a third troop of guns was added. All these came from Maj Dan Bobbitt's "D" Battery of 2nd Royal Canadian Horse Artillery (2RCHA). Bobbitt was close with 2RCR, born the son of a Royal and having served a number of years as a Gunnery Instructor at the Artillery School at Gagetown. His guns could deliver massive destructive power if absolutely necessary, but could also place relatively precise fire down to meet the mission goal of applying force delicately, though not as delicately or precisely as TF 1-07's Leopard tanks. Among the most important things Bobbitt's guns could add were illumination rounds. These parachute flares could light up the night sky for a variety of purposes.

The artillery was a different kind of tool requiring an altogether different kind of leader. Dan Bobbitt was that man. Unlike the other sub-unit commanders with a specific area to dominate, his job was to co-ordinate supporting artillery and air support throughout TF 1-07's area. His guns would be spread across Kandahar province and possibly beyond. So, he had to have eyes on the entire province and a grasp on where every Canadian, NATO, and Afghan unit was located and on what it was doing at any time. He also needed to know about all units in the air and the location of civilians everywhere. It was a huge mental task and a monumental responsibility for one person. Bobbitt, a stocky, good natured, imperturbable gunner with many years' experience, had help from his battery 2i/c Capt Derek Crabbe. It was Crabbe who ran the elaborate staff and the sophisticated tracking and information management system, tied closely to the Tactical Unmanned Aerial Vehicle (TUAV) Squadron, which located everyone, everywhere. To cope with the challenge of supplying and managing the men and women of a sub-unit scattered over a vast area, Bobbitt counted on yet another command force of personality, Battery Sgt-Maj, MWO Chad Wagar. The BSM was especially important at Wainwright for helping to bond together the stock of reserve gunners brought in to bring the battery up to full three-troop strength.

It was also clear by 2006 that the greatest threat to Canadian lives and to the mission itself were improvised explosive devices (IEDs). The battlegroup had to be able to move freely if it was going to provide security for reconstruction, and that magnified the IED risk. It was up to Maj Jake Galuga and his reinforced 42 Field Engineer Squadron from Gagetown to make sure Walker's entire battlegroup could get where it needed to go. Galuga was LCol Walker's engineering advisor and his combat sappers provided a range of services to the battlegroup so that the nuisance attacks from Taliban rockets and mortars and the far more serious land mine and IED threat did not stop the mission. Based on experience from 2006, the squadron deployed more heavily armoured engineer equipment to recover damaged vehicles and to quickly build mine-free combat roads around and behind Taliban strong-points. Not unlike Bobbitt, Galuga would have to lead a unit parceled out to the infantry companies over a large area. It was his task to keep a grip on route conditions, IED danger areas, Forward Operating Base (FOB) defences, and the state of a very hard used fleet of engineer vehicles.

The balance of the battlegroup and the command echelon came from LCol Walker's 2RCR. It provided the signals, electronic warfare, and first-line maintenance troops to the battlegroup. Most important of all, Walker provided the team of conductors for this vast orchestra in the form of his headquarters and operations staff. The headquarters team worked and planned under the direction of the battlegroup operations officer, Maj Eric Pelicano. A veteran of four tours overseas including Bosnia and Kosovo, Pelicano brought a wealth of experience with him. Having served at the national operational co-ordination centre in Ottawa, his management skills and experience were vital to making the battlegroup's moving parts function smoothly and in synch with each other. One major challenge facing the battlegroup staff was that the Afghan Development

Zone had continued to grow, increasing the range of the Task Force's communications net. To overcome this, the battlegroup was linked together by a sophisticated network, complete with redundancies in case of emergency. Making the vast and complex apparatus work 24/7 was the job of Signals Officer Capt Jim Gash and his crew of communications troops.

Pelicano managed a talented and experienced command post staff. 2RCR came with a first-rate stock of Army Operations Course qualified staff captains. The "staff" designation no longer carried the negative connotations that it did during earlier wars. Most of these officers had led platoons on prior missions and understood the machine they were now responsible for co-ordinating. All of them would later shine in Afghanistan, but two already stood out as sources of calm and careful thinking in circumstances of high stress. Capt Rob Tesselaar was responsible for planning future tasks. Capt Mike Plaunt, the senior staff captain who managed the CP, was responsible for handling ongoing operations, including crises. He was another former infantry sergeant commissioned from the ranks, a soldier's soldier and completely the opposite of the staff officer stereotype. Like all the officers and NCOs in TF 1-07 he had been overseas in the midst of war many times before. Plaunt's cool, professional, unflappable voice on the CP radio became familiar during *Maple Guardian*. It would save lives in the months ahead.

At the disposal of the Headquarters staff was a critical and fairly new technology: the TUAV Squadron, which deployed the Sperwer and other unmanned aerial surveillance vehicles. Made up of a mixed bag of air force personnel with flying and aircraft technical skills as well as air-defence artillery soldiers with tracking and communications know-how, this type of unit had been deployed in Afghanistan since 2004. It was especially critical for observing roads and for tracking bomb-layers as they attempted to hide in the multitude of high mud-walled residences that exist all over the country. In an operation where the main enemy tactic was to plant bombs on roads when they hoped no one would see, these very quiet "eyes in the sky" were critical life savers.

The battlegroup included another new type of sub-unit: Capt Shawn Arbing's Tactical Psychological Warfare Team. While the name might conjure up images of sinister efforts to manipulate the minds of the insurgents, these teams are more in the business of corporate communications. As experience had shown, many southern Afghans were unaware that NATO and the UN had arrived to assist them. Arbing, Sgt Randy McCourt, and their small team of Eastern Canadian reservists first had to counter a skillful Taliban Information Operation (IO) campaign that tried to convince the locals that ISAF was just another brutal foreign occupier like the Soviets. The Canadian team then had to convince Afghans in the south that this group of largely white men in armoured vehicles really was there to help.

That message was delivered in visible, material terms by the true centrepiece of this whole Canadian effort: the Provincial Reconstruction Team (PRT). The job of the soldiers, diplomats, CIDA officials, police officers, and other Canadian officials in the PRT was to help make Afghan governance of Kandahar a reality. The military portion of the Canadian PRT was as much a product of Bosnia and Haiti as it was of early American efforts in Afghanistan. TF 1-07's PRT was commanded by LCol Rob Chamberlain, a former gunner officer from 2RCHA. Like all senior officers in the Canadian Army, Chamberlain was a veteran of multiple peace-building missions in tough places. He was no stranger to assisting the suffering while the bullets were still flying. As a young artillery troop leader, he ran humanitarian aid convoys through the barricades to Sarajevo in the ugly days of the early 1990s.

Chamberlain commanded a polyglot organization that looked and behaved like no other unit in the Canadian Army, or any army. In fact, it was not a unit at all, but a collection of bright, energetic minds plucked from regular and reserve units all over Canada. At its core were five teams trained in Civil-Military Co-operation (CIMIC), a concept dating back to the Second World War. Then, the job of civil affairs troops had been to work with local leaders to restore governance and rebuild infrastructure in devastated areas after the battle line moved forward. As it was in the 1940s, the CIMIC Detachments' strength was a body of reservists with skills from the civilian world. They were backed by a Military Police Platoon and a Royal Canadian Mounted Police team. Both of these would have the onerous task of tackling the massive challenges of reforming the Afghan National

Police (ANP) and the Ministry of the Interior, both of which instilled among Afghans more fear and contempt than respect. Foreign Affairs' expertise and dollars would add weight to the police reform effort. Combat Engineers, a medical team, maintainers, cooks, and logisticians were all attached to make the PRT a self-sufficient entity. It worked from Camp Nathan Smith in downtown Kandahar City, separated by miles from the ISAF base at Kandahar Airfield.

The need for a degree of separation had been demonstrated by LCol Hetherington's PRT during TF 3-06 and would prove invaluable in the months to come. To make that possible the mechanized infantry company from the Quebec-based Royal 22e Regiment (R22eR) secured the urban camp and protected mobile PRT teams working on rebuilding tasks outside the wire. Chamberlain's largest, single cohesive unit, the "Vandoos" were the first troops from 3R22eR to deploy in the south.

Michael Callan, manager of CIDA's Kandahar Unit, called the PRT "a platform" on which was based the representatives from Canadian government departments that would help build and professionalize the Afghan government. In order to build trust among local leaders and the population itself, these officials had to distance themselves from the ISAF forces based at Kandahar Airfield and from American counter-terrorist activities. Unfortunately, none of those departments was able to both staff their positions in Kandahar and send people to Wainwright to train alongside TF 1-07. It would not be until the New Year that Chamberlain's PRT soldiers would meet their fellow civilian department colleagues.

Nonetheless, Chamberlain took advantage of the month-long *Maple Guardian* exercise to forge his eclectic collection of individuals into a cohesive unit with a distinct personality. His soldiers had to be compatible with civilian officials, southern Afghan culture, and the more gradual pace associated with international development and government reform programs. So he used the exercise to introduce his troops to that slower operational tempo attuned to civilian agencies with long-term objectives. More than any other part of TF 1-07, their progress could not be immediate and would be measured in how seamlessly they could blend their efforts into what previous PRTs had already accomplished and what would follow.

The National Support Element (NSE) of TF 1-07, that included the supporting base, maintenance, supply, Line of Communication troops, and most of the Task Force Headquarters staff, also joined the exercise at Wainright. However, the Task Force commander, BGen Tim Grant, did not; he was already in Kandahar taking over from BGen Fraser. With few exceptions, then, all the pieces of the Task Force were in place for the final exercise.

Maple Guardian

The CMTC training, which lasted for several weeks in the bitter cold of an early prairie winter, focused on two things. The main effort was a massive confirmation exercise that included all mission components and simulated a "force on force" environment. This was enhanced by a complete outfitting of all Task Force personnel involved with Weapons Effects Simulators. WES gear consists of a laser system fitted to weapons that discharges a short pulse of light when the weapon is fired, and a series of receptors attached to various parts of the body. These allow for the noise and smoke of battle to be simulated effectively, adding a strong dose of reality when the system lets a soldier know that they have been hit by hostile fire. Such equipment had been in use for decades in the Canadian Army but only in very small numbers. The second and equally important goal of Exercise *Maple Guardian* was to train units on the most recent tactics, techniques, and procedures (TTPs) coming out of Afghanistan, based on the experience of the first two rotations to Kandahar.

For much of the exercise, the infantry companies spent their time in isolated FOBs with few of the limited amenities available at Wainwright's mock-up of Kandahar Airfield, such as shower pods and a TV in the mess tent. It was an appropriate introduction for the vast majority of their time would be spent outside the wire, living in their vehicles and "out of bags." Also outside the wire and wearing WES gear were dozens of Afghan-Canadian actors hired to populate the villages and exercise scenarios in this Alberta re-creation of Kandahar Province. That way there would be no doubt if reckless use of weapons produced civilian casualties. The Afghans, all Pashtun speakers and former residents of southern Afghanistan, added an extreme realism to the exercise. When TF 3-06 went through the CMTC the previous year, "civilians" in the exercise were played by what most modern armies use—soldiers out of uniform, and veterans of previous deployments. But senior CF officers wanted to make the training more realistic. This made eminent sense. The demands of disciplined war-fighting in Kandahar Province, where the line between hunting militants and protecting innocent Afghans was mission-critical, allowed no room for error and little time to adjust.

Most soldiers were unaware that real Afghans awaited them in the mock-up villages and walled compounds in Wainwright. India Company was first to meet them when they received a warning order to respond to a simulated suicide bombing in a crowded market. Maj Quick's staff and platoon commanders issued orders to their rifle sections to secure the site, making sure the Taliban were not using reports of mass civilian casualties to lure the Canadians into a trap. Then they would oversee the treatment and evacuation of casualties by International Red Cross staff and Afghan ambulance attendants. This exercise scenario, which involved soldiers trying to create a stable environment in which civilian agencies could deliver their service and expertise without Taliban interference, developed in realistic person-to-person terms. Quick's soldiers would also be on the lookout for evidence that would lead them to the suicide bomb-making cell.

India Company rolled out of the mock-up of Kandahar Airfield mid-afternoon. Their task was to get to the blast site without tripping deliberately-set IEDs, laid with the intention of killing the rescue team. While driving through the cold afternoon, bouncing across country to avoid known danger areas, word crackled across the radio that two powerful IEDs had ripped through a Charlie Company convoy on the other side of the training area. The simulated blasts set off the WES gear in several vehicles, indicating over a score killed and wounded. In a case of dramatic foreshadowing, India Company was now too far committed on its own mission to turn around and intervene. Charles Company and its attached engineer troop had to help themselves, as Quick's men rolled on to deal with their own human catastrophe among Afghan civilians.

The Afghan-Canadian actors who added the crowning touch of realism to *Maple Guardian* were unsung heroes in their own right. Some did the work for the money, although it was hardly the best pay and the working conditions were difficult. On many days the temperature sat in the minus double digits. The Afghan-Canadians found themselves standing as crowds in a mock village in the frigid wind, or lying as blast victims on the frozen ground for hours on end. A good many of these Afghan-Canadians suffered through the cold out of a sense that they were helping their country get back on its feet. And their efforts were not without serious risk; their identities had to be protected so their families still in Kandahar would not be murdered by the Taliban.

The first day's efforts went well enough, and the next day the soldiers and actors were busy again. This time ISAF intelligence identified an IED assembly facility in a village in Charles Company's area. Maj Henderson's troops were to accompanying an Afghan National Police detachment to cordon off the village and search the suspect compounds. The Patricias were to establish an outer cordon keeping Taliban out and an inner cordon to keep any members of the bomb-making cell in, while the ANP officers searched the village. The exercise was designed to remind participating soldiers that their mission could only work if Afghans saw their own government performing professionally and serving on their behalf. The Canadians were there to provide security for the Afghan police.

Unbeknownst to Charles Company, the search exercise was also intended to test their understanding of the need not just to be careful, but to be perfect when in contact with the enemy. While setting up their cordon, Henderson and his men could see Afghan civilians gathered around one of the suspect buildings. Apparently, the Taliban early warning system picked up the Patricias' approach and, as in recent cases in Kandahar, the militants herded townsfolk around the building as human shields. Now, Henderson's men had to move into town and safely move the crowd away from the building before the ANP searched it. As the lead platoon closed in they saw some armed men among the crowd keeping them at the scene at gunpoint, but the Patricias were as yet too far away to do anything about it without firing indiscriminately into the crowd.

When the Charles Company platoon was finally close enough, the Taliban weapons were hidden and the militants blended with the crowd. There was no choice but to press on with the task of backing the crowd up several hundred metres and carrying out the search. As this was being done, the lead Afghan police officer into the building triggered a booby trap bomb and set off his WES gear. Patricias on the inner cordon saw some members of the crowd break and run for it, but none was seen with weapons. This was a crucial moment in the exercise—and an essential validation point in the long period training: do they shoot or not? In the end they chose to not fire. In such terrifying circumstances any human being might bolt. A positive identification of known Taliban or of a weapon, and clear demonstration of an intention to harm someone with it, was needed before shots were fired.

This intense scenario put the Canadian infantrymen's nerves and discipline to the test. Later that evening, during the post-exercise debrief, it was hammered home to all that one innocent Afghan life taken at their hands was mission failure, because the Afghans are the mission. Above all, Canadian troops had to prove themselves worthy to the Afghan people and morally superior to the enemy that held them hostage to fear. The lesson remained with every soldier on the scenario. Every one of them would replay the scenario repeatedly and for real in Kandahar. Thus, the inclusion of Afghan-Canadian actors in these validation scenarios was a critical piece of this mission-specific training.

As cold and miserable as the month at Wainwright was, it yielded enormous benefits. For LCol Walker the most important of these were that it put "every one of us through 'IED university,'" and it brought "all parts of the team together in the field for the first time." Assembling a battlegroup from units based in Gagetown, Petawawa, and Edmonton was not the ideal way of doing business, but *Maple Guardian* showed it could be made to work. As the battlegroup DCO, Maj King observed, everyone needed to "get away from their regular base training areas and into the CMTC 'Box,' away from home, away from the family distractions so they could focus and get in the zone we would need to be in, over there."

Maple Guardian also revealed many glimpses into TF 1-07's future, among them the magnetic, larger-than-life personalities of seven key majors. They inspired their troops in this gruelling exercise in the bitter cold, and would inspire them more in the intense heat and danger of southern Afghanistan.

The TF 1-07 Battlegroup trained hard in Wainwright, knowing they were going to Kandahar to follow up Operation *Medusa* and spread ISAF presence far and wide across the province. If it was going to succeed, this rich collection of leaders would have to summon every ounce of inspiration and command ability they could muster. The proof that it was possible was evident on the snowy, wind-blown prairie in eastern Alberta.

PREPARING OUR "HEARTS AND MINDS"

There were two more types of training to undergo in December 2006 before TF 1-07 deployed to Kandahar early in the New Year. For some years the Peace Support Training Centre (PSTC) at CFB Kingston had run training sessions of varying length to prepare soldiers for the cultural and social environment into which they would deploy. This type of training was particularly critical for troops headed to an isolated Islamic society that viewed all foreigners with suspicion, and where leading by example of good behaviour was critical to winning the respect and faith of Afghans. The PSTC also trained soldiers to understand how those cultural and social conditions connected to the specific threats they would face in their area of responsibility (AOR). When small numbers required the seminar training, they travelled to Kingston. But for larger units, trainers from Kingston or contractors travelled to the unit location.

In December 2006, a contracted team of Islamic and Afghan Pashtu culture and language specialists travelled to Gagetown to teach soldiers, down to the infantry privates, how to avoid offending local sensibilities, how to exchange pleasantries, and how to conduct a meeting with courtesy and win the respect of village elders. A good many officers and NCOs already possessed a wealth of transferable experience meeting with community leaders in a host of other countries, but this would be the toughest cultural divide faced by anyone yet. Therefore, all ranks learned about values and commonly held beliefs of the Afghans. The training team also delivered sessions on the phenomenon of suicide bombers, including the nature of the enemy that produces such a weapon system and the tell-tale signs that a desperate person may be about to martyr themselves.

Every bit as important as cultural training was mental preparation. From the tours in the Balkans, Rwanda, Haiti, and elsewhere it had become clear that the dangers inherent in such intense and diverse operational environments put great strain on soldiers. This, in turn, could lead to widespread and serious operational stress injuries (OSIs), psychological illnesses that resulted from traumatic incidents experienced by soldiers during operational tours, including, but not limited to, post-traumatic stress disorder (PTSD). Realizing that battlefield psychological injuries were just as common as physical ones was a positive development in CF training. Hard-learned lessons from the high tempo of the last 15 years had changed the way soldiers were prepared for deployment, as well as how they were supported once they arrived overseas and later when they returned home. TF 1-07 benefited from the steps taken over the previous decade or more to expand mental health services for troops at home and overseas.

As early as the 1980s, troops preparing for overseas missions had attended Deployment Assistance Groups (DAGs) to make sure they were ready to deploy. Over time, the DAGs carried out by base social workers, mental health nurses, and padres became more thorough. They assessed the soldier's psychological well-being to ensure that each soldier was physically and mentally fit to participate in the mission. The DAGs also considered their social circumstances, including the preparedness of their family to deal with their deployment. Based on the outcome of the DAGs, the troops were categorized as either "good to go"; ready, provided certain issues were addressed before deployment; or, not fit to deploy unless more serious problems were resolved. This system allowed the CF to address many problems before they arose in-theatre and ensured that soldiers were fitter and better able to deal with the stress of operations once they arrived there.[1]

Thus, well in advance of TF 1-07's departure, troops selected for the mission underwent various rounds of medical and psycho-social screening to determine their eligibility to deploy to Afghanistan. Troops also underwent mandatory drug screening in October 2006. Soldiers who failed the drug testing, or were deemed ineligible to deploy for any number of reasons, were transferred out of their sub-units to 2RCR's Golf Company, where they assumed rear party duties.

Knowing what to expect and how to cope with it can go a long way toward preventing a soldier from becoming a stress casualty. This was the message delivered to battlegroup soldiers in December 2006 by West Point psychology professor LCol (Ret'd) David Grossman. His most important theme was that it is a soldier's job to get help when they see PTSD symptoms in their friends or in themselves. He advised troops about what to expect, both physically and mentally, during and after battle in order to "inoculate" them against OSIs.

The other essential part of mental and spiritual preparation for facing violence and suffering was the padre team. Four padres were assigned to TF 1-07, commanded by Maj Malcolm "Mac" Berry, a reservist from the 8th Canadian Hussars in Sussex, NB. The role of the padre or chaplain in the military institution remains what it has always been—to be the spiritual advisor and counsellor to the soldiery and to advise commanders on the mental and spiritual health of the troops. The padres, together with military leadership at all levels, were key to reminding soldiers that this mission in a profoundly Muslim country and culture was not "a war against Islam, but a mission to save Afghans from extremists and criminals who seek power over the weak." Padres also dealt with the difficult problem faced by most soldiers: the use of deadly force. Both Canadian criminal law and social norms forbid the act of killing. Yet the last resort of Canadian troops is to use deadly force against armed and dangerous enemies. One of the most important jobs for the padres then is helping individual soldiers come to terms with this moral dilemma. They must remind them that to use measured violence to stop people who aim to do others harm is just, in the same way a police officer at times must shoot to kill a criminal who threatens the lives of innocent people.

The padres also perform the traditional function of providing religious ministry in the field to soldiers of all denominations and faiths. The number of soldiers openly practicing their religion has dropped dramatically since the Second World War when all soldiers attended church parades. Now the troops come to the padres when they need them. The greatest demand on the padres comes when friends die in action. It was safe to say that in the final days of preparation, every soldier in TF 1-07 hoped the padres would not be required for such work.

The availability of psychological support for troops overseas also had changed during the 1990s. Historically, the padre addressed not only the spiritual needs of the troops but also their mental health concerns and family circumstances. During this period, however, uniformed mental health care workers also began deploying abroad to places like Rwanda where they carried out critical incident de-briefings among Canadian soldiers. Beginning in 1999, CF mental health nurses and later social workers deployed to Bosnia to provide services to the troops in the field, travelling around the Canadian AO giving stress management briefings. Teams made up of mental health nurses, social workers and psychiatrists have also been sent to Afghanistan, especially when the Canadians re-deployed to Kandahar. At Kandahar Airfield they de-briefed soldiers involved in critical incidents and provided stabilization for those showing signs of combat stress. Treatment could consist of short periods of sleep, "talk," and medication before returning them to the field. Occasionally, they travelled outside the wire to FOBs, usually in the company of the padres who know the troops.[2]

Post-deployment treatment for returning soldiers suffering from emotional, psychological, and social problems was expanded during the 1990s. In 1999, the Department of National Defence (DND) stood up five Operational Trauma and Stress Support Centres (OTSSCs) across the country, along with satellite services that reached into numerous military bases. The majority of their clients were soldiers suffering from PTSD and associated conditions like depression and substance abuse. Because some soldiers were reluctant to seek treatment for OSIs, the OTSSC developed a partnership with the Operational Stress Injury Social Support (OSISS) program. Established in 2001, OSISS includes a peer support network funded by DND and Veteran Affairs Canada (VAC) that uses either currently serving members or veterans who have suffered from OSIs themselves and recovered to offer social support for soldiers trying to reintegrate. Receiving support from others who have had similar experiences is thought to help soldiers overcome the stigma that has accompanied mental illnesses and to encourage them to seek care.[3] Fred Doucette,

OSISS's Peer Support Coordinator for New Brunswick and Prince Edward Island, has received "informal referrals" from various sources, including base mental health departments, padres, VAC, unit leadership, and friends of members who were showing signs of stress.[4]

More dangerous missions that often required longer periods of training before deployment also meant higher levels of stress for the families of deploying members. During the 1990s, DND and the CF successfully addressed many long-term problems confronting military members and their families, particularly low pay and pensions, and inadequate housing. Moreover, during this period troops began to receive extra pay and allowances for overseas deployments, most of which was non-taxable. These included the Foreign Service Premium Allowance, a Separation Expense for married or "official" common-law spouses, and the Hostility Premium for those who deployed within a designated Area of Operation.

Beyond these concerns, the military has understood for many years that providing support for the families of deployed soldiers—"the strength behind the uniform"—improved morale by relieving their anxieties about how their loved ones fared back home while they were overseas. Traditionally, this support has been provided at the unit level, especially by rear parties. Frequently, they helped out with such things as snow removal and household repairs. During the early 1990s, other services became available to military families, especially with the advent of the Military Family Resource Centre (MFRC). A not-for-profit grassroots organization begun by military spouses who wanted more services and support, they receive part of their funding from the Director Military Family Services on behalf of DND and the CF, although they operate outside the military's chain of command. The centres are governed by volunteer boards of directors made up of military members and spouses, and are located at bases across the country. They provide CF families with various services and programs, including child care, short-term counselling, and deployment support. The Gagetown MFRC (GMFRC) in Oromocto opened in 1992 and was responsible for central and north-western New Brunswick, including Woodstock and Edmundston. By 2007, 42 centres had been established.[5]

The military has also worked to strengthen ties between deployed soldiers and their families by improving methods of communication between them. Traditionally during deployments, CF personnel had to rely on the mail service, which could be slow and unreliable, especially for those deployed in remote areas like Eritrea. Or the soldiers used the commercial telephone system, which they sometimes had to pay for themselves. More recently, facilities have been set up to allow troops to reach home via telephone, e-mail, and video teleconferencing between overseas bases like Kandahar and local MFRCs.[6]

Steps have also been taken to help troops make the transition from overseas missions to garrison duty and family life back home. In the past, soldiers coming back to Canada were given little or no time to "decompress"; in many cases they simply got off the airplane, met their families, and went home. With the more intense nature of the mission in Afghanistan the CF implemented in July 2002 a "third location decompression" (TLD) program. Troops returning from *Operation Apollo* spent between three and five days in Guam winding down and preparing physically and psychologically for their return home. After reviewing the benefits of the program, in light of intensifying operations in Afghanistan, TLD stops became standard practice in 2005, initially in Dubai and more recently in Cyprus.[7]

The CF has also instituted post-deployment medical screening to assess the soldiers' mental and physical state so that a proper diagnosis can be made and counselling or other services arranged for those needing it. These are usually carried out about three months after the troops return, by which time the normal transitional symptoms a soldier experiences either have been resolved or may be moving into a more serious state. The soldiers complete detailed questionnaires that assess their overall physical and mental well-being, including symptoms of PTSD, depression, anxiety, substance abuse, and family/marital problems. The results are then computerized and sophisticated screening tools used to identify those that might need help. Once the scores have been tabulated the soldiers go through an interview and recommendations are made for further follow-up. The screening also provides the CF with a comprehensive profile of the returning troops which can be used to assess the effectiveness of their current practices.[8] Although some soldiers showing signs of distress are still reluctant to seek psychological services, the majority of those needing help carry through with the recommendations and receive help and support. Fred Doucette stated that the change in attitudes toward OSIs over the last decade has been "quite remarkable." In part, this was attributable to injured veterans from earlier missions in Bosnia, Rwanda and elsewhere making their plight better known.[9] According to Doucette, the war in Afghanistan has also "legitimized" OSIs, partly because of the public's greater awareness of the mission and the CF's role. Finally, mental injuries have now become more widely understood "as the cost of doing business" by the army's leadership, many of whom cut their teeth in missions like Bosnia.[10]

As early as June 2006, 2RCR received briefings from Base Gagetown's mental health department on such subjects as how to identify the signs and symptoms of general, combat-related, critical incident, or reunion stress that would result from re-joining their families, as well as general guidelines on how to care for oneself upon return home. Closely associated with this were measures taken to prepare military families for the deployment so members of the task force could remain focused on the tour and not have to worry about their families back home. Family briefings took place in early December throughout the Atlantic region. Members of the task force command element and rear party, along with representatives from such organizations as the Deployment Support Centre (DSC) and MFRC, met with the troops and their families to inform them about the nature of the mission and the availability of services to family members while the troops were overseas. The GMFRC also did more focused pre-deployment briefings for military families. As well, in January 2007 2RCR developed the 8th edition of their *Family Support Handbook*, and circulated it to the deploying military members, their families and friends. It provided them with detailed information and advice on what the families could do to prepare for the member's coming absence, what support services were available within the community, and a summary of important contact numbers.

These preparations culminated in a huge Red Friday rally at Base Gagetown's gymnasium on 19 January 2007. Despite the wintery weather, it was attended by hundreds of troops from the base, many about to deploy, their families, and members of the local community. One of the highlights of the rally was the creation on the snow-covered playing field of the largest human Canadian flag ever organized, by hundreds of military and civilian participants holding up sheets of red Bristol board for the photographer suspended high above the crowd. It was an inspiring display of support for the troops about to leave for Afghanistan.

Mission-specific training wrapped up in December, at which point all were granted leave for the Christmas season. They would need the break, for early in the New Year there were final kit checks before TF 1-07 boarded planes to ferry them to Kandahar. Some took comfortable civilian airlines, others the equally comfortable CF Airbus passenger aircraft to a staging area in the Middle East. There they would acclimatize to the heat and marry up with weapons and tactical equipment. The final leg of their journey to Kandahar was in the cramped, canvas-webbed seats of a noisy, stomach-churning but ever reliable C-130 Hercules.

SETTLING IN

Under the overcast skies of late January and early February 2007, chalk after chalk of C-130s unloaded the troops of Task Force 1-07 (TF 1-07) onto the tarmac at Kandahar Airfield. As the fresh troops deployed, over the next few weeks LCol Omer Lavoie's battle-weary soldiers of TF 3-06 boarded the same C-130 transport aircraft for their return home.

TF 1-07 arrived in Kandahar with the rain, that came down in amounts not seen in ten years. It caused natural mountain cisterns to fill, water-courses to run in spate, and roads to wash out. While International Security Assistance Force (ISAF) troops struggled to keep their base from flooding, Kandaharis rejoiced. The end of the drought brought renewed hope and new opportunity to a destitute people. It also gave TF 1-07 a real chance to jump-start the rebuilding process through the first two months of the deployment.

As TF 1-07 settled in at Kandahar Airfield, the insurgency was in seasonal remission. After their severe pounding during *Operation Medusa,* the Taliban needed the winter months to re-organize and regenerate. What ISAF and the Afghan government called the "Tier 1" force—the hardcore Taliban fighters deeply committed to the extremist cause—was either lying low in Kandahar or had fled west into Helmand Province or east into Pakistan. These men came primarily from refugee camps and *madrassas* (religious schools) along the Pakistani border, but many were foreigners: Chechens, Saudis, Palestinians, among others. The "Tier 2" Taliban or the "part-timers" included local Taliban and drug-trafficker militias, as well as young, angry, often unemployed, local men. They melted back into the local population and waited for the next fighting season to start in the spring. It also helped that refugees from the 2006 fighting in Zharey and Panjwayi Districts were back in their villages, and that Canadian and Afghan troops were now permanently installed in those areas. For all these reasons, Taliban activity in Kandahar Province was at low ebb when TF 1-07 arrived.

But no one thought that the Taliban was down for the count. Their resurgence in the summer of 2006 had demonstrated not only resilience, but also their deep roots in the area. Intertwined with local clans and the drug lords, the line between them completely blurred, the Taliban was also present in the "hearts and minds" of the population. More feared than loved to be sure, they nevertheless remained a powerful force in Kandahar Province. That would not change unless ISAF and the Afghan government asserted their authority over the countryside. This was the challenge, and the opportunity, that awaited TF 1-07 in early 2007.

But of all the things happening in the countryside that winter, nothing was more important than the rain. Among the memories many TF 1-07 soldiers have of their first months in-theatre was the Afghan New Year (*Nowroz*) festivities featuring traditional music, dancing, and a feast of local delicacies. Few Afghans could have known then that this New Year's celebration marked a real new beginning, but the rain might have seemed like a good omen. The time was ripe for change. More importantly, it was time for the Canadian mission in Kandahar to refocus on its central mission—reconstruction—because the hopes of Kandaharis would not be realized without it.

For the moment, the attitude of Kandaharis toward Canadian and ISAF forces was still uncertain. Many had been won over, especially in Kandahar City, but in the countryside others were undecided. The post-*Medusa* environment can perhaps be described as an armed election campaign in which the people of southern Afghanistan faced a tough decision. Two potential state systems were campaigning against one another: the insurgents, who offered a tyrannical, authoritarian system of feudal servitude, and a more hopeful, but still unproven, government of Afghanistan, backed by the UN and NATO. With which authority would they enter into a new social contract?

The key issue was human security: whichever side could provide the greater protection for families and help sustain their simple livelihood would win. Afghans voted with their feet—and often their lives. And it was not simply a choice between good and evil. Support for the Taliban and a willingness to take up arms as a Tier 2 fighter might have reflected anger about corrupt police. Likewise, farmers enslaved to drug lords might have had little choice other than to join the insurgency. On the other hand, supporting ISAF and the new government might mean gaining a new road or irrigation rebuilding project, or the chance to plant wheat or grapes rather than opium. But Kandaharis would cast their votes that way only if the return was good enough to provide for families and only if the work was safe enough. Some wanted tangible proof that life under the new government and its police would be better than under the Taliban. Others merely wanted both sides to leave them in peace. This "election campaign" would be fought bitterly in 2007.

To win that "election" the Canadians and newly readied Afghan troops had to push the security zone deeper into the agricultural heartland. However, if 2006 had proved anything it was that southern Afghans needed more than a guarantee of security to win their support for the government. The Canadians needed to carry on the painstakingly slow process of earning trust, delivering aid, and advancing reconstruction while simultaneously reforming and expanding the provincial government. This is the story of the subsequent march from Route Summit into western Zharey District and beyond. The aim was to dominate that vital oasis and create a security zone around the most populous areas where the Provincial Reconstruction Team, the Afghan government, and aid agencies needed to work. It would prove a difficult task.

THE FACE OF WAR

TF 1-07 troops began taking over 1RCR Battlegroup's positions and LCol Hetherington's PRT in late January and into February, allowing time for the outgoing leaders to bring their replacements up to date on the situation. Most TF 1-07 sub-units were in place by 16 February: the day before the 2RCR Battlegroup and headquarters officially took over security duties in Kandahar Province. On that day, as if to remind the newly arrived Canadians of why they were needed, a young boy and a man were brought to the main gate of

Patrol Base Wilson, home of the district police station as well as Maj Dave Quick's India Company HQ.

The 12-year-old boy, from the UN refugee camp north of the highway, was a mass of third-degree burns and blast wounds. He was the victim of an IED, probably intended for the foreign aid workers who frequented the camp. The injuries called for more than the rudimentary first aid available at the police station or even from India Company medics. Injured Afghans generally went to the International Red Cross-supported Mirweis Hospital in Kandahar City. The injured man could make it to the civilian hospital, but time was of the essence for the boy. Maj Quick radioed for a medevac helicopter and within minutes it was on the way to lift the boy to the base hospital at Kandahar Airfield, a procedure normally reserved for soldiers with traumatic battle wounds.

The incident left a deep impression on many who witnessed it. This was their first real encounter with an enemy who used terrorist violence to achieve their aims. For Canadian soldiers trained in the laws of armed conflict, the deliberate targeting of civilians was more than just unlawful; it was evil. To the India Company troops, maiming a child was certainly a strange way for the Taliban to convince Afghans that they deserved to rule.

THE TASKS AT HAND

The immediate task for the military component of Canada's Joint Task Force Afghanistan was to secure, patrol, and expand the Kandahar Afghan Development Zone (ADZ). This included the city itself and the greenbelt districts adjacent to it. The concept of securing decisive population and economic hubs and then spurring government reform and development came out of the 2006 Afghan National Development Strategy. These ADZs, in turn, drew upon the time-honoured "expanding inkblot" method of state-building and counter-insurgency employed successfully by the British in Malaya in the 1950s. The strategy called for areas to be rendered comparatively safe from violence and coercion, while local security forces were stood up and economic and social life revitalized. In theory, the normalcy and prosperity that took root in those first inkblots would become contagious and spread to neighbouring communities.

To make the ADZ inkblot secure and viable, military and civilian planners understood that the Canadian battlegroup and the Afghan National Army first had to reduce Taliban military activity in the countryside. The battlegroup's role in this strategy was to continue whittling away at Taliban access to the Kandahar ADZ by rooting out sleeper cells, bomb-making teams, and enemy agents living and operating within it. Given that the drug-traffickers and the Taliban were intertwined and that many government and police officials were corrupt, clearing the Kandahar ADZ would take time.

This part of the mission was also closely attached to the second TF 1-07 task, which was to "deliver immediate reconstruction" to communities in need, and to the third objective of building the capacity of the Government of Afghanistan. The latter was a hugely complex job of untangling corruption in existing government, training and mentoring officials, and setting up new parts of the provincial public service. It was the toughest and most critical part of Canada's mission and the part whose results were the most difficult to measure.

To facilitate these tasks, the battlegroup had to open road access from the country to Kandahar City. While this would enhance security, it also would restore economic ties; in fact, these two objectives were closely entwined. In particular, as LCol Walker explained to his company commanders and soldiers, they had to ensure the safe flow of commercial traffic on Highway 1 between Kandahar City and Helmand Province to the west, and improve the flow of all civilian traffic. Walker later recalled that "restoring civilian freedom of movement was key to getting life back to something like normal in Kandahar."[1]

Highway 1 was part of the 3,000-kilometre Afghan national highway known to most as the Ring Road. Keeping open the section west of Kandahar City meant never allowing Taliban military forces to gather in strength there as they had done the year before. Doing that meant patrolling all of the farming villages in Zharey and Panjwayi Districts, keeping Taliban cells off balance. Closely tied to this effort was the task of improving Afghan governance by supporting the police in their bid to spread the rule of law into the countryside. In essence, Walker's battlegroup planned to clear and patrol Zharey–Panjwayi to render those areas safe for the ANP to establish stations and checkpoints there.[2]

The other goal behind these presence and security patrols was to negotiate a new relationship with the people of Zharey–Panjwayi, to encourage them to be part of a new Afghan government solution to the country's problems. Every patrol had to include conversations with locals, of the kind begun before *Medusa,* but now on a much larger scale. In a process sometimes referred to by the hackneyed counter-insurgency phrase "winning the hearts and minds," Walker's troops were trying to put hope back in the hearts of Afghan people and to give them peace of mind.

It was clear, even in the comparative calm of that rainy February, that the Taliban would strongly resist this process; they would come back and fight. Walker's troops would have to disrupt that intended return, and separate hardcore Tier 1 insurgents from the farmers and other part-timers pressed into service as Tier 2 fighters. And when it came to a fight—as it surely would—violence would have to be meted out with extreme care and discrimination.

To help meet these complex goals, the 2RCR Battlegroup became the first Canadian rotation to partner with an ANA Kandak (Battalion) for the duration. The 2nd Battalion, 1st Brigade, 205th Hero Corps (2/1/205) of the Afghan National Army (ANA) had been training with a Canadian Operational Mentoring and Liaison Team (OMLT) since mid-2006 and was now ready for operations. Led by LCol Shereen Shah Kohbandi, a veteran soldier with a powerful command presence and a keen understanding of the Zharey–Panjwayi area, this battalion was, many believed, the most capable and professional Kandak in the entire ANA. Its rifle companies were ready to help plan and conduct joint patrols with the battlegroup. No one doubted that it would face a tough fight against the Taliban, but Shereen Shah's toughest job would be proving to Kandaharis that his troops were competent, high-quality public servants of an Afghanistan worth believing in.

Securing Zharey–Panjwayi: Phase One

The process of securing the Canadian area of operations (AO) area west of Kandahar City began immediately after the battlegroup arrived. Walker wasted little time after deploying into the Forward

Operating Base (FOB) at Ma'Sum Ghar in February and taking over the strong-points up and down Route Summit. His troops immediately began pushing patrols throughout Zharey–Panjwayi and as far west as the Helmand border. All of TF 1-07's units focussed on asserting the Canadian presence throughout the area and getting to know the people they had come to help.[3] In a gesture of goodwill to lay the groundwork for re-opening relations with locals, LCol Walker shut down the regular test firing of weapons and registration of artillery around Route Summit. His troops took every advantage of the winter lull to restore freedom of movement around the ADZ for UN workers and their counterparts in the PRT. The PRT needed to get back on track with its National Solidarity Program (NSP) tasks before the traditional fighting season began in May—after the poppy crop was harvested and men and money became available for the insurgents. Restoring stability was also vital so that the people of Zharey–Panjwayi, driven from their homes during heavy fighting the previous summer, could settle back in and get ready for a planting season that promised to be the best in a decade.

Maj David Quick's India Company took over their strong-points and started patrolling the eastern end of Zharey District. In the absence of Taliban activity, the infantry soldiers and their attached engineers roamed freely about the area on foot, talking to locals through translators whenever possible, carefully studying the terrain, and learning how the people of Zharey lived. Quick's troops soon realized that the tense standoff atmosphere that prevailed during the previous tour was gone. They therefore used this grace period to patrol deeper into Zharey.[4]

Company Sgt-Maj (CSM) Steve Jeans recalled that they quickly learned which villages were used by the Taliban as bases and safe-areas, and which were unmolested. Some of the villages with signs of Taliban activity also seemed to be more affluent and tied to opium production. This confirmed what the Canadians already suspected—that the line between the Taliban and the drug-traffickers was so blurred that it perhaps no longer existed. Quick's company also soon developed an estimate of how the Taliban moved in and out of the area, which would prove quite accurate in a few months' time.[5] Among other things, they learned how local farmers worked the irrigation system, and how to tell the difference between farmers opening up small canal gates at night and a Taliban IED cell planting explosives in the roads.

While Quick's troops spread out from Route Summit, Maj Alex Ruff's Hotel Company linked up with the Strathconas' "B" Squadron tanks, led by Maj.Trevor Cadieu (Broomfield's tankers were not scheduled to arrive until March). The infantry-armour combat team patrolled virtually everywhere in Zharey–Panjwayi. They protected themselves from IEDs by travelling with armoured engineers and the latest counter-IED equipment, and enjoyed the benefit of being the first ISAF soldiers into a number of villages. Ruff and Cadieu sought to reassure locals, afraid of a Taliban return, that the Canadian battlegroup could go wherever it wanted, whenever it wanted, and was not deterred by IEDs and mines. The sight of a large column of heavy armoured vehicles in rugged, remote, and close terrain impressed the population.

These February patrols were tightly wedded to an operational plan to keep Canadians mobile and to expand the presence and effectiveness of the Afghan National Police. The idea was that Canadian presence would underwrite the authority of the ANP and protect them while they pursued their path toward professional improvement, as the United States committed considerable financial and human resources to ANP reform. Newly recruited policemen were coming out of regional training centres kitted out with new equipment and uniforms. The hope was that a much improved ANP would be at the centre of the security solution in areas cleared by ISAF in the New Year. But it takes years to fashion an effectice police service and so far only modest progress had been made in rooting out corruption in the ANP and in the Afghan Ministry of the Interior which oversaw them. ANP units and leaders in Kandahar in early 2007 had improved from a year earlier, but unevenly. Now they were a widely mixed bag of the capable, professional, and effective, as well as the pitiful, crooked, and worse than useless. Unfortunately, this reality was largely still unknown to the Canadian Task Force.

As far as TF 1-07 was concerned, new ANP units and commanders arriving would make a positive difference. And that would go a long way toward Canadian Department of Foreign Affairs efforts to mentor and support the governor of Kandahar Province, to whom police commanders were responsible in the eyes of Kandaharis. February and March was thus a period of gradual awakening in the Canadian Task Force that the ANP were still a long way from being able to do their jobs properly.

Fortunately, Canadian patrols, district *shuras*, and Community Development Councils (CDCs) made it clear that local Afghans differentiated between their own corrupt police and the skilled and well-intentioned international soldiers, who were actually providing far more security in Zharey–Panjwayi than the locals were accustomed to. Thus, Canadians and ISAF were respected now as part of the solution. So unlike 2006, when the locals took up arms against ISAF as well as the corrupt ANP, resentment now focused solely on the ANP and its shakedowns at checkpoints. This was a major step forward.[6] However, for the soldiers of Hotel and India Companies, tasked with setting up those checkpoints, lingering problems with the ANP were a major disappointment. The battlegroup's solution was to take over direct control of policing in the Area of Operation by pushing Military Police (MP) detachments out into the field to monitor and mentor ANP stations. The PRT had started this first inside the city at the beginning of the year, but it was difficult to achieve in the rural areas until the battlegroup established its presence there. Sorting out the police remained the pre-eminent challenge for Canadians throughout TF 1-07, but in early 2007 many believed that the police problem was on the way to being solved.

Although things were much quieter during the initial phase of TF 1-07's deployment than they had been the previous fall, the Taliban were not entirely inactive and violence was present from the outset. In early February two incidents captured headlines at home in Canada and brought to the forefront the need for the utmost care in the use of weapons. The first occurred during an ambush of a Canadian convoy in Kandahar City. Several rocket-propelled grenades (RPGs) struck vehicles, fire was exchanged, and a policeman was killed by a stray 25mm cannon shot. A civilian, who failed to heed warnings not to approach the disabled convoy, was also shot. No matter that the convoy was in a running fight; everyone recognized greater care was needed, especially inside the densely populated city.

The second incident happened a few days later when a man approached a convoy wearing what appeared to everyone as a suicide bomber's vest, complete with wires protruding from his shirt. The man appeared distraught and he chanted while the crew commander of the lead vehicle signalled for him to stop and move away from the convoy. Warning shots did not drive him off, a burst over his head and then at his feet failed to deter him. The crew commander decided he could not take the chance. The next bullets cut the potential bomber down. After setting up a cordon around the man and bringing up explosives specialists to investigate, a bundle of wires, but no bomb, was found under the dead man's shirt.

Just what he was doing with a shirt full of wire and why he failed to heed warnings to get off the road may never be known. It smelled like a deadly set-up. What was clear, however, was that the Taliban immediately launched into a well-scripted information campaign pushing the message that Canadians did not care about where their bullets landed. This version was given global media attention, especially in Canada where doubts were raised about the professionalism and training of the troops. If this was the nature of the Taliban enemy, and if information was to be their key weapon, then every Canadian in Afghanistan was reminded again how force must be applied carefully. The decision to use it would always be split-second and, given that an enemy was trying to kill them, soldiers had to be prepared to kill to protect themselves and drive out that enemy. No man knew it more clearly than LCol Walker, the crew commander in the lead vehicle on that day who shot down the decoy bomber.[7] After that incident, no soldier of TF 1-07 could claim that their CO did not understand the difficult challenges they all faced. Walker made the only decision possible to protect his convoy that day. When the story spread quietly among TF 1-07 soldiers, they actually felt more confident that their rules of engagement could protect them.

* * *

And so, as Ruff's Hotel Company, Cadieu's tank squadron, and one of LCol Shereen Shah's infantry companies rolled down Highway 1 into the heart of Taliban country on 23 February 2007, the perils of accidentally shooting civilians were fresh in their minds. They would need all the judgement and fortitude they could muster. The objective of Ruff's small force—one of the first joint Canadian-Afghan, infantry-armour operations in Kandahar—was Howz-e-Madad, a cluster of hamlets south of the arterial road. Home to notorious Taliban leader Mullah Manan, it was known to be tightly in the Taliban's clutches. Like almost every patrol Canadian troops conducted during this tour, Ruff's group had multiple tasks. First, responding to intelligence, it was going to conduct a search for a large weapons and explosives cache reported to be in the area. Second, LCol Walker wanted Ruff to defy Taliban-imposed limits on ISAF and ANA mobility, by driving this large force all the way into Maywand District and having his first *shura* with the chief of police. By doing so, Ruff would be showing the Afghan, Canadian, and ISAF flags in the furthest, western reaches of Kandahar Province.

The combined force rolled westward, gun turrets sweeping the brown winter landscape for possible threats. In February this greenbelt was not yet green. After final crops were harvested in the fall, and the foliage dropped from the trees, the mud-walled houses and yards blended in colour with the fields and roads, making the entire landscape south of the highway appear desolate. If anything, the north side was worse: mostly barren, gravel desert, too far from the Arghandab River to be watered and cultivated like the ground south of the highway. The open terrain on both sides of the road thus offered clear vision at good distance into empty grape and poppy fields. Eventually, the column deployed in fields around the suspect house and walled yard where the explosives cache reportedly was located. The Canadian troops and tanks set up a security cordon, allowing Afghan troops to do the search and seizure without fear of being ambushed.

The tip proved accurate and, before long, Afghan troops emerged with mortar bombs and rockets. Ruff's attached engineer troop and a bomb-sniffing dog team cleared the area for traps and extracted the explosive ammunition, while the rest of the Canadian-Afghan combat team readied to move back out of the hamlet. Whether stirred by the seizure of their bomb-making supplies, or by the presence of this patrol deep in their territory, this was the moment that the

Taliban force struck. They suddenly sprang a series of small ambushes all around the area. What followed was almost a replay of one of the Wainright training exercises.

The potential for disaster was high, not least because the Taliban force was large, but also because it struck between the Canadian and Afghan companies in the midst of a populated area. Local civilians scurried to escape. However, Ruff's men returned fire as they were trained: carefully. One Taliban section opened up on Hotel Company's 4 Platoon with RPG and automatic weapons fire. The RPG operator was killed instantly by an accurate burst of return fire. But it was the Afghan company, the engineer troop, and the dog team that was in the centre of the largest ambush. For the first and definitely not the last time on this tour, LCol Shereen Shah's men demonstrated their bravery and small unit tactical skill, as they returned fire and pursued the ambush party, killing four. Meanwhile, one of the Canadian engineer sections and Capt David Nixon's LAV became the focus of Taliban attention, receiving a volley of rockets and rifle fire. Nixon had the option of dropping into the safety of his turret and directing his 25mm cannon and coaxial-mounted machine-gun to return fire, but that would have fallen in the midst of the village. Instead, Nixon opted for precision. He remained exposed in the hatch of his LAV and knocked down several enemy riflemen with the C-6 machine gun on the turret.[8]

The whole firefight was over in minutes, but was highly noteworthy. A combined Canadian-Afghan force had successfully conducted a cordon and search operation, and had fought the Taliban on their home turf in the presence of unarmed civilians. There seemed little doubt that the ambush was sprung with the intention of provoking a disproportionate response, possibly even artillery fire or air strikes to flatten the village. But this day the Taliban were foiled. Not one civilian was hurt, and because force was returned "in-kind" or with small arms fire, there was no damage to property. It was a small-scale action compared to the battles for Pashmul six months earlier, and it got no attention in the Canadian media at all. But some might argue it was warfare Afghan-style: close infantry combat in a fashion which southern Afghans respect. The event sent a strong message to the people of western Zharey. The Canadians and their own soldiers were prepared to come right into the Taliban heartland and look them in the eye.

The small battle was also important because it strengthened the confidence and mutual respect between the ANA and the Canadians. It proved that they could indeed patrol and fight together, safely and successfully. One of the key figures in that co-ordinated action was Maj Ruff's 2i/c, Capt Mike Archibald, who acted as the key rear comms link. Using all the technology available to him, he kept track minute by minute of the location of every Canadian and Afghan soldier in the fight and kept it flowing on the radio. That prevented soldiers from the same team from firing at each other in the heat of action.

These first small clashes between the battlegroup and the Taliban indicated an important change from the year before, when Berry's convoy was attacked. Instead of trying to disrupt the work of the PRT, the Taliban now seemed to be focussing their attacks on ISAF combat troops, intending either to kill them or to trick them into firing on innocent Afghans. It was clear that the Taliban wanted to turn western nations against the Afghan mission, by making the costs too high or by making their troops appear to be reckless killers.[9] These attacks also respresented a feeble and unsuccessful attempt to limit ISAF's mobility in Kandahar. As a result, the Taliban were drawn to the battlegroup like moths to a flame, while the PRT focused on reconstruction. This was exactly how the ISAF mission had been conceived a year before. The Taliban were following ISAF's script to the letter.

The PRT Gets Down to Business

Meanwhile, the work of LCol Rob Chamberlain's PRT, the UN, and other agencies in the Kandahar ADZ took off like a rocket. The winter quiet and the Taliban's focus on the battlegroup meant that the PRT could move freely and ramp up the pace of its work. Guarded by LAV-mounted infantry platoons from the Royal 22e Regiment, Civil-Military Co-Operation (CIMIC) detachments, Mounties, Corrections Canada workers, CIDA officials, and Foreign Service officers flowed across the area with the kind of mobility not seen since Glyn Berry's time. *Shuras* did not make news back home, but they were essential in Kandahar and were pursued vigorously by PRT during February and March. The PRT also moved with a clearer sense of purpose, building on the previous eight months of negotiation and relationship-building, and community and infrastructure needs assessments.

The reconstruction focus was two-fold. Kandahar City needed to function like a normal urban centre if the local economy was to take off. A thriving city was vital to the PRT's other main task: restoring Kandahar's agricultural capacity. Farmers needed a functioning city, complete with food production facilities, water, sewers, and power if their crops were going to find a market. So the PRT devoted a lot of attention to restoring basic city services, training municipal government, getting young people into schools, and paving the way for businesses to get back on their feet. The irrigation system had to be repaired to take advantage of the heavy winter rain. So too did the secondary road network. Farmers needed a working road grid if they were to move produce into the city. The PRT had its work cut out for it.

Finding out what to do fell to Maj Shawn Courty's CIMIC operators. These teams became the eyes and ears of CIDA and the National Solidarity Program in the high-risk areas inside the ADZ. The NSP normally was administered by a combination of UN workers and Afghan Ministry of Rural Rehabilitation and Development. That approach had to be modified for Zharey and Panjwayi Districts. In those areas, CIMIC detachments often met directly with the CDCs. By using uniformed members of the PRT, working alongside local groups, it was possible to push the NSP even into areas not fully secured. The key was careful local consultation, something badly needed in districts caught in a squeeze between the Taliban, drug-traffickers, and corrupt officials. The NSP concept of allotting small amounts of project money directly to village elders made it difficult for the money to enter the wrong hands or be otherwise wasted. In these instances PRT projects were a compromise, but still much better than the poorly planned quick-impact projects of the earlier years.

Thus, one of the core functions of the CIMIC detachments in early 2007 was co-ordination between the various groups who were trying to help in Kandahar. PRT soldiers in the communities served as monitors and information gatherers, detailing what Kandaharis wanted, recording what was missing or needed, and ensuring that the rebuilding projects paid for were actually delivered. Project follow-through and ensuring accountability were critical means of ensuring that Canadian reconstruction dollars did not end up lining the pockets of warlords or corrupt government officials. The PRT detachments also tracked who was reliable in the province—particularly government officials and police. Given that the lack of educated and capable people to lead Kandahar's regeneration was a serious challenge to the mission's success, establishing an organization dedicated to monitoring human resources was critical.[10]

The third major piece of the Kandahar mission was also back in full swing by early 2007. PRT political director Gavin Buchan, along with LCol Chamberlain and his adjutant, Lt Mark Timms, worked with Governor Khalid's provincial administration to move beyond the security issues and get on with the business of governing, reconstruction, and rooting out corruption. Buchan stood at the centre of a brand-new civilian mentoring and advisory team, working on government reform and mentoring. RCMP Superintendent Dave Fudge laid into the job of police reform. A Correctional Services of Canada detachment, led by Louise Garwood-Filbert, was on the ground and wading into the onerous job of improving the quality of Sarposa Prison. Like the rest of the PRT, thanks to the work of the battlegroup Garwood-Filbert's officers could now reach the prison in safety and start their task. So, in February 2007, the PRT hit the ground running and did not stop.

The Maywand Deployment

Security and development work in the Kandahar ADZ during this period was greatly assisted by developments in Helmand Province. Regional Command South's plan was to disrupt the insurgency by patrolling into previously undisturbed Taliban-held "no-go areas." The Helmand River from Lashkar Gah northward into the Sangin Valley was known to shelter Tier 1 Taliban survivors from the fighting around Pashmul in 2006. It was also there that the lion's share of southern Afghanistan's opium poppy was grown, and where the Taliban/drug-trafficker marriage of convenience was strongest.

The task of breaking this stronghold fell to the British Army brigade. Working with Estonian and Danish contingents, Special Forces, and several ANA Kandaks, it launched *Operation Achilles* in the first months of 2007. Their ultimate objective was to create another ADZ around the Kajaki hydro-electric dam on the Helmand River. Getting the turbines back on line would provide electricity to large swaths of southern Afghanistan, including Kandahar Province. The impact of this was potentially highly significant, not least by powering water pumps that could triple agricultural capacity. Once they established a secure environment, the British PRT based out of Lashkar Gah could begin delivering projects. Forcing the Taliban to fight for Helmand Province during those critical late winter months bought Canada's Task Force enough time and stability to build the trust and consensus in Kandahar's rural districts so necessary for rebuilding there.

Nevertheless, in March TF 1-07 deployed a heavy mechanized combat team to the open desert in the District of Maywand near the Helmand border to support *Operation Achilles*. Alex Ruff's Hotel Company got the job, joined by Maj Broomfield's newly arrived "A" Squadron of Lord Strathcona's Horse, operating the Leopard tanks. They drove west in late March, covered by Bobbitt's artillery and parts of Jake Galuga's 41 Engineer Squadron. Reminiscent of the Western Desert campaign in the Second World War, their job was to dominate the open desert of Maywand and the main routes through it. They were at once to keep ISAF troops and supplies flowing west and to prevent any Taliban from escaping east. With their LAVs and Leopards, the Hotel Company Combat Team had the armour and off-road mobility to own the desert.

For the British, Estonian, and Danish troops in Helmand, this was war. The Taliban fiercely resisted ISAF and Afghan government expansion into their logistics base. But on the Canadian side of the Helmand frontier LCol Walker encouraged Ruff to seize the opportunity to spread the reform and rebuilding message to the scattered farming villages of Maywand. It seems that the combat team's counter-insurgency and peace-building training paid off. Although this heavily armed team had the power to do the worst when the situation warranted, that power was seldom used during *Operation Achilles*. Instead, the mere presence of this mobile team seemed to be enough to keep the Taliban at bay.

The primary role of Ruff's armoured and mechanized infantry combat team was to guarantee the safe passage of ISAF convoys travelling from ISAF's main southern base at Kandahar Airfield to Task Force Helmand. At times they also came to the rescue of lighter US and British convoys, especially when vehicles became immobilized by mines and IEDs. On one occasion Dave Broomfield's tankers were called in to assist an American 82nd Airborne Division convoy which ran into a nest of mines and IEDs, losing half a dozen of their light Humvees. Two of the Strathcona's tanks, equipped with mine ploughs and commanded by WO T.W. Hopkin and Sgt T.P. Hiscock, cleared a safe lane through to the US convoy and to each of its damaged Humvees. The lightly equipped US airborne troops were deeply impressed. It would not be the last time that Boomer's tanks proved their value in this way.

Apart from improvised bombs and mines, the only way the Taliban could take on the Hotel Company Combat Team was with 107mm rockets. And so, rocket attacks became part of the routine in Maywand in March. The threat seemed real enough until everyone realized that the rocketeers were poorly trained; none came close to hitting much of anything. Most landed while the formation was in "leaguer" (formed into a square or other shape for all-round defence) at the end of the day.[11] The combat team set up a new leaguer in a new location each night. Taliban units tried with limited success to keep tabs on the Canadian's armoured phalanx, and had to be content with the occasional rocket attack when it stopped astride their main east-west communications route.

"Leaguer-life" was only for "heavy-metal" soldiers. The infantry soldiers, tankers, engineers, and gunners in the combat team spent those weeks "sleeping in a bag, eating out of a bag, and crapping in a bag." No one showered for four weeks, while temperatures climbed steadily during the day, and plunged to near freezing in the desert night. CSM Wayne O'Toole kept the morale and discipline up in spite of it all. So too did tank Squadron Sgt-Maj Bill Crabb, who ran the sophisticated system for keeping the constantly moving force supplied. Fuel, ammunition, water, food, spare parts for the aging Leopards, and anything else Crabb could lay his hands on to keep the soldiers' spirits up, found Ruff's team no matter where they leaguered-up in western Kandahar Province. Maj Ruff kept them busy, too, pushing the governance reform and reconstruction agenda. The infantry and tankers provided security for his meetings with village elders. The Canadians pushed meetings of the Maywand *shura*, so that a CIDA project aimed at agricultural infrastructure could move on repairing irrigation canals and reservoirs, to provide water during the coming crop season. The combat team also conducted joint vehicle checkpoint operations with the ANP.

This latter task focussed the attention of everyone in the combat team on the lingering problem of ANP corruption. The Maywand detachments still had a long way to go toward reform. Within minutes of setting up joint traffic-control checkpoints and stopping trucks, the policemen were taking payment from drivers in produce or cash. Ruff and his troops immediately put a stop to it, but the moment their backs were turned the practice resumed. Ruff saw it as simply "part of the culture out there, the police weren't shaking drivers down so much as they were just taking melons and bags of almonds." While such corruption may have been the norm, or even necessary so the policemen could support their families, it was still unacceptable. By this time, Canada's Task Force Afghanistan Headquarters was already making plans to permanently ensconce mentors with police detachments and substations. But it would be some months before the manpower was available in quantity to effect significant change. For now, Ruff's combat team had to accept frustration and try to lead by example.

In late March, as the battle for the Sangin Valley and the hot pursuit of fugitive Tier 1 units in Helmand continued, the need for NATO resources increased. The combat team's convoy escort duties through the desert grew in tandem with the rising British demand for supplies and reinforcements. In early April Ruff handed over responsibility for this task to a British brigade-group. Taken together, *Operation Achilles* in the Helmand Valley and the Canadian role in it had served the purpose of keeping the combat aspect of the ISAF mission contained largely in the west, at least for a few more months, so that Kandahar's regeneration could continue on its new upward trajectory.

Meanwhile Back in Z-P

While Ruff and his combat team worked Maywand in March, the balance of the battlegroup continued to push patrols deeper and deeper into areas of Zharey–Panjwayi that only months before had been considered Taliban strongholds. Maj Chris Henderson's Charles Company 3PPCLI first worked into western Zharey to support ANP checkpoints before moving to the south side of the Arghandab River, into the area known as the "Panjwayi peninsula." This was cultivated farm country in the fork of the Arghandab and Dowry Rivers. At the north-eastern base of this triangle of land was a five-acre forward operating base (FOB) at Ma'Sum Ghar, manned by the Canadians and the ANA. Six kilometres west was another FOB (initially held by US and ANA troops), on an unassuming mound of earth known as Sperwan Ghar. When the US-Afghan force headed west to join *Operation Achilles*, Henderson's combat team took over the FOB. The sandy pile may have looked inconsequential, however, Henderson's Patricias quickly found out that its height and its location at the base of the Panjwayi Peninsula made it decisive ground. Thus, these two craggy outcrops, on an otherwise flat fertile plain, formed the geographic focal points of the battlegroup's operations during 2007. Backed by tanks, artillery, and engineers. Henderson's troops also moved into patrol base checkpoints along the main road traversing the southern bank of the Arghandab. There they supported ANP checkpoints recently taken over from the more professional ANA units.

North of the Arghandab and 14 kilometres west in Zharey District lay an equally nondescript, sandy mound rising oddly out of the river flood plain. The locals call it Sangsar Ghar, after the cluster of hamlets in the centre of Zharey. To avoid confusing the hill with the hamlets, Canadian maps labelled it Ghundey Ghar, even though in Pashtu both Ghundey and Ghar translate as "hill." In the next months all of the elements of TF 1-07 came to know the Ghundey Ghar and the Sangsar area well. In March, part of Steve Graham's Royal Canadian Dragoon Reconnaissance and Surveillance Squadron established some of its Coyotes atop the commanding mound, while the rest of his squadron's modern surveillance equipment was spread around the Canadian area. Between commanding the high ground, the tremendous reach of their surveillance equipment, and regular patrolling, Walker's battlegroup cast a security cordon around the densely populated areas of Zharey—Panjwayi.

In March the battlegroup held and patrolled that area in the face of an increasing threat from suicide car bombers and IEDs. Several of these struck 6 Platoon of Hotel Company on one memorable day late in the month. The platoon had been detached from the rest of the company to patrol and provide security around Ma'Sum Ghar and Sperwan Ghar. According to MCpl Tracy Price, commanding one of the platoon LAVs, being separated from the rest of the company "sucked" and they felt like they were not part of the team. Their mood changed on the 26th.

After transporting a Danish liaison team from Ma'Sum Ghar to the company leaguer out west, Price's three-LAV patrol was ambushed on return outside Patrol Base Wilson. When an RPG round passed in front of him and the group's middle vehicle just ahead was struck by machine-gun fire, Price reacted instantly. Radioing "Ambush Right," Price engaged the enemy with his turret-mounted machine gun, suppressing their fire. Once the convoy was safe, Price took stock. He realized he was in good spirits: they had just gone through their first action, their training had kicked in, he had returned fire effectively, and no one had been hurt. However, his luck did not last long.

As the LAVs entered Kandahar City, they were struck by a suicide car bomb hidden in a parked taxi cab. It went off just as Price's LAV passed by, enveloping the vehicle in a blast of flame and debris. The explosion set off a small fire inside the LAV's engine compartment, which was quickly doused. Meanwhile, Price dropped down into the turret to check on the rest of his crew. The driver had a separated shoulder and broken wrist. However, while scrambling around inside the LAV Price realized that his right arm had been badly injured. Fortunately, the wound was cauterized by the blast and the pain numbed by the excitement of the moment. After his gunner bandaged his wounds, Price radioed the other vehicles to report the attack and injuries. They then proceeded to an ANP checkpoint about 10 minutes away. By the time they arrived Price's adrenalin rush was subsiding and he could now feel the pain in his broken arm. On return to Ma'Sum Ghar, he was given a shot of morphine and joked with the medical personnel about not smelling good, this being his fourth day without a shower. For Price the most frightening part of the whole ordeal now followed: medevac by a Black Hawk helicopter. As he recalled later, "I got through the ambush and suicide bombing and we're all alive, and now I'm going to crash and die in this helicopter." After treatment at Kandahar Airfield, Price was flown to the American military hospital at Bagram, then Germany, and finally to Canada.[12]

But while Taliban bomb-cells targeted Canadian battlegroup convoys and the more vulnerable ANP, PRT activity continued to increase. Among other things, UN Habitat workers and Maj Quick convened the newly elected Zharey District *shura* (the Panjwayi District *shura* was elected the previous fall) and began the complex process of building consensus for NSP and other development program project ideas. Municipal governance, however imperfect yet, had started to rebuild. Likewise, PRT detachments started operating out of the Zharey District Centre at Patrol Base Wilson and out of Ma'Sum Ghar. Their job in these sensitive areas, where local trust had yet to be restored, was to push on with setting up CDCs for the NSP.

* * *

The bulk of TF 1-07's activities in its first two months in Afghanistan was to meet with Kandaharis to explain that the Canadians and ISAF were there to keep the Taliban from interfering as they tried to get on with life. These early efforts to build trust were complicated by the presence of a special ANP unit sent from the north to conduct a token number of poppy field eradication operations. The overwhelming word from the people of Zharey–Panjwayi and Maywand Districts was that poor, tenant farmers faced serious consequences (coercion or inability to buy food) if they did not produce the opium crop later in the spring. Canadian soldiers got the message; if you want stability, steer clear of poppy eradication. That suited Chamberlain's PRT and the Canadian opium strategy at large. The Canadian aim was to gradually supplant opium with traditional crops, while simultaneously eliminating the traffickers and insurgents who depended on the sale of opium. After the Kabul-based poppy eradication team finished its token work and left, trust between Canadian soldiers and local farmers built rapidly.

The first fruits of this emerging trust appeared in March, when residents in Zharey–Panjwayi offered important information about the location of IEDs and other intelligence on the Taliban. An increasing flow of intelligence is a significant measure of success in counter-insurgency. In this case it indicated a major shift in local attitudes and a vote of confidence in the battlegroup and the ANA. Up to that point, every Canadian involved in *shuras* and meetings with individuals in Zharey–Panjwayi had been able to sense the fear latent in the population. They feared what would happen to them if they talked to Canadians or if they expressed confidence that the Afghan government and the PRT could make good on their promises. Most of all, they feared what was coming when the winter lull ended and fresh Taliban units arrived from Pakistan.

Despite those deep-seated fears, in March some people took the risk and offered little hints about IED locations. In fact, it was those little hints that seemed most honest: "ISAF might want to check out that piece of road" or "foreigners had been seen in that hamlet the other week, milling around a certain house." This could only be pressed so far, and with good reason. The Taliban made a habit of severely punishing those who spoke up. Hangings, slitting of throats, and beheadings had been reported.

Apart from the professionalism and friendliness of the Canadian soldier, TF 1-07's main weapon against this climate of fear was Capt Shawn Arbing's Tactical Psychological Operations Team (TPT). Since the Taliban sought to carefully control what rural people saw and understood of the world around them, it was critical for ISAF and the Afghan government to clearly communicate their intent to the people. To the Canadian Army, unused to having to "sell" itself to the people it was deployed to help, this was something new. They had encountered competing messages from armed gangs and power brokers on a number of missions since Bosnia, but TF 1-07 was the first time the army had "fought back" systematically in an Information War. Thus, Arbing's team did not have the benefit of experience to rely on; they had to make it up as they went. What they soon learned was that sitting face-to-face with village elders was the best way to communicate the international community's desire to help and to gauge what Kandaharis actually understood of this foreign presence among them. Arbing, Sgt Randy McCourt, and their small team travelled with battlegroup patrols, helping to get out the message that the westerners were there to help.

The Taliban were no more content to let Kandahar slip from their control in early 2007 than they had been a year earlier. So, their lashing out against police checkpoints and Canadian patrols came as no surprise to the battlegroup. Watching developments on either end of Zharey revealed the shape of things to come. The fear, and the distance between the troops and locals, was strongest in what Dave Quick called an "egg-shaped cluster" of villages and hamlets between Nalgham and Sangsar. This was Mullah Omar's former home and the birthplace of his Taliban movement. In this place, some families had money. In this place, the fear among other families was deepest. And it was here that a Taliban IED cell, supported by some guerrilla and rocket cells, opened for business in March.

And so in March, India Company foot patrols probed around and into that area to keep open the dialogue with local leaders and to honour promises to come back for follow-on discussions about projects. These return visits made a profound impact whenever they occurred. Quick saw that the stock of his company went up in east Zharey as word of their integrity grew. It also grew when the locals saw how the Canadians could be discriminate and careful with their fire when the Taliban did try to take them on. When an ANP patrol was ambushed and mortared as it attempted to get back to the district police headquarters at PBW, India Company's LAV captain Neil Whitman led a Canadian team to cover their withdrawal by returning fire on the ambush positions only, despite coming under Taliban mortar fire. Dan Bobbitt's artillery was ready if needed, but it was not called in.

As they had a few weeks before, locals scurried out of the way, expecting the hammer to drop on the Taliban ambush party and 155mm shells to slam into civilian homes, which was doubtlessly part of the insurgents' aim. But the Taliban would not get their wish. Instead, Whitman stayed on the defensive, watching only for clear and obvious enemy targets. However, none presented itself. During the night Maj Quick and Sgt-Maj Jeans prepared a foot patrol to clear the homes from where the ambush was launched. By then, of course, the Taliban were gone.

But the significance of the entire incident was not lost on local villagers. The heavy handed tactics of *Operation Enduring Freedom*, and the conventional warfare of 2006, had passed. Now the Canadians seemed both fearless and careful. Respect and trust deepened.

The Belly of the Beast

Steve Graham's recce troops and Galuga's engineers were getting similar local reactions to their patrols into the west end of the Nalgham–Sangsar area. Graham called this region "the Belly of the Beast." In the middle of the month, IED attacks on Canadian convoys increased, thankfully with no serious injuries. But just as elsewhere in Zharey–Panjwayi, something new was happening here. In village *shuras* attended by Graham, and in encounters with locals while on patrol, the people let Canadians know where some—but not all—IEDs were buried. It was a good start, but as Graham's patrols pushed deeper into the Belly of the Beast, many would be discovered the hard way.

On 20 March the lead vehicle in one of these patrols hit an IED that blasted the vehicle's undercarriage. The Coyote did its work and saved all on board from injury. The patrol then secured the site and called in what might be called "CSI: Kandahar": specialist engineer teams with the knowledge and tools to investigate these incidents. IED blasts always yielded hard information on who the bombers were and how to defeat their threat. The particular IED cell that laid this bomb was crafty, having laid multiple explosive devices in the general area. All of these were located quickly and disarmed.

Part of the team responding on 20 March included an ex-US soldier who handled a bomb-sniffing dog. That day, he and his dog performed their life-saving work with great courage. The well-trained dog moved ahead on the road to the vicinity of a suspected IED near the blast site. He caught the scent of explosives and sat down to mark the exact location so that engineers could disarm it. As he sat, the dog triggered the detonator. The blast obliterated the poor animal, inflicted horrific wounds to the chest and face of his handler, and wounded a Canadian engineer. However, the dog had saved a dozen other men that day and they all knew it. And the information gathered from the site and from locals would help Graham and his squadron close in on the perpetrators.[13] But the "Beast" had yet to be tamed.

BEWARE THE IDES OF MARCH

By the end of March TF 1-07 was hitting its stride. It had barged into enemy territory with heavy armour, moving about at will and inviting attacks which the Taliban could not deliver. It had used that aggressive posture to establish itself more firmly in the critical area of Zharey–Panjwayi, building trust with local Afghans in the process. And aid, development, and confidence-building were well underway. As winter gave way to spring, the Taliban would either have to find a way to fight back or surrender their status in Kandahar Province. The stage was set for a showdown. It was not long in coming and would deliver a brutal shock to TF 1-07.

THE PROMISE OF SPRING

Spring is a season greatly anticipated in southern Afghanistan. Not only have the cold and damp of winter abated and a verdant green begun to creep across the fertile river valleys, but the poppy harvest looms. In recent Afghan history the cycle of war and peace has revolved around the collection, refining, and shipping of opium. Once that labour-intensive process was completed, usually by early May, the war chests of local drug lords, criminal gangs, and the Taliban would be replenished for the year and there was money to fuel conflict. Just as important, the myriad hands of the harvesters themselves would now be idle and Tier 2 Taliban fighters could be bought for a summer's campaign. In the spring of 2007 the objective for the international community, the Afghan government, and TF 1-07 was clear. They had to take advantage of the quiet, the plentiful water, and the surge in the International Security Assistance Force (ISAF) and Provincial Reconstruction Team (PRT) activity to break the cycle before the peace of April dissolved into another summer of fighting.

In April the adobe-coloured flats framed by rock walls that TF 1-07 had inherited only weeks before had turned green as winter rains brought life to Kandahar Province. The Arghandab River and its tributaries remained high, and the water flow in the portions of the underground *karez* irrigation system that still functioned was also plentiful. And as usual, the poppy fields were yielding a bountiful harvest. But what set this spring apart from those of the previous decade was the sudden expansion of traditional cash and subsistence crops. Fields that had lain fallow for a decade were now sprouting with wheat, grapes, melons, potatoes, onions, almonds, pomegranates, and apricots. With Kandahar starting to mend, markets for these cash crops began to re-appear.

The rains of the winter of 2006-07 could not have come at a better time. Almost two years' worth of United Nations road repair meant that produce could now actually make it to the city for sale and processing. A private Canadian development company, Drew Gilmour's Development Works, that first helped Afghans build sewer systems, roads, and wells, now began to build bakeries and other food-production facilities to process the harvest from five of Kandahar's villages. Five million dollars from the Canadian International Development Agency (CIDA) made Gilmour's work possible. CIDA had been the prime source of development and aid work funding in Kandahar for over a year now, putting priority on long-term sustainable economic development and quality-of-life programs. Much of this was targeted at breaking the cycle of war through economic development and employment.

Meanwhile, back in Ottawa, Michael Callan took over as manager of CIDA's Kandahar desk and pushed a district-level version of the National Solidarity Program (NSP). In the spring of 2007, Callan's office supplied money to the district *shuras*, stabilized by regular battlegroup and PRT representatives, to fund larger irrigation canals and reservoir construction, hiring local, unemployed men as part of the cash-for-work program. Several major bridge construction jobs to reconnect farm communities to the road grid were part of the program, too. Reviving agriculture and markets spurred commerce. A walk down Kandahar streets and markets in April 2007 revealed stalls with goods to sell and people looking to buy. On one busy intersection there even stood an internet café. The spring of 2007 was so far bearing out New Year hopes.

Western observers who climbed the winding track to the observation post at Charles Company's forward operating base (FOB) at Sperwan Ghar in April 2007 would have been able to detect little of this crucial change. But anyone who had spent time in Afghanistan could immediately pick out the differences. Grape vines now grew on trellises, a farming method far more efficient and profitable than the traditional practice of short plants on earthen mounds. Grapes offered a viable cash crop alternative to opium poppies. CIDA was funding the efforts of the Central Asia Development Group to establish dozens of test and training sites that showed Afghan farmers how to use the new methods, even producing guidebooks in Pashtu.

The total bill for the new grape industry was a paltry $99,000 over a year, yet the snowball effect had potential to be worth much more in turning tenant farmers away from opium. On the well-patrolled and -observed road between the grape fields, children played soccer where children had not had the luxury of playing for some time. To the hardened Patricia paratroopers on watch at Sperwan Ghar, the shouts of happy children in the cool evening convinced many of the importance of their task.

Other traditional cash crops got similar attention. CIDA and the PRT also put money into an American NGO called Roots for Peace operating in western Kandahar. Roots for Peace was planting pomegranate seedling orchards. The seedlings were raised by Kandaharis, who then replanted them in their fields. It was another small-scale but potentially powerful reconstruction job, and like the new methods for grape cultivation re-establishing pomegranate orchards required little money.

The crucial elements of the rebirth of Kandahar's agriculture were water and labour, as well as people willing to run the risk of living in Kandahar to show farmers how to thrive. In the spring of 2007 CIDA and the UN Development Program therefore pushed to get water into more fields. The 10-year drought had forced many tenant farmers to consolidate their limited water supply on a tiny portion of land on which they grew opium to pay the rent and buy food. But the result was never quite enough, so that farmers were often forced to take out high-interest loans from their absentee landlords, which reinforced the cycle of abuse and servitude. To break this cycle, CIDA focused development on getting wadis, *karezes*, canals, and more modern pipelines into the older fields so that farmers could radically increase crop production back to pre-Soviet War and pre-drought levels. The UN, the Canadian PRT, and NGOs were fixing roads and culverts so that farmers could move their crops to the city. The next stage of this long-term effort was even more technical training and mentoring on how to improve crop yields. It helped that Afghan farmers were hungry for knowledge about how to improve their plight. All of this ran counter to the interests of local drug and war lords, and the Taliban, who depended on a climate of fear and dependency in the countryside to support their lifestyles and their wars. Bravery in the Afghan struggle was, therefore, something demanded of even the most humble farmer and his family.

Because of the urgency of this work, by April 2007 PRT activity in the province had gathered a noticeable momentum. Even more promising was how, in the presence of improving stability, international assistance in Kandahar accelerated locally based renewal. Afghans, regardless of ethnicity, regardless of whether northern or southern, are a tremendously entrepreneurial people. As the Taliban threat declined or shifted to attacks on ISAF troops and Afghan soldiers and police, industrious Kandaharis took on much of the rebuilding process themselves. This was part of the UN plan. Investment and development assistance from outside turned into a progressive movement that could be felt on the streets of Kandahar City, even if the blast and smell of a suicide car bomb attack still occasionally drifted across the city.

POLICING AND CORRECTIONS

But development and economic activity was not sufficiently advanced in the spring of 2007 to convince all Kandaharis that the future lay with the Government of Afghanistan: there was still a great deal to do. By 2007 the United States of the Americans had assumed responsibility for Afghan police reform, and made serious funding available for training, organization, and equipment. ISAF members like Canada took more control over police support in their own respective Areas of Responsibility. Indeed, Gavin Buchan could not hope to achieve any kind of collective reform of the Kandahar Provincial Government if the police were not part of the process. So, in many ways the busiest people in the region were those in the RCMP detachment. Like other components of the Kandahar PRT, the Mounties were just now getting around the city frequently enough to effect widespread change. Their job was part of the "capacity-building mission," designed to turn the Afghan National Police (ANP) in the Kandahar City sub-stations into a real police force that could serve and protect the citizenry. The team was led by RCMP Superintendent Dave Fudge who, like so many of TF 1-07, was a veteran of several overseas deployments to failed states, including the former Yugoslavia.

Indeed, the RCMP are one of the few police services in the world with the organization and know-how to deploy abroad to train new police forces in war-shattered societies. Fudge brought with him a wealth of wisdom on the challenge of building professionalism among police in areas where corruption was a survival mechanism and respect for the rule of law had to be re-earned as much as rebuilt. His efforts were backed by a platoon of Canadian Military Police.

While Fudge and his fellow officers offered professional training and mentoring for Afghan police in the city, the countryside was a different matter. The scale of the problem was immense, not least because in early 2007 ISAF did not have enough troops to provide security for local police detachments, nor resources to monitor their behaviour. Plans for co-locating more Canadians with the ANP were in the works but could not be staffed till the fall.

The corrupt and antiquated Afghan prison system was another challenge. Prison reform in 2007 was always overshadowed by the hot-button issue of the Canadian policy of turning over detainees to the Afghan judicial and detention system. At the beginning of April, the Correctional Service of Canada team, led by the dynamic Louise Garwood-Filbert, finally got in the door of Kandahar's prison system and got the administration on board with a reform process. Based on experience in the former Yugoslavia, it was clear from the very outset of Canada's deployment to Kandahar that rebuilding the police and courts would fail without similar attention to the prisons. Garwood-Filbert's job was to rebuild Kandahar's prison system from the bottom up. With a team of three, plus a Vandoo escort when travelling around town, she was responsible for improving conditions at Sarposa Prison, various police detention centres, and the infamous National Directorate of Security (NDS) facility. Canadian corrections officers set out to bring Kandahar's jails up to UN and International Red Cross standards, and to train prison staff and police guards in the philosophy of civil society in which all citizens, including prisoners, have fundamental human rights—a tough job in a land where the concept of basic human rights had broken down. That started with basic prison administration: tracking who was incarcerated and why. Basic humanitarian needs of inmates, including the provision of fresh air and beds in cells, fresh water, and medical care, also required attention.

Then came training courses for guards on everything from basic sanitation to proper treatment of prisoners.

By the end of April 2007 many of those basic UN benchmarks were on their way to being achieved. Mirroring the experience of so many Canadians in Kandahar, Garwood-Filbert found that the will to improve certainly existed. The warden and staff at Sarposa, for example, were eager (as they described it) "to pull themselves out of the darkness they knew as Taliban." By month's end plans were afoot to begin literacy training for staff and inmates and to build a nursery for female inmates and wives of prisoners forced to work for food. Humanitarian initiatives for inmates' families were supported with particular vigour by Kandaharis whose local brand of Islam encourages the faithful to take up the cause of the forgotten.[1] It seemed that hope for Kandahar as a whole was most visible in this unlikeliest of places.

THE TALIBAN TRIES AND FAILS

But in such a war-torn land hope did not come cheap. Rebuilding efforts proceeded unmolested in part because the Taliban seemed to realize that attacking targets built with the input and labour of locals, rather than by outside contractors, would turn the people against them. Reconstruction was also not so much the target because Taliban units in Kandahar faced the more immediate problem of Canadian patrols roaming their safe areas and their transit routes. So the target of Taliban efforts was to attack the security forces, which allowed all the rebuilding to proceed. Indeed, the Taliban had been trying to hit ISAF and the Canadians in some meaningful way all winter. In April 2007 they finally got lucky.

On 1 April, Sgt D.H. McIlvenna was escorting a supply convoy on its return run to Kandahar Airfield (KAF) after delivering its cargo to the combat team still operating in Maywand in support of *Operation Achilles*. The Canadian heavy logistics vehicles (HLVWs) of the convoy rolled along on their six massive tires, with the crews perched in cabs high above the road. Snipers and mines in Bosnia, and IED threats in Afghanistan, had led to an add-on armour package for these otherwise soft-skinned 10-ton trucks. The height and armour saved the crew of the third vehicle in McIlvenna's convoy from the

C-9 gunner from Alpha Company 2PPCLI during Operation MEDUSA. Taliban violence during the first Canadian battlegroup deployment to Kandahar in early 2006 demonstrated the need for a fourth infantry company in the Task Force. The 2PPCLI added the extra company to the 1RCR Battlegroup in the latter half of 2006, as 3PPCLI would be contributing to the 2RCR Battlegroup in 2007. *Photo: DND/Combat Camera*

Maj Bill Fletcher SMV, holds an Orders Group ("O" Group) for the officers and NCOs in his Charles Company combat team in the open desert of south-western Afghanistan. Soldiers from LCol Ian Hope's 1PPCLI spent much of their tour surging into Helmand and Uruzgan Provinces in early 2006, paving the way for British and Dutch task forces that followed later.
Photo: DND/Combat Camera

Infantry section from LCol Omer Lavoie's Battlegroup during Operation MEDUSA. The section is halted in a traditionally planted, mounded grape field in Panjwayi District. Behind them sits an infamous "grapehut" used by farmers to turn Kandahar's re-nowned grapes into raisins—and also used by Taliban fighters as bunkers during the battles for Bazaar-e Panjwayi and Pashmul in September 2006. *Photo: DND/Combat Camera*

Construction contractors from Kandahar City work on the southern end of Route Summit under direction of Maj Mark Gasparotto. This photo was taken from Forward Operating Base Ma'Sum Ghar built by Gasparotto's 23 Field Squadron, Royal Canadian Engineers in the fall of 2006 to establish permanent ISAF and Afghan National Army presence in Zharey-Panjwayi. *Photo: DND/Combat Camera*

CFB Gagetown family, friends and co-workers turned out on 19 January 2007 for a Red Shirt Friday rally to send Task Force 1-07 on its way to Afghanistan. *Photo: DND/Combat Camera*

Handover ceremony. LCol Bob Chamberlain, incoming commander of Canada's Provincial Reconstruction Team addresses the troops at Camp Nathan Smith in Kandahar City while his predecessor, LCol Simon Hetherington, looks on. *Photo: DND/Combat Camera*

Infantrymen from 2RCR and their LAV III light armoured infantry fighting vehicles during a pre-deployment live-fire exercise at CFB Gagetown, New Brunswick. Training emphasized protecting Afghan civilian lives and applying deadly force with extreme caution. *Photo: 2RCR*

Combat Engineers or "sappers" from Maj Jake Galuga's 41 Field Squadron, Royal Canadian Engineers from CFB Gagetown. Experience in Kandahar in 2006 led to the deployment of a much larger engineer component with TF 1-07, including more mine detection and counter-IED equipment and more heavy armoured engineering vehicles. *Photo: DND/Combat Camera*

LAV III infantry fighting vehicle in Zharey District. The wheeled vehicle is small and light enough to manoeuvre down narrow farm community lanes and cover long distances efficiently on packed gravel and asphalt. Its armour has saved lives against IEDs, anti-tank mines, and suicide car bombs. *Photo: Cpl Dan Pop, PRT/Combat Camera*

Capt Larry Sanford (left) and Maj Alex Ruff (right) on top of the gravelly low hill at Ghundey Ghar. Ruff commanded Hotel Company, which often joined with most of the battlegroup's supporting tank squadron to form an infantry-armoured combat team that projected ISAF and Afghan Army presence all over Kandahar Province. *Photo: DND/Combat Camera*

Left to right: engineer Maj Jake Galuga; Lt George Williams, battle adjutant in LCol Rob Walker's mobile tactical headquarters; and Capt Allan Best, Battlegroup Information Operations Officer. Williams, a former master sniper, managed the TAC HQ packet through dozens of small battles, ambushes, IED strikes, and suicide bomb attacks. The trio stand at Strong Point Centre early in the tour. *Photo: Capt Martell Thompson, 2RCR BG*

Canadian-Afghan Forward Operating Base (FOB) Ma'Sum Ghar looking north towards the Arghandab River and the town of Pashmul. In 2007 it was home to 2nd Kandak, 1 Brigade, 205th "Hero" Corps of the Afghan National Army, their Canadian mentor team and "A" Squadron, Lord Strathcona's Horse (LSH) and the heavy troop of 41 Engineer Squadron. *Photo: DND/Combat Camera*

High-level *shura* in Kandahar City led by then Provincial Governor Assadullah Khalid (top of the photo without a turban). Also present in blue is Gavin Buchan, Glyn Berry's able successor as senior Canadian Foreign Affairs officer in southern Afghanistan. In uniform is LCol Bob Chamberlain, commander of the Canadian PRT. *Photo: Cpl Dan Pop, PRT/Combat Camera*

Maj David "Boomer" Broomfield, "A" Squadron LSH commander, interviewed by Canwest reporter Richard Foot in April 2007. All Canadian Forces members were authorized to speak to the media. Foreign Affairs, RCMP, Corrections Canada and CIDA officials were more restricted, putting a military emphasis on the Canadian multi-departmental mission in Afghanistan. *Photo: DND/Combat Camera*

FOB Sperwan Ghar observation post manned by infantry soldiers from Charles Company, 3PPCLI and gunners from Dragon Battery, 2RCHA. The hilltop position provided an excellent view of north central Panjwayi District and the Arghandab River.

Photo: DND/Combat Camera

Hotel Company LAV atop the Canadian temporary patrol base at Ghundey Ghar. The small hill offered a commanding view of the western end of Zharey District's most productive farming country and Highway 1 running west to Helmand Province.

Photo: DND/Combat Camera

LCol Rob Walker (left), 2RCR Battlegroup Commanding Officer and his Reconnaissance (Recce) Squadron commander Maj Steve Graham (centre), brief visiting LGen Michel Gauthier (right) on the situation in Zharey. LGen Gauthier headed Canadian Expeditionary Force Command (CEFCOM), set up in 2005 to direct overseas operations. *Photo: DND/Combat Camera*

Lt Ben Rogerson's 5 Platoon, Hotel Company back on the job in Zharey in May, after losing a section to a powerful IED on 8 April 2007. The two armed locals are Afghan National Police officers. In early 2007, TF 1-07 realized that training and equipping ANP detachments in rural areas still had a long way to go. *Photo: DND/Combat Camera*

Capt Rhonda Matthews and WO Lori Coady of the PRT's detachment responsible for Kandahar City conduct a Needs Assessment at Said Abad School. PRT members contracted and monitored Kandaharis working on locally designed rebuilding projects. They also coordinated efforts with other agencies, in this case UNICEF and the Afghan Ministry of Education. *Photo: Sgt Roxanne Clowe, DND/Combat Camera*

In early 2007 Canada's PRT was reinforced by Louise Garwood-Filbert's Correctional Service of Canada mentoring team, sent to bring Kandahar's prison system up to UN basic standards. Here CSC Officer Ric Fecteau meets with Sarposa Prison's warden. *Photo: Sgt Craig Fiander, DND/Combat Camera*

Canadian-designed and Afghan-installed wells and water pumps like this one in Sayad Pacha were often the first projects voted forward in rural villages as part of the CIDA-sponsored National Solidarity Program (NSP). The program empowers village councils to decide on rebuilding priorities, regenerating municipal governance. *Photo: Cpl Dan Pop, PRT/DND*

The International Arches at the Highway 4 border crossing at Spin Boldak-Wes. The road connected Kandahar City to Quetta in Pakistan. The chaotic border region was the prime transit route for the Taliban-drug trafficker alliance in and out of Afghanistan. *Photo: MCpl Kevin Paul, DND/Combat Camera*

PRT Capt Geoff Marshall, Recce Squadron Capt Francis Conliffe, and their interpreter disguised for personal safety, close a recon-struction *shura* in Spin Boldak. Starting in May 2007, the squadron and its attached PRT detachment began coordinating the disjointed international security, aid, and development effort in the border area. *Photo: MCpl Kevin Paul, DND/Combat Camera*

Recce Squadron's Lt John Maerz (centre), Cpl Martin Duperron (right) and their interpreter on an assessment visit to an Afghan National Border Police station. Linking together and improving the four different Afghan police services in the border region was the toughest job in Spin Boldak. *Photo: MCpl Kevin Paul, DND/Combat Camera*

An opium field in western Kandahar. Decades of war and drought destroyed southern Afghanistan's food production and distribution system. With only a fraction of the usual amount of water available for irrigation, drug lords extorted tenant farmers to grow opium in order to pay rent. Breaking this cycle is the key to Afghanistan's regeneration. *Photo: DND/Combat Camera*

Desert Leaguer. For weeks on end the Hotel Company/-"A" Squadron Combat Team lived out of their vehicles in the open desert of Maywand District and in the barren hill country of northern Kandahar. Sand storms and desert insects added to the nuisance of occasional Taliban rockets. *Photo: DND/Combat Camera*

Hotel Company/-"A" Squadron Combat team rolls out of the Ghundey Ghar Patrol Base. They had the mobility to go where none of the other 37 nations in ISAF could travel. *Photo: DND/Combat Camera*

Dismounted Hotel Company infantrymen on their way to Nalgham in May. This field once grew marijuana, but in the spring of 2007 was replanted with wheat with the help Canadian project funds, seeds and tractors. That summer the wheat was milled and baked in Kandahar City bakeries. *Photo: DND/Combat Camera*

Canadian Leopard C1 Main Battle Tank affixed with Cold War-era mine rollers. The heavy rollers were used to clear routes of pressure plate mines and IEDs devices without damaging roads. *Photo: "A" Squadron/LSH*

Regimental Sgt-Maj Mark Baisley and Deputy CO Maj Russ King take a much-needed break during probing patrols into the Taliban stronghold in Nalgham–Sangsar. These two forces of personality were the glue holding the widely dispersed Battlegroup together. *Photo: Maj RJ King, 2RCR*

WO John Pudar's Leopard tank, Call-sign "T11A", with mine rollers minutes after detonating an IED on 18 May 2007. The rollers worked exactly as intended, lifting into the air and settling the tank down undamaged. *Photo: "A" Squadron/LSH*

Callsign "0", battlegroup command post deployed forward to Ma'Sum Ghar. Left to right: Maj Eric Pelicano, Operations Officer, LCol Rob Walker, Battlegroup Commander, Plans officer, Capt Rob Tesselaar, and Maj Dan Bobbitt, commanding the supporting artillery. *Photo: Capt Peter Weis, 2RCR BG*

blast effects of a powerful IED. Even so, the cab and the front of the truck on the driver's side were blown apart. Sgt McIlvenna stopped the convoy and called in the contact report. In what was becoming a familiar routine for the task force, the qualified tactical combat casualty care (TCCC) soldiers raced to the blast scene to administer critical immediate care to the wounded. McIlvenna's gunner, Tpr M.S.K. Barker was out of the hatch and into the wreckage in moments flat. He checked out the co-driver, Cpl E.R. Pellerin, who was not seriously hurt but refused to leave his comrade who was. So, Barker and Pellerin worked to stabilize the driver, whose foot was clearly smashed and who appeared to have head and spinal injuries. Meanwhile, veteran Strathcona sergeant Mike Bolger leapt out of his vehicle to secure the blast site and clear a lane so that the convoy medic, Cpl Sonya Briére, could reach the scene without triggering other hidden IEDs. Within moments Briére was in the shredded truck cab, getting the driver ready to be moved. Sgt Bolger passed the details back to Sgt McIlvenna so he could call in the nine-liner to get a medevac helicopter.

This was the second convoy attack Bolger had endured in a short span of time. Only two weeks earlier a smaller supply convoy he commanded was hit by a suicide car bomb. Two Afghan civilians were killed and a teenage boy's stomach torn open by the blast. Bolger and his TCCC-qualified driver got the boy patched up and sent off to hospital. So in many ways, 1 April was just another day on the job for the battlegroup and for the National Support Element truckers, supply techs, and mechanics who ran the roads, keeping the battlegroup squared away with "gas, bombs, bullets and beans."[2]

The first day of April also brought the battlegroup nearer the Belly of the Beast around Nalgham and Sangsar. Patrols at both ends of Zharey District's fertile triangle, combined with intelligence provided by locals, confirmed that this area was a Taliban stronghold. In fact, tension in the area had peaked in the last days of March. Steve Graham's Recce Squadron helped the Ghundey Ghar ANP detachment search a number of suspected houses in the vicinity where bomb-makers were thought to be hiding. On several occasions Taliban riflemen had opened fire on them. In each case the recce soldiers returned fire, watched the areas where enemy fire came from, and gathered more information about the way this Taliban cell conducted its business. On several evenings, the Taliban had fired rockets into squadron positions on the mound. The Taliban rocket position was located because, by this point, the Canadians had taken over the night. Mounted and dismounted recce patrolmen watched closely as the IED cell moved around the area with their weapons and explosives during the night. They watched the houses and walled yards they slipped into. Clearly, a Taliban bomb-making team or IED cell was operating in the fertile triangle area of Zharey, trying to score more hits on ISAF and halt their patrols in the area. This cell had to be stopped. The Canadians had to be certain, however, that the time and location was right so they could take on the bomb-making cell with precision. This kind of basic intelligence work was the bread and butter of Graham's Recce Squadron. However, the most important new tool the Canadians had to help locate hidden explosives was the increasing faith and trust of the local population, who came forward with clues.

Owing to such constant and detailed surveillance and to locally generated intelligence, far more IEDs and mines were "defeated" than were effective. And every time an IED detonated, "CSI: Kandahar" gathered a little more evidence about the bomb-makers. The challenge facing Walker's battlegroup was how to neutralize this threat. The Taliban, on the other hand, grew frustrated that their attempts to blow up a Canadian vehicle in this cat-and-mouse game were failing. So, they opted for a more direct approach: ambushing patrols and convoys.

Acting on a tip, Graham launched a patrol on the last day of March to clear IEDs in the west end of Nalgham. His troops found two anti-tank mines and brought in the sappers up to remove them. Suddenly, the patrol was struck by volleys of poorly aimed RPGs. This was followed by rifle and machine-gun fire. In the din of action, some Canadian troops could discern a Taliban mortar firing on them. Return fire was directed only at visible targets. For the most part, the Taliban lined a wall overlooking the road and they could be seen from a number of vantage points held by Graham's team. The man who could see the most was Graham's attached artillery forward observation officer (FOO), who watched as five Taliban fighters ducked behind the wall. At their distant fire base Maj Bobbitt's gunners were "spooled up" and they readied their 155mm howitzers. Bobbitt had trained his team to apply artillery fire accurately, and taking no risks with Afghans' lives and their property were his critical benchmarks. The target on the afternoon of 31 March fit the profile of accept-ability, and Bobbitt's guns fired a half-dozen carefully directed shells. The whole event was finished in minutes. A quick survey revealed that "the shoot," as artillery missions are known, was a tremendous success. No Canadians or local civilians were even injured during this brief encounter: the only damage was to the Taliban along the wall.

Graham's patrol pulled back to their observation posts to watch and wait. Before long, Recce Squadron soldiers on top of Ghundey Ghar saw about one hundred families flee the area for neighbouring villages. ANP and patrolling aircraft spotted others leaving. The locals, understandably perhaps, expected that the ambush would only be the prelude to a massive battle on the order of what had occurred the previous September. Certainly, they expected retribution from ISAF and the forces of the government. There was, indeed, a second act to this drama, but not one to which the Afghans were accustomed.

After darkness fell, the surviving Taliban cell members and their commander (who had been observed before) came into the open to retrieve precious weapons and explosives. In these circumstances the high-tech equipment and skill of the Canadian Army could be used with extreme precision and efficacy. As the Taliban were tracked with powerful image intensifiers, a combination of snipers and another six rounds of artillery from Bobbitt's guns completed the destruction of this Taliban cell. Undoubtedly there were more cells lurking and more were likely to come to Zharey later in the year. But the bomb-laying work of this particular cell had come to an end.

The next morning, 1 April, patrols pushed back into the hamlets on the west end of Nalgham. They found homes that clearly had been evacuated in a hurry, and others that were empty of families but had been used by the IED cell. The handful of locals they encountered told them that the Taliban had ordered people to leave their homes because a big battle was coming. But if the Taliban had intended to lure the battlegroup into another destructive battle like Pashmul— to sacrifice Nalgham to achieve a larger goal of proving to the locals that ISAF could only bring death and destruction—they failed.

Days later, when the population returned, village elders told Steve Graham that after the last Recce Squadron patrol in late March the Taliban had gathered villagers together and killed one with a knife as a warning to those who talked to Canadians.[3] The struggle to break this reign of fear still had a long way to go in Zharey District.

The same was true in Panjwayi District. During those same days in early April, Major Henderson's Patricias' standing patrols on the road on the south bank of the Arghandab were hit by Taliban rockets and rifle bullets, prompting return fire at the rocket-launching sites. The whole battlegroup was keenly aware that the Taliban were doing all that they could to lure the Canadians into blasting indiscriminately into the night and into populated areas. Again they would not get their wish. Henderson's soldiers fired a few short bursts directly at where the rockets came and then ceased fire. They also asked Bobbitt's howitzers to fire illumination flares over their positions to drive off the rocket-firing party. If they chose to stay in the open, lit up by the flares, the Taliban rocket team could be fired on with precision. In the glare of the parachute flares the rocket firing stopped. All over Zharey–Panjwayi the Taliban attempted to prevent Canadian and ANA patrols and to drive them to the safety of their FOBs. But their small-scale ambushes, IED strikes, and rocket attacks did nothing to stop patrols reaching deeper into Taliban territory and connecting with more villagers.

THE DEVELOPMENT FRONT

Nor did the targeting of ISAF and Afghan government forces stop the PRT and UN agencies from their rebuilding efforts. Community Development Council (CDC) elections, negotiations, and planning supervised by UN workers the previous year all paid off that spring. Whether the Taliban liked it or not, these new forms of municipal government were getting things done, in Zharey in particular. In early 2007, 12 major irrigation canals were restored, allowing abandoned fields to be watered for the growing season. South of the Arghandab in Panjwayi, Community Councils agreed to 19 separate repair jobs that fixed 400 kilometres of canals. CIDA and the United States Agency for International Development (USAID) paid for it all, but took no credit—and got no media attention as a result. In keeping with the spirit of restoring faith in government, the money for the work was allotted through the Afghan Ministry of Rural Rehabilitation and Development and matched to small amounts of money raised by the CDCs themselves. CIDA and USAID were also reluctant to draw attention to these projects to protect the people in those communities.[4]

The CDCs were part of the continual dialogue with Kandaharis to foster genuine hope for prosperity and confidence in their government. Critics often condemned ISAF in these years for not negotiating with the Taliban. However, given that only a year before many local farmers had been the Tier 2 Taliban, ISAF, aid agencies, PRTs, and battlegroup soldiers were, in effect, talking to the Taliban all the time in early 2007. It was never explained this way, in large part because the UN and CIDA officials involved were too busy working on the program and not yet certain of the outcome. On the other hand, there could be no mistake that the "Peace Through Strength" (PTS) program amounted to negotiations with Taliban fighters. The program was led, necessarily, by the Afghan government to heal connections with its own citizens and is ultimately an amnesty program for Tier 2 Taliban fighters. Like all other reconstruction efforts, the UN and NATO philosophy was that Afghan government agencies, and especially the local *shuras*, led the process in order to "build their capacity." In other words, the program reinforced the authority and respect of community and district *shuras* because former Taliban fighters had to be sponsored by that *shura* and provided with support before re-entering the community. Often this involved hiring those young men, who a year before had been conscripted into the Taliban insurgency to work on the various reconstruction projects. ISAF deliberately kept out of this process of community-level healing.

ISAF and the Canadian battlegroup supported the effort from a distance by continuing to patrol and improve security, and by drawing the Taliban onto themselves so that the main effort of rebuilding could go on. They also contributed to the negotiation process by providing security at *shuras* in dangerous areas. And then there was the Small Rewards Program whereby the impoverished and frightened people of Zharey–Panjwayi received a cash reward when they turned in weapons and ammunition, or information about the location of weapons caches. In this way, as the spring season progressed, more and more weapons and explosives were turned over to the ANP, ANA, or ISAF and destroyed by Canadian engineers. Thus, the IED-making process was being shut down before the explosives could actually be improvised into a device.

TRAGEDY IN MAYWAND

Even out in "the Maywand" where the joint Hotel Company/"A" Squadron Combat Team roved, CDCs were pushing ahead with rebuilding. Farm communities there relied on the *karezes* to pull water from nearby mountains. In early 2007 UN, CIDA, and USAID funds allowed the Afghan government to hire unemployed young men to repair 20 of them, and even built a brand-new one. As was the case in Zharey–Panjwayi, the Taliban could not afford to make enemies in these communities by attacking their own home-grown rebuilding efforts. But they could make life more difficult for the troops protecting them.

In late March and early April 2007, the Taliban had suffered a serious defeat in the Sangin area of the upper Helmand River Valley, west of Maywand. British, Afghan, Danish, Estonian, and American troops had pushed them out of safe areas in the Helmand greenbelt, turning them into desert fugitives. Tier 1 Taliban units could not stop the ISAF advances. Whenever they attempted to stand and fight conventionally they were destroyed. Instead, as elsewhere, they resorted to IEDs and minor ambushes. They also attempted to cut the flow of British reinforcements coming into the area by attacking the main road from KAF through Maywand to Helmand. Their attempts failed; most of the new units had been safely escorted into the province by the end of the first week of April.

It was while patrolling in support of that traffic to Helmand that TF 1-07 suffered its most serious losses of the whole rotation: the Easter tragedy. The morning of 8 April 2007, Majors Ruff and Broomfield gathered their junior leaders together in the desert leaguer to brief them on the day's coming events. After 36 straight days of living out of their vehicles in the open desert, their part in *Operation Achilles* was about to end. Ruff's combat team would return to KAF for hot showers, clean sheets, clean laundry, a call home, and a Tim Hortons coffee. It was even "Roll-up-the-Rim to

Win!" season at Canada's favourite coffee shop, the universal sign that winter was turning into spring. The return to civilization and real food could not come soon enough; in the Maywand desert it was summer already, with the daytime temperature reaching well over 40 degrees. Ruff and Broomfield nonetheless cautioned their men to remain alert. Before they could head back to KAF they had one more large ISAF convoy to escort through the desert and turn over to an Estonian combat team near the Helmand Border. And so they rolled out of their last leaguer in the Maywand with happy hearts on that sun-drenched, desert morning.

Lt Ben Rogerson's 5 Platoon had the duty of establishing the comms link to tie together both ends of the long convoy route through Maywand. They had performed this task many times before. En route to carry out this task the three LAVs of 5 Platoon came to a crossing point over one of the vital *karez* systems. The lead vehicle halted to check for threats, but none was obvious. There was no reason to be especially cautious; Afghan forces had been working throughout the area and for Rogerson's men such obstacle crossings had become routine. Unfortunately, on this day their luck ran out. The first vehicle, containing Sgt Donald Lucas and his section, went down a route where a Taliban IED cell had buried a powerful charge consisting of what later appeared to be multiple anti-tank mines stacked atop each other. The size and type of IED was not unusual in Kandahar Province, but this one detonated under the troop compartment at the rear of the LAV. The massive explosion blew call-sign 22Bravo into the air, ripping off its rear door. The explosion killed Sgt Lucas, one of the best section commanders in 2RCR, and five of his soldiers instantly. Cpl Shaun Fevens, guarding the left rear from an air sentry hatch, was blown clear and landed in a scorched heap 50 feet away. The LAV turret commander, gunner and driver were all wickedly shaken and bruised but alive.

Rogerson, the tall, lean, quiet, young commander of 5 Platoon, needed all his calming presence in the minutes that followed. His first task was to report the strike to Maj Ruff, who passed it on to battlegroup headquarters in Kandahar. Rogerson then leapt from his vehicle to clear a safe lane to the wreck as well as the area around it to ensure that no further IEDs could harm the wounded or the rescuers.

Only when he was satisfied that no more of his men would be hurt by coming forward to help did he wave them on. Cpl Robertson, LAV gunner in 22Bravo, was roughed up but mobile. He was the first to reach Shaun Fevens. Ironically, it was Fevens himself who took charge of his own care. Despite his wounds, Fevens—who had taken the TCCC course—calmly explained to Robertson how to deal with the blood flowing from his smashed legs and arm.

Platoon Warrant Officer Richard Yuskiw, in the last vehicle of the packet, dismounted his soldiers to start clearing a safe LZ for the chopper they knew they needed. Platoon medic, Cpl Rob Wickens, went to work stabilizing the critically injured Fevens. Rogerson and Yuskiw steadied the lot and kept them focused away from the dead and on saving the living. Rogerson also took on the horrible task of checking to see whether any man was still alive inside the back of the smashed vehicle. He confirmed what he sensed, that all his men were killed in an instant.

It did not take long for help to arrive in the form of 41 Squadron engineers, to clear the area of further explosives, and Maj Ruff's command party, including CSM O'Toole. By then the main task was to carefully remove the friends they all had lost. It was the most horrible and difficult task to ask soldiers to do and O'Toole was the man who would make it work. The calm and quiet professionalism demonstrated by all involved during those hours was noted by many. O'Toole also ensured the area was cleaned after the engineer explosives specialists finished their investigation. Ruff picked up the last washer found and keeps it on his key chain in memory of his men.[5]

Back at the battlegroup Command Post at KAF, and on the radio net for the whole task force, news came slowly as Yuskiw and O'Toole painstakingly made absolutely sure of the status of all casualties and verified names precisely. There could be no errors when handling such details. Gone were Sgt Don Lucas, MCpl Chris Stannix, Cpl Brent Poland, Cpl Aaron Williams, Pte Kevin Kennedy, and Pte David Greenslade. As the names were confirmed in the Command Post, a cold wind blew among the buildings. Men and women maintained their composure, though, and put away their personal feelings. They were all helped in this by the calm and reassuring professionalism of the battlegroup's LAV Captain, Dave Nixon. He set the tone immediately with his calm, collected voice on the radio: this was a situation they had all prepared for, there were critical things that needed doing, and the dead and wounded were best served by making sure these were done properly. Once the situation in Maywand was sorted out they had an evacuation to deal with. In the meantime, the entire Kandahar base went into a communications lockdown. The last thing anybody wanted to happen was news to leak that Canadians had been killed before the families were all notified. That way there would be no uncertainty about the dead soldiers' identities and only six sets of family and friends need be devastated.

That day, like all days, came to an end. The dead and wounded were lifted to KAF by American Blackhawks, and the living—due to the capriciousness of war fewer in number than anyone expected— returned as planned, pouring their exhausted frames into showers and starting to peel away 36 days of grime. A ramp ceremony was planned for later that Easter weekend, the 90th Anniversary of the Battle of Vimy Ridge. Ironically, because Kandahar is a half day ahead of Canadian time, and because news travelled home slowly, many in the battlegroup watched on TV in the CP or in the Canada House recreation centre in Kandahar as Prime Minister Stephen Harper announced the deaths in 5 Platoon. By then Cpl Shaun Fevens had already talked to his mom in Nova Scotia to let her know that he was all right, but that there would be some news breaking soon about deaths in Afghanistan. Within a few minutes of that brief call, Mrs. Fevens was dealing with national media interested in her son's miraculous escape.

As the story broke, the media at KAF went looking for the background to the event, searching with particular tenacity for something faulty or someone incompetent to blame. Rumours flew about how the men in the back were killed by ammunition "cooking off" due to unsafe stowage. None of the rumours was true, and no one except the men in 5 Platoon knew how their platoon leader had crawled across ammunition boxes in the shattered LAV to check on the vital signs of their dead comrades. Those who best knew the dead knew they did not suffer. And while the media focussed on more Canadian deaths in Afghanistan, no one covered the first ever Kandahar half-marathon that ran that very day; no stories were filed on the irrigation system restoration, or the road and culvert repairs that propelled the largest agricultural growth in southern Afghanistan in a decade. Nothing that gave meaning to those deaths made the headlines in Canada.

On 9 April 2007 Canada's Task Force Afghanistan and hundreds of other ISAF troops fell in on the tarmac of Kandahar Airfield to bid farewell to their friends. There were soldiers' quiet tears as the flag-draped coffins were marched slowly to the waiting aircraft, accompanied by the haunting skirl of the bagpiper's lament. This was the only time they could afford for grief. So much had been accomplished so far on this tour, but even more remained. Tomorrow, the battlegroup had to get back to work.

THE WAR GOES ON

Many troops in TF 1-07 had no chance to break at all from their routine, and little time for sentiment. LCol Rob Chamberlain's PRT soldiers held a short memorial parade at Camp Nathan Smith and pushed on with making Kandahar City's sewers, water supply, and sanitation services function: warm weather brought disease and there was still much work left to be done. Meanwhile, Maj Henderson's Patricias kept their vigil in the Panjwayi Peninsula so that irrigation work, and alternative crop training, could continue. In Zharey, Sgt Lucas's 2RCR comrades in Dave Quick's India Company never relaxed the pace of their foot patrols, reaching into more and more hamlets that had yet to see western soldiers coming to their aid. Quick was probing right to the edge of the Nalgham–Sangsar stronghold. Almost every night his platoons were in a different location in central Zharey, much to the surprise of the locals and doubtlessly the Taliban scouts who came across them.

On the other side of the "Belly of the Beast" Graham's recce troops also kept up with their probing patrols. Grand plans were made to surge into the centre and plant ANP checkpoints in this Taliban stronghold. Indeed, that would be the tactic used to break Taliban dominance in those villages six months later. But in April 2007, the ANP were not ready or available for the task. The Task Force was working on a plan to create police versions of the Afghan National Army's OMLTs or mentoring teams, but the extra Canadian soldiers, police mentors, and the preparation needed would not be ready for some time. As it stood, Rob Walker's battlegroup and Shereen

Shah's Kandak would have to cope with whatever spring offensive the Taliban could muster.

Over the next several days, Quick's company in eastern Zharey patrolled hard on foot by night and established temporary, defensible patrol bases by dawn. They held *shuras* with members of nearby villages, hearing their views on work that needed to be done and on which police detachments were a problem. The process repeated itself every few days. In fact, India Company lived on the move, only returning to FOBs to resupply before heading out again. Quite often, WO Bill Hunter, the PRT detachment leader in the district, came along on those patrols so that impromptu *shuras* could also convene CDCs in villages where the UN had already established them or could help start new CDCs in others. He also used the time traversing Zharey to map out the entire district irrigation system so that work on it could be co-ordinated into a district-wide water management plan.[6] India Company's continual night movement was impossible to catch and ambush with IEDs, so the Taliban in the area laid low. But the process was intensely physically demanding for the troops as daytime temperatures were hitting 40 degrees Celsius.

Having lost one of their cells at no cost to the Canadians and with no civilian casualty events to exploit the Taliban on the western end of the Nalgham–Sangsar nest were probably more concerned with the relentless pressure from Graham's Recce Squadron. In the second week of April he pushed vehicle and foot patrols into northern Nalgham, initially with the aim of setting up a new ANP post, until he decided that simply was not possible. Nonetheless, they carried on with presence patrols to demonstrate to locals that the Taliban hold on this nest area was slipping. Interestingly, the people who moved out of the way of the anticipated battle at the beginning of April had returned, convinced the Canadians meant them no harm.

The sum total of patrol and meeting reports in early April created a firmer picture of the complexity of life in the Nalgham–Sangsar nest. The fear was evident among many residents. The Taliban were still using the area as a base and were moving more bomb-making cells and fighters into it to prepare for some kind of spring offensive. It was unclear in mid-April just how many, but many signs also pointed to teams of foreign fighters entering the area. But unlike Pashmul the year before, thousands of people were still in their homes and working in their fields. Canadian and Afghan troops would have to deal with this looming threat very carefully. Most of all, they could not let the Taliban mount an offensive from that area, as it would disrupt the tempo of reconstruction taking place over large swaths of the province. But that goal could be achieved only if the Taliban kept up their pattern of attacks—hitting the Canadians instead of the reconstruction and the locals who supported it. Unfortunately, the troops of TF 1-07 would pay the price.

By 11 April, Graham was ready to pack in this series of patrols in Panjwayi and haul his squadron back to Ghundey Ghar. The success of their recent defeat of the IED cell proved to them that discipline, skill at arms, and good relationships with local Afghans could make a difference in earning the faith of Kandaharis and breaking the Taliban/drug-trafficker reign of fear. The Easter tragedy sobered them, but did not shake their resolve.

LColWalker's TacHQ party arrived at Ghundey Ghar on 11 April to be briefed on Graham's latest patrol. The briefing had just gotten underway when it was interrupted by radio chatter and a concerned look on the face of Capt Sean Piers, the Recce Squadron's battle captain. Not a kilometre away, near the scene of Hotel Company's February gunfight, one of the squadron's Coyotes had struck an IED. The blast blew off the front axle and injured the driver. The news, though disturbing, was not enough to end the briefing. IED finds and strikes were the norm in the area and this event seemed almost routine. Piers co-ordinated the recovery of the wounded and the blasted vehicle, and sent out a team to gather evidence on the bomb-makers. Graham had just resumed his briefing to Walker and his staff when another explosion occurred, this one powerful enough to be heard by everyone at Ghundey Ghar.

One of the Coyotes in the rescue force responding to the first blast had detonated a second IED. This one was no simple anti-tank mine or propane cylinder. Like the IED encountered by Hotel Company out in Maywand, the explosive material in this bomb was enough to throw the Coyote armoured vehicle into the air, twirl it like a toy, and drop it on its side. The power of the blast and collision with the earth separated the turret from the hull. The crew commander,

MCpl Allan Stewart, was killed instantly. The vehicle's gunner, Cpl Matthew Dicks, was badly injured but alive. The air sentry in the rear hatch was once again blown clear and landed on his back. Crewmen from the other Coyote in the patrol dismounted to assist.

First on the scene of the second explosion was the patrol commander, WO K.W. Nykorak, who started searching the area lest there be even more IEDs, traps, or an ambush awaiting the rescuers. Darkness was gathering as reports were received of new foreign-fighter cells moving into the area. Cpl Dave "Gio" Gionet and Tpr Shane Dolmovic, both TCCC-trained, raced into the carnage to help the wounded. They reached the turret first and quickly realized Allan Stewart was gone; Dicks was alive but trapped by the wreckage. Gionet and Dolmovic had to move fast because a fire was raging in the shattered vehicle. Within five minutes, SSM Bill Richards was on the scene with a medic, an Explosive Ordnance Disposal (EOD) team, a Badger armoured engineer vehicle and, perhaps most importantly, his calming and commanding presence. Ordinary people would have buckled under the strain of that scene. One of Richards' friends was already dead, one of his troopers lay in critical condition under a burning LAV filled with fuel and ammunition, and no one had yet reported on the driver, Tpr James Pentland, who was probably trapped in his compartment. Dozens of peacekeeping missions, a mass of cultural and personal experiences, and professionalism drove the soldiers to make incredible efforts to save others, especially their comrades. That night, many summoned energy buried deep inside themselves and rose to the challenge.

Richards added men to the defence perimeter and called in the details while the debris was cleared away from the turret. Dolmovic and Gionet got Dicks out of the gunner's hatch and moved him to safety, where the medic could work on him. As the hull burned, fuel dripped from leaking tanks, and sparks flew around, Dolmovic went for the driver's hatch to try and find Pentland. He was there, all right: unconscious and bleeding badly. But the driver's hatch was blocked by the engine hanging out over it. Not to be foiled, Dolmovic went through the open turret ring and crawled forward through dripping fuel, roiling smoke, and spitting sparks. Other members of the patrol worked at extinguishing the fire and shutting down the wrecked

Coyote's electrical system. When he was unable to free his friend, Dolmovic turned over the task to the stockier Gionet. But even Gio could not move the steel that trapped Pentland in his seat. Gionet remained inside with the smoke and fumes trying to stop the bleeding, while Sgt-Maj Richards tried to pull the engine away with a cable attached to a Badger engineer vehicle. About the time that the engine was pulled free, Pentland's pulse stopped. Gionet feverishly administered CPR until he practically passed out from inhaling so much smoke and diesel fumes. Then Dolmovic took over and kept at it until the medic confirmed what they all knew. Their friend James Pentland was gone.

It is expected and hoped that in the terror and confusion of combat and human suffering soldiers will continue to function. Bill Richards and his troopers did more than perform their jobs well that night. Richards, in particular, lived up to the highest standard of professional and dedication as he co-ordinated the work of dozens of men and women who came to the aid of James Pentland.

All of these events filtered back on the crackling radio at the squadron CP. The senior officers present, LCol Walker and Maj Graham, ended the briefing so they could attend to the serious matter before them. As events at the scene of the two blasts went from bad to worse, reports came in from other Canadian units in the area that as many as one hundred Taliban combat troops, bomb-makers, and Chechen fighters had moved into Zharey District. At that time the numbers seemed ridiculous; however, during the coming weeks they proved an underestimation. Moments after that report came in, Walker and Graham understood that the situation in Kandahar changed drastically that night. The casualty rescue, vehicle recovery, and site investigation to get the vital information needed to hunt the bombers would take more time. If anything approaching the numbers of Tier 1 Taliban fighters reported by intelligence estimates arrived on the scene to ambush the recovery effort, a tragic IED strike could turn quickly into a major action. It was time to call in the cavalry. Without hesitation, LCol Walker scrambled an additional force of tanks with mine-clearing equipment from Ma'Sum Ghar. It would not take them long to cover the distance and bring their might to bear.

A short time later, no less than "Boomer" Broomfield himself led the Strathconas' tanks into the perimeter around the blast site. Any attempt to ambush the rescue effort would be revealed by the Leopards' powerful array of night sensors and dealt with by their weapons. No one on that wretched night in the desert near Ghundey Ghar questioned the value of deploying tanks to Afghanistan.[7]

What remained was to once again get the dead and wounded back to KAF and then home.

A second ramp ceremony in less than a week was a tough blow for the Task Force. But once again, like the post-battle burial parades of Canada's past wars, the event provided soldiers with those critical few hours to think about their friends and to grieve before putting it all in a box, putting their helmet back on, and getting back to work.

Despite the casualties, TF 1-07 had accomplished much in only three months. They had taken large steps forward in building trust with the people of Zharey–Panjwayi, both with their ability to bring help to communities and by displaying courage and careful discrimination in action against the Taliban. If this upward trend was to continue beyond April, the threat from the Nalgham–Sangsar area had to be contained. And with the poppy harvest looming in early May time was of the essence. A significant drop in insurgent activity after mid-April was the most telling indicator of the Taliban's dependence on that harvest. Everyone knew that when the harvest ended in early May, the Taliban and their criminal cohorts would resume their war in Kandahar. The few times they did strike it was at easy targets. Tragically, one of those was a van carrying UN aid workers from Nepal. Chamberlain's Quick Reaction Force from the PRT base in Camp Nathan Smith helped retrieve the dead.

DRAGON FIRE

While the Canadians worked hard in the comparative quiet of Kandahar Province through late April, the war still raged in Helmand. ISAF asked the Canadians to assist that effort and Task Force HQ sent a troop of Maj Dan Bobbitt's prized M777 155mm Howitzers. When the troop from "Dragon" Battery 2RCHA arrived at British FOB Robinson in late April, the threat was still very high. As the Canadian gunners disembarked from their helicopters they had to run a gauntlet of Taliban mortar and rocket fire. For the next few weeks rounds left the barrels of the two M777s at a rate not seen by Canadian gunners anywhere else in TF 1-07. The stress on the guns—so new that the Canadians were the first to deploy them operationally—was high, and no weapon is completely fool-proof. On 13 April, one of the "Triple 7s" suffered a premature firing. The crew had been fixing a priming problem when the powder charge exploded out of the breech. The gun detachment commander, Sgt Sydney Barnes, and several of the crew were burned by the flash. As medics treated the old gunner sergeant's wounds, another call for support came crackling through the radio from British soldiers locked in a firefight. Barnes brushed the medics aside and ran to the troop's other gun to ready it. Bobbitt wrote later that Barnes's "singular focus on his mission is in the finest traditions of the Artillery corps and of the Canadian Forces."

The artillery troop stayed on in Helmand for several more weeks until the Taliban were broken in the area and the threat had passed. When they boarded their helicopters only a few short weeks later, they sauntered onto the strip and loaded up for the return ride as if on exercise. Things were changing even in Helmand.

MAINTAINING THE MOMENTUM

Back in Kandahar the situation in late April remained quiet, but tense. Everyone had worked hard to ensure that the young men of the province had reason to stay on their farms or at the very least had employment in reconstruction projects once the poppy harvest ended. Only time would tell if it was enough. The waning days of April were used to the utmost to make sure those young men had productive alternatives and to prove that life was getting better for all Kandaharis. Even representatives from Nalgham and Sangsar were turning up at the Zharey District *shura*. Maj David Quick noted that representatives from other villages complained that the Nalgham–Sangsar members were only coming to cash in on PRT project money, but from ISAF's perspective, in the grand scheme of things, that was just fine. On behalf of the government of Afghanistan the PRT was bringing public works to all Afghans. And by doing it through traditional village and district *shuras*, the PRT and the government were reinstating the grass-roots governance system that previously had been hijacked by Taliban strongmen.

But some things defied quick and easy fixes, and improving the quality of policing remained the biggest challenge. In Kandahar City, regular PRT patrols and mentoring visits kept the ANP sub-stations there performing to a higher standard. The challenge was trying to get similar results in the western greenbelt. To that end, India Company on the north side of the Arghandab River and the Patricia company on the south sent out a series of assessment patrols in the latter part of April to determine the status of rural ANP units. Each patrol was aided by a section of Canadian Army MPs: the first tentative step toward Police Operational Mentoring and Liaison Teams (POMLTs) that later became a standard practice. Not surprisingly, what they found was that some detachments and checkpoints were led by corrupt officers and manned by drug addicts with little interest in doing their jobs, while others were quite good. Small bands of new constables, recruited and trained more recently and led by a handful of committed leaders, were doing excellent work. In other cases they found keen new constables seeking ways to work around corrupt commanders. Quick and Henderson therefore found problems, but they also found something to work with.[8]

While the battlegroup took the pulse of the police problem, the PRT used the late April lull to conduct CDC *shuras*, mostly in Zharey–Panjwayi, but some in districts where the Taliban's footprint was light. In many of those, CIDA co-ordinated with UN Habitat officials to get more CDCs started in remote villages largely untouched by either the Taliban or the government and ISAF. PRT patrols could not always reach them to verify whether those CDCs were actually making progress on projects, and doubtlessly sometimes frightened UN workers reported non-existent progress. But in many other cases this surge brought to remote rural villages the first connection to the far-off national government in Kabul that anyone had ever seen.[9]

Closer to the danger area of Zharey–Panjwayi, soldiers like WO Bill Hunter sat at the *shuras* and confronted representatives of the very absentee landowners that the development program aimed to undermine. The process was slow and required infinite patience. But Hunter and his opposite number, Kendall MacLean in Panjwayi, were both laid-back rural Maritimers from reserve units. They had the right personalities for the job, blending plenty of patience with stiff resolve to shift project funding away from the landlords and into the hands of the locals. It was, after all, the residents of Zharey–Panjwayi who were trying to get the irrigation work done that would make meaningful differences in the farm hamlets.

While TF 1-07's soldiers worked the rural areas of Kandahar Province, Gavin Buchan and the Canadian Department of Foreign Affairs was busy in April holding *shuras* with district leaders and strongmen outside the current area of Canadian and Afghan government influence. Buchan was laying the ground work for a critical new expansion of the Kandahar ADZ. Some observers of Canada's and NATO's Afghan rebuilding mission suggested that while the development scheme was laudable, there was no hope for success without addressing the question of Pakistan and the border between the two countries. In fact, the highest echelons of Canada's Department of Foreign Affairs—not to mention the Americans and NATO as a whole—were well aware of this problem, and in the spring of 2007 they all worked the channels with Islamabad. The results of that sensitive diplomatic work cannot yet be disclosed, but Canadian troops knew that things were moving when Recce Squadron received orders late in April to close down in Zharey and head to the border at Spin Boldak. This new demand spread the battlegroup very thin indeed, and it came just at the moment when the fighting season was about to start. Everyone in the battlegroup—not to mention Afghans watching from the sidelines—was holding their collective breaths to see what the next few weeks would bring: a repeat of the major battles of 2006, or something completely different?

The Home Front 6

"I can tell you that the whole community is in shock."[1]

Those eleven words by Col Ryan Jestin, commander of Base Gagetown, accurately reflected the mood in the garrison community of Oromocto, New Brunswick, in the wake of the Easter deaths in Afghanistan. A town that only months before had sent its sons and daughters off to war with great fanfare had now been rocked to its core. While everyone knew an event such as this was possible, there was a sense that "the unthinkable" had happened.

But while the tragedy touched many deeply, it did not hit a community wholly unprepared to deal with loss. Just as the long period of training prepared the soldiers for their mission, an equally long process helped the "Home Front" to deal with the rigours and demands of a combat deployment overseas. While the task force carried out its mission in Afghanistan, a large network of people and agencies in Canada provided support for both the troops overseas and their families back home. In fact, in early 2007 some parts of Atlantic Canada were communities at war, a condition they shared with a handful of other places: Edmonton, Alberta; Petawawa, Ontario; and Valcartier, Quebec.

Although many of the troops who made up the task force had participated in earlier overseas deployments, members and their families were dealing with new circumstances that created significant stress. First, with its higher risk of casualties, the Kandahar tour was much more dangerous than most previous deployments, including earlier rotations to Afghanistan. Second, because of the army's higher tempo of operations over the last decade, many of the troops, especially senior non-commissioned members (NCMs), had served on numerous deployments, some in Afghanistan. When combined with the lengthy training period that preceded the deployment of Task Force 1-07, the troops were separated from their families for many months. Added to these were the challenges unique to the changing military family lifestyle, including frequent moves to new bases, the recruitment of older members who already had families, and, in the case of dual serving couples, the chance that both members might be posted or deployed simultaneously, or that a wife/mother might be deployed, leaving a solo parenting father behind to care for the family. All of these circumstances placed stress on both the members and their families, so extraordinary steps were taken in Canada to both support the troops in-theatre as well as their families back home.

"THE ARMY TAKES CARE OF ITS OWN"

In many respects, the army itself provided the first line of support to the Home Front. In fact, that was one of the primary missions of the "rear parties," the elements of a deployed unit left behind in Canada. Their job was to help manage the affairs of the unit while it was overseas. Each of the units that deployed elements with the task force, including the Princess Patricia's Canadian Light Infantry, Royal Canadian Dragoons, and Lord Strathcona's Horse, set up their own rear parties. However, because the 2nd Battalion of the Royal Canadian Regiment (2RCR) generated the battlegroup headquarters and had the most direct link into theatre, 2RCR's Golf Company acted as rear party for both the task force and the battalion's battlegroup. Within the chain of command they were responsible to Headquarters, Land Forces Atlantic Area (LFAA) in Halifax, who in turn reported to Canadian Expeditionary Force Command (CEFCOM) in Ottawa. The "old hands" of Golf Company, who hand served in Afghanistan in 2005, understood the importance of their task to both troops in the field and loved ones at home.

Golf Company had four main tasks.[2] The first was casualty management, which meant co-ordinating the repatriation of killed and wounded to Canada. The rear party notified the next of kin of all casualties, and provided assisting officers for the families of soldiers killed in action. When an incident occurred in-theatre, the rear party was notified immediately and in the event of a death it assembled a

Critical Incident Response Team, which included the rear party commanding officer and adjutant, the base surgeon, a padre, a representative from Base Gagetown and Public Affairs, as well as an assisting officer. A Notification Team that included a notifier, usually a senior officer from the unit or base, a padre, and an assisting officer would then inform the soldier's next of kin. When more than one death occurred during an incident, as was the case in the 8 April attack on Hotel Company, the teams were co-ordinated so that notification was carried out at the same time. On at least one occasion the RCMP helped the military find the residence of a member's next of kin.[3] Following notification the names of the casualties were made public.

The assisting officer remained with the family constantly over the next several weeks, acting as the main point of contact between the military and family. Among other things, this officer arranged for the family's travel to CFB Trenton for the repatriation of the deceased soldier and home again afterward, and assisted the family with funeral plans. Thereafter, the assisting officer continued to be available to help the family when necessary.

It was Capt John Hill, an officer with the transport section of 3 Area Support Group (ASG) at CFB Gagetown, who was assigned to the family of Sgt Donald Lucas in April. Hill quickly realized that assisting officers were "all about the CF supporting military families." He underwent a three-day training course that gave him the tools he needed to carry out his role. This included information about family benefits and a list of contact people, as well as how to work with grieving family members. He also remained in close contact with other assisting officers. Hill accompanied the Lucas family for two weeks in Ontario and Newfoundland before returning to Gagetown. Over the next few months he assisted Mrs. Lucas on almost a daily basis. For Hill this was more than a duty or job—it was about helping a family during a very difficult time. He knew that should his family find themselves in similar circumstances, someone else would do the same for them.[4]

In the case of a wounded soldier, notification of next of kin came from the soldier himself whenever possible, in order to reassure his family that he was alright. MCpl Tracy Price from Hotel Company's

6 Platoon had been wounded in Kandahar City in late March. Shortly after arriving at the medical facility at Ma'Sum Ghar, he first called his parents in Boisetown, N.B. When his mother answered she said how thoughtful it was of him to call on his father's birthday. When his father, who had served with the Black Watch and 2RCR for almost 30 years, came on the line the real reason for Price's call became clear: he had been wounded, it was not serious, and he wanted his father to drive to Fredericton to be with his wife when she got home. He then called his wife at work to let her know what had happened.[5]

A new addition to TF 1-07's rear party structure was the casualty management cell. It was developed following Roto 2's mass casualty incident on 4 September 2006, when one soldier was killed and dozens wounded, which overwhelmed the existing casualty management system. The cell was set up to provide liaison between the unit, families, and the medical system by providing escorts for wounded soldiers returning to Canada, as well as drivers to transport repatriated troops and their families from the airport, and to and from medical appointments. Once wounded or injured soldiers had recovered, the cell assisted them to return to work.

The casualty management cell was made up of previously wounded or injured soldiers and so they knew about the challenges facing returning injured soldiers. Being handled by comrades who had themselves been wounded and evacuated helped the soldiers to deal with the disappointment of not seeing out the tour. According to MCpl Price, leaving Afghanistan after he was wounded was the hardest thing he had ever faced during his military career. Joining the casualty management cell allowed him to stay in contact with the mission and "remain part of the loop." Once he had returned to duty, Price became the cell's 2i/c and among other things escorted an injured soldier home from Germany.[6]

The rear party also trained and provided replacements for the casualties, injuries, and administrative repatriations in TF 1-07. Providing replacements turned out to be a challenging task. When troops designated for the mission failed their drug tests in October 2006, their slots had to be filled by soldiers being prepared to act as replacements during the later phases of the mission. And with the loss of a whole section from Hotel Company on Easter Sunday, most of the 2RCR replacement cadre was sent overseas. Thus, more replacements had to be quickly found and readied for deployment.[7] It was a constant scramble to keep up.

Finally, through its Family Support Cell, the rear party provided an important link between the unit, the deployed soldiers, and their spouses, families, and friends back home. They did this by keeping the unit and families up-to-date on the task force's activities, and offering advice and assistance when it was needed. They also notified deployed soldiers about emergency situations involving family members. In this capacity, they worked closely with other groups within the network, including the Military Family Resource Centre (MFRC), Deployment Support Centre (DSC), and spousal committees.

Base units reinforced this system by sponsoring the families of their members deployed to Afghanistan. For example, base maintenance personnel assisted the families of troops assigned to the Task Force's maintenance company, helping them to move, shovelling snow, and making small household repairs. As Capt John Hill put it, "the Electrical and Mechanical Engineers look after each other."[8] The base also organized a network of padres who could reach into communities across the region. This was important because a large augmentation force of Atlantic region reservists were deployed as part of TF 1-07.

A number of other base organizations supported military families. Working in partnership with base units, the Gagetown MFRC provided information, services, programs, and activities developed specifically to support the military community. By 2007, the centre had more than 40 employees and 90 registered volunteers who included military spouses and parents, retired military members, and community youth. Together they serviced over 3,000 families. Although deployments were nothing new for the centre, the size of the battlegroup from Gagetown required extensive preparations that began nine months before the troops departed. This included professional development sessions that made sure the staff were ready for this demanding rotation. No matter what was going on behind the scenes, they always had to appear calm to visitors and children in the day-care rooms. Their emergency child-care providers also received more training prior to going into the homes of families experiencing emergencies.

Throughout the deployment, the Gagetown MFRC offered adult programs designed to help spouses cope with separation and plans for reunion. Many family members remarked on the stress that came from following news about the mission, to the point where some no longer watched the evening news. Instead, they relied on others to keep them up-to-date. Others reported how late-night telephone calls or unannounced visitors kept them on edge.

More frequent contact with troops in-theatre through weekly satellite telephone calls and e-mailing alleviated stress levels, although loss of contact when members went outside the wire also caused anxiety. Soldiers often developed ways to communicate that would not compromise operational security to let their family know when they would be out of touch. The centre's very popular Tuesday coffee evenings provided a setting where military family members could come together with strangers and form friendships, enabling them to spend time with others dealing with the anxieties of separation. Between 30 and 50 people regularly attended these get-togethers. Short-term counselling was provided for those individuals and families in crisis.

The Gagetown MFRC ran programs in local schools to assist children with the emotional stress of having a parent deployed, including how to cope with anger, known to the children as "dragon days," and finding safe places for themselves when they became afraid. They also held family social events, such as Easter parties, barbeques, and their annual strawberry social which drew 600 people. The centre provided free deployment childcare that enabled parents to do their grocery shopping or just have time for themselves. It's mail drop-off location allowed families to send packages overseas free of charge. Their video-conferencing service provided more direct contact with deployed members in-theatre at Kandahar Airfield and Camp Nathan Smith, especially during holidays, anniversaries, birthdays, and school graduations.

The Military Family Resource Centre also kept in touch with the families of reservists throughout the region. Many of them did not live in military communities like Oromocto and, although they received support from their own families and friends, frequently outsiders could not really understand the stress military families went through during the deployment. The MFRC kept reservists' families up-to-date with events with monthly newsletters and visits to reserve units, where they presented pre-deployment and reintegration briefings to members and their families. They also provided reservists' spouses in Saint John, Woodstock, and Edmundston with emergency child respite care.[9]

A more recent addition to the military family support network was 3 Area Support Group's Deployment Support Centre. DSCs were initially established at Valcartier and Petawawa, where the operational tempo was higher than Gagetown and a brigade structure existed. The Gagetown DSC was stood up when it became clear that there was no direct link between military families and the chain of command. Located in the same building as the MFRC, the DSC was staffed by hand-picked military members, most of whom had been on overseas deployments and knew about the experience first-hand. According to Capt Mark Milligan, the DSC Co-ordinator, they wanted staff who "were empathetic ... who could get down and play Lego with the kids but yet when they put their uniforms on they had a military bearing . . ." He said the MFRC presented a very positive environment and they needed to fit in as partners. The DSC staff wore civilian clothing to avoid unit and rank bias among the soldiers and their families.

During the deployment the DSC played several roles. Much of their work consisted of making referrals for family members looking for services within the community, helping those who were having administrative or pay problems or who needed to contact deployed members quickly in the event of an emergency. The DSC was able to call directly into theatre and usually put the family member in touch with the soldier within two and a half hours. This kind of direct contact also helped to defuse family problems before they became crises which in the past sometimes required compassionate repatriations. From October 2006 to August 2007, the DSC handled almost 600 assistance requests.

The DSC also kept a detailed database of information on deployed members that assisted the base and MFRC in a number of ways.

They helped to keep track of family members' contact numbers when they planned to be away from their primary address for more than 24 hours, so that the military could reach them quickly, if necessary. They also provided important information during next-of-kin notifications that made that process work more effectively. The information might range from the make, colour, and license plate number of a family member's car, to details about a family's special needs that would be helpful to notification and assisting officers.

Finally, although many of the task force units had their own rear parties, some did not. The DSC therefore worked with Unit Family Support Representatives to ensure that members from units throughout the Atlantic region and their families received the same level of support as those from Gagetown.[10]

Gagetown found other ways to show support for military families. In July, the Base CANEX held Fun Days which featured food, entertainment, rides for kids, and a petting zoo. More than 2,000 people from the wider base community attended, many of them families of deployed members. The CANEX is a division of the Canadian Forces Personnel Support Agency (CFPSA), a nation-wide organization that develops and delivers morale and welfare services to CF members and their families in Canada and overseas. Among their successful programs is the "Support Our Troops" project.

THE COMMUNITIES RALLY 'ROUND

Throughout the Atlantic region, governmental and local community organizations also found ways to support the troops overseas and their families back home. Provincial governments took steps to ensure that soldiers and military families received support. Local hospitals worked with the CF to make sure they could accommodate repatriated wounded or injured soldiers so they could recover close to their families. Over 200 students in Oromocto High School had one or both parents deployed in Afghanistan, so the local school district ensured that students throughout the area received support, especially during tragic incidents. They set up specially trained crisis events response teams—comprised of learning specialists, guidance counsellors, and psychologists—who could help students cope with

anxiety and grief, as well as comfort school staff, many of whom
also had family members overseas. Moreover, workers throughout
the school system, including bus drivers, were trained to watch for
signs of stress among students arising from the deployment. Finally,
retired teachers within the community volunteered to relieve colleagues in the classrooms should it become necessary.[11]

Communities, like New Maryland, N.B., where many military
members and their families lived, as well as individuals showed support
for the troops by placing yellow ribbons on trees, telephone polls,
and signposts.[12] Elsewhere, in early February 2007 volunteers who
had spouses, relatives, and friends serving in Afghanistan gathered at
the Dalhousie, N.B. Legion to form their own "support our troops
group." One of the main organizers was Sandra Carrier-Harquail
whose husband, WO Ken Harquail of the 2nd Battalion of the Royal
New Brunswick Regiment (2RNBR), was serving in Afghanistan.
Initially, she undertook the project to keep busy and support the two
dozen local soldiers who were part of the task force. They held regular
get-togethers every two weeks where they sponsored fund-raisers
that featured local entertainment and suppers. They also created a
parcel donation program, setting out boxes at a local grocery store
as well as the Legion for anyone wishing to donate non-perishable
items. According to Harquail, the response was "unbelievable . . .
overwhelming," with hundreds of people participating in rallies and
other events. They received donations from many local businesses as
well as endorsements from such nearby communities as Tide Head
and Atholville. "Care packages" that included sweets, local newspapers, even portable camping showers were picked up by reservists
from Bathurst and then sent on to Gagetown for distribution among
the troops in Afghanistan. Gagetown also showed support for these
efforts in August 2007 by sending a Light-Armoured Vehicle to participate in Dalhousie's annual Bon Ami Festival parade alongside the
Support Our Troops float.[13]

Other community organizations found ways to support both the
troops and their families as well as communities at large throughout
the region. Among them were churches and their congregations
within the Oromocto, N.B. area. Anticipating the high stress levels the

deployment could have on the community, especially if the warning that as many as 100 casualties might occur, local clergy began developing ways for their parishioners to cope as early as July 2006. Reverend Robert McDowell, minister of the Oromocto United Church, made up handouts outlining ways to deal with stress and planned for community dinners and homework co-ops for students. (Fortunately, these plans never had to be implemented.) McDowell also joined with Father Ken Weir of St. Vincent de Paul Roman Catholic Church to organize Neighbours for Peace services. Beginning in October 2006, these monthly ecumenical services brought together people from the United, Roman Catholic, and Anglican churches for 20-minute prayer services that would be followed by opportunities for people to decompress if the need arose. Among the 120 to 150 people that attended were military family members and friends. Padre Gregg Costen, the rear party chaplain, e-mailed copies of the services to Padres Berry and Lazerte overseas who posted them around the Canadian compound. During one service several soldiers thanked those assembled for their support from Afghanistan via cellphone. Military members from Gagetown sometimes spoke to the groups, updating them on the course of the mission.[14]

Members of the business community also took on Support Our Troops projects, such as collecting letters, postcards, and other mementoes from local students for the troops, as well as school supplies and other gifts for Afghan children which the troops then distributed. Many community organizations held Red Friday rallies to show support, including a local rotary club and grocery store who joined with the Gagetown MFRC and Town of Oromocto to hold a Father's Day rally that featured a giant human heart formed by participants. It was photographed by the town fire department and then sent to the troops as a Father's Day present.[15] Similar displays of community solidarity and support occurred in Edmonton, Petawawa, and Valcartier.

Communities drew together when deaths occurred among task force members. Reflecting the make-up of the CF, these included many smaller, tight-knit communities throughout the Atlantic region, such as Perth-Andover and Geary, New Brunswick; Stellarton,

Nova Scotia; and St. Lawrence, Newfoundland. On 25 April 2007, a memorial service was held at Gagetown to honour the eight members of the battlegroup who died on 8 April and 11 April, and bring a sense of closure to the military and broader communities. The moment was particularly poignant for communities in New Brunswick. Sgt Lucas and his five men were all based at CFB Gagetown and the two Petawawa-based RCD troopers who died on 11 April were native New Brunswickers. More than 4,000 military personnel and civilians attended the moving service held in the field house of the base gymnasium, among them LGen Andrew Leslie, Chief of the Land Staff, and the Hon Greg Thompson, Minister of Veterans Affairs.

Involvement in overseas wars has always been a divisive issue in Canada, and the Afghanistan mission was no different. In time, most Canadians came to realize that this was not a "Heritage Minute" peacekeeping mission. Rather, it was a much more complex mission that involved Canadian troops in a range of actions, including combat, which at times could become quite intense. Gauging public attitudes toward the war was difficult, especially given regional variations. Many communities, especially in the Atlantic region, showed strong support for the troops. The rallies, fundraisers, and other events described here included widespread participation from the civilian community, not just troops and their families. Rev Bob McDowell described support for the troops in Oromocto as "absolute." He said the community saw itself as a garrison town, and "if the soldiers are asked to serve then the community will rally immediately behind them. That's a given." He also observed that during the deployment "the political debate about the war was almost absent. I very rarely heard anything from anybody in the community about whether or not we should be in Afghanistan . . . The issue was who the families were and rallying around those families."[16] Shelly Hillier, the Deployment and Family Support Coordinator at the Gagetown MFRC, described support for the troops and their families in the Fredericton/Oromocto area as "absolutely amazing." According to Hillier, it was important for soldiers home on leave and their families to see so many employees in stores and elsewhere wearing red shirts on Fridays and the yellow ribbons on cars and in store windows, showing them that "I'm living in an area that really cares."[17]

Nevertheless, support for the mission was not universal. Prior to the deployment small groups gathered in Fredericton, urging the government to bring the troops home. During the deployment a lively exchange took place within the "Letters to the Editor" sections of local newspapers. Several themes emerged that paralleled the larger national debate. Some local opponents to Canada's involvement in Afghanistan believed Canada's interests lay elsewhere, especially supporting more traditional UN peacekeeping operations, not the commitment to Afghanistan, which they saw as supporting America's war against terrorism. Others asserted that the mission in Afghanistan not only protected Canadians' right to free speech but was also helping to bring peace and stability to a war-torn nation. Some opponents to the mission made it clear that while they opposed government policy, they still supported the troops.[18]

Division over Canada's involvement in foreign military operations has often followed linguistic lines, with many francophones in Quebec opposing either sending troops overseas to fight or specific government policies related to war, such as conscription in 1917 and 1944. However, such sentiments were not present within francophone areas of the Atlantic region in 2007. According to Tim Jaques, editor of *The Tribune* of Campbellton, N.B., their sister newspaper, *La Voix du Restigouche*, ran stories from time to time about local francophone soldiers serving in Afghanistan. He reported that no anti-war protests occurred in his area nor did the paper receive any letters against their coverage of the mission. Sandra Carrier-Harquail of the Dalhousie Support Our Troops group reported similar impressions, stating that of the hundreds of people she met during their events only one person reacted negatively to their presence, accusing them of being "pro-war."[19]

THE FOURTH ESTATE

Canada's role in Afghanistan had received extensive national print and electronic media attention from the outset of the mission, and once the Canadians moved to Kandahar reportage became even more intensive. During TF 1-07's deployment regional media, including newspapers, also provided widespread coverage. Local newspaper correspondents, like Chris Lambie and Christian Laforce of the Halifax *Chronicle-Herald* and Marty Klinkenberg of the Saint John *Telegraph-Journal*, travelled to Afghanistan to cover the experiences of Atlantic Canadian troops first hand. Lambie and Laforce produced a book entitled *On Assignment in Afghanistan: Maritimers at War*, that was based on their time with the Task Force.[20]

Media also reported extensively on events occurring back home in support of the troops and their families. Newspaper dailies, like Fredericton's *The Daily Gleaner*, decided that with so many local soldiers deploying this was an important issue to the community and so should receive special coverage. Reporters were given more time to work on their stories.[21]

Regional weekly newspapers, such as Oromocto's *The Post-Gazette* and *The Tribune* from Campbellton, N.B., also covered the task force in some depth. Tim Jaques devoted coverage to the deployment, "because it is a combat mission, or at least a mission that includes combat, and local soldiers [are] involved. Too many people have the idea that Canada's wars are in the past, and its veterans are all from World War Two and Korea. I also thought it important that people realized what the troops were doing there."[22] *The Tribune* profiled local soldiers serving in Afghanistan and covered the activities of local organizations like the Support Our Troops group in Dalhousie.

If there were ever any doubts that the Afghanistan mission was dangerous, the casualties of 8 and 11 April shattered them. Covering the military funerals and memorial services were difficult—but essential—assignments. According to Michael Staples of Fredericton's *Daily Gleaner*, sometimes the media's presence was considered intrusive and unwelcome. But, as Staples explained, the media believed they played an important role in the nation's experience in Afghanistan, especially for Canadians grieving over the loss of soldiers. He also believed his role was more than just informing Canadians; by telling the stories of the deceased troops and their families, he was also paying homage to the fallen.[23]

The mood of the region was captured well by the response to a regular column in *The Tribune* of Campbellton called "Postcard from Kandahar," contributed by Sgt Terry Richardson from nearby Dalhousie. With 23 years of service in the regular forces, Richardson had worked recently with 2RNBR in Bathurst, N.B. until being deployed with the task force headquarters to Kandahar. There he worked with the Operational Mentoring and Liaison Team (OMLT), mentoring Afghan National Army troops at the brigade headquarters level. After receiving approval from Public Affairs, Richardson submitted to *The Tribune* weekly "Postcards" detailing his experiences in Afghanistan and thoughts about the mission, along with photos as a way of keeping in contact with family and friends back home, and letting them know what the troops were doing. Richardson, and a dozen other soldiers from New Brunswick's North Shore who helped to initiate the project, believed that most Canadians were out of touch with the kind of work on the ground that was going on in Afghanistan on a daily basis. The "Postcard" published on 18 April 2007 recounted the sadness felt by Canadian troops in Afghanistan following the deaths of the troops on Easter Sunday and two days later. As Richardson reminded his readers, "The death of a fellow soldier takes a toll on all CF members because we are a small force and we are like a large extended family." But, he continued, "we will soldier on, because that is what we are trained to do." Richardson received dozens of emails from all over Canada, the vast majority of which were very positive. The response "really surprised" him and "it was great to know people were supporting you."[24] Richardson and his colleagues would need that support in the days ahead. For while they had endured much during the first three months of their tour, and suffered deaths and injuries, much of the hard work of soldiering lay ahead in Afghanistan's summer fighting season.

While this chapter focuses mainly on the military and civilian Home Front experience in New Brunswick, similar events occurred throughout the Atlantic region, home to a large number of Canada's soldiers, both regular force and militia. The battlegroup and the supporting elements that comprised the core of TF 1-07 were unique in that they drew most of their personnel from the smallest region of the country. It is probably no great exaggeration to say that there were few communities or people within Atlantic Canada that did not know of someone who was deployed with the task force. That probably goes a long way to explain the depth and breadth of support they had on the Home Front. And why, between February and August 2007, thousands of Atlantic Canadians came together to support the task force overseas as well as the families of the troops in ways probably not seen since the Second World War.

TAMING THE WILD FRONTIER

On 5 May 2007, Major Steve Graham's RCD Recce Squadron rolled down the thin asphalt ribbon of Highway 4 from Kandahar Airfield to Spin Boldak. They were not the first coalition or even Canadian soldiers sent into the area. The amount of al-Qaeda and Taliban traffic across this border area had kept Operation *Enduring Freedom* (*OEF*) forces routinely coming and going there since 2001. Canadians had supported stability and reconstruction operations around Spin Boldak in the early months of 1PPCLI's deployment in 2006. Unfortunately, when Task Force 3-06 (TF 3-06) troops were forced to concentrate west of Kandahar City for *Operation Medusa*, they left behind a mixed bag of American Special Operations Forces, police trainers, customs and immigration workers, and development officials. These groups all worked with limited manpower, and in many cases at cross purposes. By spring 2007 progress in Spin Boldak was not faltering; it had barely gotten underway.

Indeed, the Kandahar Afghan Development Zone (ADZ) could never work so long as the Spin Boldak border area remained a separate region under *OEF* command, out of reach to International Security Assistance Force (ISAF) and UN Assistance Mission in Afghanistan (UNAMA) rebuilding programs, and—to a large extent—out of Afghan control. The southeast corner of Kandahar province is an intersection of culture, commerce, politics, and geography. The spectacular desolation of the "Reg" or Red Desert sprawls either side of Highway 4 as you drive south out of Kandahar Airfield. The Reg terminates in a scattering of wheat fields, pastures, and tiny villages clinging to thin patches of arid soil spread across a plain as flat as the Canadian prairies. Such life as can grow is sustained by winter rains and, in spring, by melting snow draining from the mountain wall on Pakistan's border. The water moves through a myriad of wadis that feed the Duhrey and eventually the Arghandab Rivers.

Weaving past rocky outcroppings and across the dry plains, the highway links Kandahar City to the border and beyond to Quetta, Pakistan. The ebb and flow of traffic and trade along this, the only paved road in the area, is interrupted by border checkpoints on both sides of the "International Arch." On the Afghan side lies the bustling town from which Spin Boldak District takes its name. It is typical of central Asian border communities that are junctions between cultures, nations, and trading partners, but it is also uniquely Afghan. The entrepreneurial spirit found all over Afghanistan may be strongest in Spin Boldak. It is home to the colourfully decorated "jingle" truck-transport industry that carries goods to and from Pakistan. It is the black-market vehicle and auto parts capital of Afghanistan. It is also the scene of extreme poverty and water shortages magnified by the thousands of refugees from decades of war and Taliban repression, who live in Internally Displaced Person camps or squatter settlements between Spin Boldak and the neighbouring village of Wes. Sometime during the two-decade exodus, the communities merged into one.

If Afghanistan is the crossroads of three continents, then Spin Boldak is its front gate. Legitimate trucking and automotive family businesses and refugees rub shoulders with smugglers, Taliban and al-Qaeda members, as well as Special Operations Forces and intelligence agents from a variety of nations observing the stream of humanity across the border. In 2007, four separate Afghan police forces operated in the district. Lacking mentors, the Afghan National Police (ANP) and the Afghan Highway Police (AHP) were the least effective. Before 2007 they maintained law and order in Spin Boldak intermittently and on their own terms. They profited by maintaining a "live and let live" truce along the Taliban and drug trade lifeline to Pakistan. The Afghan National Border Police (ANBP), with a recently attached US Army Embedded Training Team (ETT), and Afghanistan's fourth police agency, the National Directorate of Security (NDS: Afghanistan's intelligence agency) appeared to be more effective, at least on the counter-terrorist front. As in so many of Kandahar's districts, none offered real police services to their communities.

UN and NATO mission staff had learned from decades of peace support operations that a critical part of rescuing any failed state involves re-building healthy relationships with neighbouring nations. When those neighbours recognize that the once-failed state beside them has been stabilized and is no longer a threat, they are less likely to support terrorist groups, political parties or other efforts that undermine their neighbour's civil society.

In the case of Afghanistan and Pakistan, a decades-old state of near complete lawlessness had existed on both sides of the long, often ill-defined, border. Its remote and difficult terrain provides an ideal hiding place for anyone seeking to avoid authority. Since Pakistani independence, both nations have blamed each other for providing refuge to their respective criminals and enemies. That mistrust has been exacerbated by charges that the Pakistani Inter-Services Intelligence Directorate (ISID) openly supports the Taliban or at least is willing to look the other way while its proxies destabilize the vulnerable Afghan state from sanctuaries inside Pakistan. In October 2006 the US Institute for Peace insisted that "the United States, NATO, and the UN must agree to send a common message to Islamabad: that the persistence of Taliban havens in Pakistan is a threat to international peace and security that Pakistan must address immediately."[1] At time of writing, that difficult problem had not been solved.[2]

Of course, deep mistrust between neighbouring nations usually exists alongside common ground and interests. The challenge for the UN and NATO in 2007 was to persuade Pakistan and Afghanistan that co-operation on the common problems of drug-trafficking and Taliban violence offered mutual rewards, especially in improved regional trade relations. Creating a stable and secure border with efficient customs services collecting revenue and limiting drug and weapons traffic could be a powerful incentive for both countries. Western diplomats had been working quietly to that end, especially since ISAF began expanding across Afghanistan in 2004. By 2006-07 they had succeeded in bringing Pakistani and Afghan leaders to the discussion table. The diplomatic element of the mission is seldom mentioned in Canada because of its political sensitivity.

But diplomats from Canada and allied nations scored a major success in 2007 by taking the matter of border security co-operation beyond just talk to working on it at the ground level. In an area as tense as Spin Boldak, packed with armed power-brokers, the diplomats needed soldiers to make it work. And Steve Graham's Recce Squadron was ready, willing, and able to take on the border security problem from the bottom up.

The squadron's job involved nothing less than getting a grip on the organized chaos of Spin Boldak. That could not be done solely on the Afghan side of the border. In fact, chief among the partnerships the Recce Squadron was sent to build was one with the Pakistani Army and Border Police. Together they were to pinch the flow of weapons and insurgents into Kandahar.

LCol Rob Walker called Steve Graham his "soldier-diplomat," high praise in a theatre where all combat team commanders constantly served as "diplomatic" envoys. Graham's 2i/c, Capt Francis Conliffe, proved equally capable. The two were young, but were always accompanied by Squadron Sgt-Maj Bill Richards, whose greying hair, moustache, and commanding presence filled the role of the wise elder backing the two officers: an ingredient essential in *shuras*. All of their negotiating skills honed in western Zharey would be tested even more in Spin Boldak. Graham brought with him a PRT detachment led by Capt Geoff Marshall, a reservist from 1st Battalion, (Carleton and York) Royal New Brunswick Regiment. His job was to spread the National Solidarity Program (NSP). Marshall also had to figure out how much US Quick Impact Project money had been thrown around in the district and how to tie it into the NSP. Given that the Afghan government exerted so little sovereignty over the border area, the job of spreading government services and credibility while improving security was daunting to say the least.

In an area where foreign armed forces routinely came, fought, and left, it was essential to get across the message that the Canadians had arrived to help the new Afghan government and the people—and that they were there to stay. To do that, Graham's squadron was reinforced with Capt Shawn Arbing's Tactical Psychological Operations Team (TPT). The TPT would conduct community outreach activities to explain what ISAF was and what it intended to do.

Graham's team also included an important contingent of Afghan forces: the freshly minted recce company from the 4th Kandak of 1 Brigade, 205th "Hero" Corps. In the spring of 2007 LCol Wayne Eyre's Operational Mentoring and Liaison Team (OMLT) had taken responsibility for all of 1 Brigade as part of a dramatic increase in the number of newly trained and mentored Afghan Army and police units in Kandahar Province. 4th Kandak was especially important as it was the Combat Support Kandak that included supporting recce, artillery, engineer, and logistics troops needed to enable the ANA to become self-sufficient. Part of Graham's job would be to mentor the ANA Recce Company while they in turn provided the Afghan professional military presence that proved so successful in Zharey and Panjwayi. Fortunately, the Canadian deployment to Spin Boldak also coincided with dramatic improvements in the quality, training, supply, and professionalism of the local 1,200-man 4th Brigade of the ANBP. By May, its US Army ETT had gone a long way towards weeding out corruption and turning the border police into a more serious threat to Taliban and drug-traffickers.

The first Recce Squadron tasks were to liaise with the Afghan, US, coalition, and Pakistani forces, and to use their surveillance equipment and skills to gather information on border activity. Not only were these part of the normal functions of reconnaissance units, they were also the kind of tasks associated with "traditional" peacekeeping. But the chaotic nature of Spin Boldak District and the frontier meant that the squadron had to be war-fighters and peacekeepers at the same time.[3]

As in so many of Kandahar's districts, the establishment of a Canadian ISAF and effective Afghan Army presence worked more quickly than had been expected. They bypassed the corrupt District Development Assembly (made up of absentee landlords) and convinced the locals of the value of getting involved in new Community development councils (CDCs). Capt Marshall and his Civil-Military Co-Operation (CIMIC) team found that the basic infrastructure for education and health care already existed in Spin Boldak, but it needed much repair and expansion to cope with the swollen population.[4]

Outside of Spin Boldak–Wes, however, it was a different story; in effect, there was no infrastructure. Nearly every village the squadron patrols visited was in dire need of a well. Most were close to wadis harnessed to irrigate crops, but very few villagers had clean drinking water. Many hauled drinking water by donkey or on their backs from sources hours away. In such places, it took little time for Geoff Marshall to get consensus from village councils that a central well must be their first NSP project. Steve Graham recalls that the process of visiting villages, asking them what they wanted, returning to consult, and then returning again to provide security for the drilling team, had a powerful impact on the impoverished people in the rural areas. Foreigners passing through and making promises in return for information was nothing new. But, foreigners who offered to help and then returned to honour their promises was a novel experience. The most significant impact of all came when the Afghan Recce Company soldiers accompanied Graham's men, as they did regularly from mid-May onward. In remote borderland villages that had never seen a government official before, this was an occasion of momentous significance. The sight of a clean-uniformed, well-disciplined soldier proudly wearing an Afghan flag on his shoulder, providing security for the installation of a village's first Afghan government-funded well, made a highly positive impression on the population. Graham recalls that his own soldiers were always received warmly on these patrols, but that the ANA recce soldiers were "showered with hugs and kisses and cheers."

Even in Spin Boldak–Wes, the population seemed to swing quickly toward the government once the corrupt police and district *shura* were marginalized. Previously, locals had tried to remain neutral, as there was much money to be made along this lawless border. But corruption and criminal economies are inherently unstable and dangerous, and the people of Spin Boldak seemed eager to turn to the better alternative the Canadians and the Afghan government offered.[5]

Monitoring the border 24/7 with their sophisticated surveillance devices, the Recce Squadron quickly determined the pattern of Taliban cross-border movement. Much of it went right through the main crossing point at the International Arch. Solving that problem fell to Canada's Department of Foreign Affairs and the US State Department, who worked at brokering a deal to build new and more efficient international border checkpoints with a

streamlined transiting and search process. The whole system sought
to make travel easier for legitimate traffic and force criminals and
insurgents to use the more difficult mountain paths. Clearly, negotiations would take time, and in 2007 the process was still in its
infancy. Nonetheless, this quiet diplomacy progressed to the point
that it caught the UN Secretary-General's attention. UN envoys
travelled to Kabul and Islamabad to encourage the process and came
away with the sense that "a collaboration has begun to prevail in
Afghan-Pakistani relations on both sides of the border."[6]

The expansion of ISAF and ANA patrols, NSP building projects,
and local government reform did not please the Taliban. The unofficial
truce that had prevailed while the Taliban dominated the district gave
way in May to a spike in attacks against ANBP posts. Taliban bomber
cells also targeted the Recce Squadron but could not score a hit.
The wide-open terrain meant that Graham's patrols and re-supply
convoys never had to follow the same route. It was like trying to lay
an ambush on the Prairies.

Cracking the Egg: The Battle for Nalgham–Sangsar

The first days of May in western Kandahar Province remained
quiet as the opium poppy harvest continued. But every Canadian
and Afghan soldier stationed in Zharey and Panjwayi knew that
when the harvest ended things would change dramatically. Indeed,
for months Taliban spokesmen had been pushing one message to
westerners and Afghans alike: a massive new Taliban offensive was
about to begin, and it would finish what they had started the summer before—the recapturing of Kandahar. Although the prospect
of another *Operation Medusa* captured headlines in Canada, ISAF
commanders and intelligence staffs knew that message was over-
blown. Nevertheless, they also knew that the Taliban had brought
in fresh Tier 1 units from Pakistan to open the summer "Fighting
Season." It was up to the balance of the 2RCR Battlegroup to make
sure the insurgents could not stop PRT momentum in Kandahar
province. Walker's troops would not have to wait long or look
hard to find them. Everything they had learned about the area
and about insurgent behaviour in the past three months told the
Canadians the Taliban were in Nalgham and Sangsar. However, the

battlegroup was not going to sit and wait for the spring offensive. Instead, it manoeuvred to disrupt the Taliban's plans before they could start.

Alex Ruff's Hotel Company infanteers, Strathcona tankers, and their attached gunners, engineers, and maintainers prepared for another series of patrols to clear out IEDs and open the roads straight into the Belly of the Beast. This was meant to support establishing a better Afghan National Police (ANP) presence and to demonstrate to the people of Zharey that ISAF could not be intimidated by Taliban bombs.

Ruff had wanted one of the high-tech American Husky Route Clearance Package of vehicles to open safe lanes for him, but none was available. However, the Canadians did have an ace up their sleeves; their Leopard tanks had been shipped to Afghanistan with all of their high-intensity war-fighting kit, including dozer blades and mine-ploughs. These devices were not appropriate for patrols in villages. The last thing Rob Walker wanted his battlegroup to do was rip up the very road network they were trying to open for commerce. Then, battlegroup DCO Maj Russell King, and Strathcona Squadron 2i/c Capt Craig Volstad remembered the "mine-rollers" gathering dust in Ma'Sum Ghar. The heavy steel rollers, mounted on the front of the tanks, could detonate anti-tank mines and pressure-plate IEDs without tearing up the roads. To avoid alerting Taliban bomb-makers the rollers were moved up to Patrol Base Wilson (PBW) on trucks. Then, in the wee hours of 7 May, behind the high walls of the Zharey District Centre, the tankers fixed the rollers onto the two Leopards commanded by Sergeants Jordison and Sewards.

Before dawn on 7 May, the column of Strathcona tanks, Hotel Company LAVs and two platoons of LCol Shereen Shah's Kandak rolled onto Highway 1. The morning light was breaking as the column turned south at Howz-e-Madad. Sgt Jordison's Leopard, call-sign T16, led the way with his mine rollers deployed. If the broad aim of the operation was to prevent Taliban interference with reconstruction and keep the main highways open, then the timing was nearly perfect. Minutes after the patrol turned south towards Nalgham and only a few hundred metres off the highway, two large blasts went off well ahead of T16, as two rocket propelled grenades (RPGs) fell short. The patrol had found the Taliban. Around the same time T16 stopped in the narrow, walled lane, a Taliban ambush party opened up with RPGs and a medium machine gun on a US-contracted jingle truck carrying supplies west on Highway 1 to Helmand. The fire hit the mark, smashing up the truck and killing one American contractor. But now a Canadian mechanized combat team was between the would-be ambushers and their base in Nalgham.

Ruff and Volstad left the ANP to deal with the attack on the highway, and prepared to confront the Taliban on the road to Nalgham. Hotel Company's 4 Platoon dismounted from their LAVs for a close-in fight. Then another rocket sailed clean over Jordison's tank. His gunner spotted a black-turbaned man ducking behind what looked like a prepared fire position down the road, but he could not be sure he saw a weapon and nobody wanted to fire indiscriminately into people's homes. But the same man popped up again and shot an RPG that landed 20 metres in front of Jordison's tank. T16 had the position fixed in their sights and instantly returned fire with a High Explosive Squash Head (HESH) round from the 105mm main gun. The RPG shooter and half the small mound he hid behind vanished in a cloud of smoke and dust.[7]

The action around Jordison's tank convinced Capt Volstad not to push the tank-LAV column down the narrow, canalizing road. Instead, he called for permission to "breach," or essentially blast through, the wall on the road and move cross-country through farm fields around the ambush. When the action seemed to peter out, his request was denied. It would be pointless to risk local anger over crop damage if the firefight was over. But it quickly heated up again when Jordison's crew spotted four more armed Taliban watching their approach from a grape hut up ahead on the road. The Canadians had heard the stories from *Operation Medusa* about how the Taliban had used grape huts as nearly indestructible pillboxes. Jordison hesitated to open fire at first because a number of farmers between his tank and the Taliban were scrambling to get out of the way. As soon as the path was clear he opened fire with his coaxial machine gun, forcing the Taliban to duck behind the high grape mounds. Meanwhile, Alex Ruff's dismounted infantry cleared through the field ahead of the vehicles.

Suddenly Jordison's tank took fire from the front, and two more RPG rounds smoked towards the column from the south-east side of the road, flying straight over Volstad's command tank. The Canadians now had Taliban with anti-armour weapons in front and beside them positioned in a grape hut-bunker. "Game-on," Volstad thought to himself and ordered, "Breach left!" His own tank fired a HESH round, blowing a hole in the adobe mud wall on the roadside. Into the breach went a Badger Armoured Engineer Vehicle with a dozer blade to plough a lane through the adjacent grape field, followed by tanks and LAVs. The open ground of the field offered a much better view of the Taliban ambush area and a better approach to the thick-walled grape hut.

Unfortunately, before long the Badger and Jordison's tank with its rollers bogged down in the loose, well-cultivated earth. Anyone experienced driving tracked vehicles off-road knows that this is par for the course. It took only minutes for other tanks in the column to winch them out and restart the drive, but in general the new route proved too soft to use all the way to Nalgham. It also would cause more damage to carefully-built grape mounds and irrigation wadis than first expected. The main road was the only option for this approach to Nalgham, but the Taliban were not apparently aware of that yet. There seemed to be nothing they could do to prevent themselves from being outflanked, although they tried.

Meanwhile, a Taliban RPG team opened fire on Volstad's tank from a mud wall 300 metres east of where the tankers and engineers were dozing their safe lane. Communications failure inside Volstad's tank made it difficult to return effective fire promptly. Without air conditioning, the temperature in Canada's Cold War-vintage tanks reached 60 degrees Celsius. Apart from heat exhaustion, the enormous volume of sweat pouring from the crew shorted out their headsets. So, Volstad shouted fire orders to his gunner. The long barrel traversed and locked onto the point on the wall where the RPG flash had come from. In an instant, a HESH round made that section of wall disappear. When a Taliban survivor made a run for it with an RPG launcher, a second tank round hit him directly.

And so the morning unfolded in a series of Taliban pin-prick attacks on the armoured and infantry column. Greg Vander Kloet's

4 Platoon also got into a fire-fight with a Taliban section and took out most of them. By late morning it seemed the Taliban wanted to lure the combat team deeper down that road. They would not get their wish. Before noon, Maj Ruff pulled his team back to PB Wilson.

A total of six Taliban fighters had been killed and two arrested. The only Canadians harmed were two tank crewmen who collapsed from heat exhaustion; special crew cooling vests were on the way but would not be available for a few more weeks. More important, the Canadians demonstrated to the Taliban and to the locals that they could and would fight without laying waste to villages. This was also the first prolonged, "hatches down," tank battle fought in Kandahar. Yet, for all the 105mm tank rounds and machine-gun bullets fired, and all the off-road driving done, not one civilian was harmed and property damage was minimal. In fact, before the column withdrew, the Badger repaired an irrigation wadi broken during the breaching attempt.

* * *

The combat team planned to go straight back to Nalgham the very next day, because Ruff did not want locals to think the Canadians had been driven off. Rather, he wanted to get into the heart of the Nalgham–Sangsar area and send a strong message that the Taliban reign of fear was being challenged. Maj Russell King, acting battlegroup CO while Rob Walker took his mandatory two weeks leave, agreed that Ruff and Volstad must return, although this time by a different route. The goal of these patrols was not to destroy the Taliban at all costs, but to keep them off balance and unable to interfere with reconstruction efforts. So, if the Taliban wanted to dig in and fight a major battle on the main road south from Howz-e-Madad, King and Ruff decided that the combat team would take a different road into Nalgham.

On the early morning of 8 May the infantry-armoured combat team barrelled down Highway 1 again, this time past the previous day's route, and turned south on the main road to Ghundey Ghar. Sgt Sewards's T12B led the way with mine rollers down to sanitize the route. The column drove south, past large numbers of villagers, who came out to see the parade of Canadian armour, until they reached the edge of a large open area on the south-west corner of Nalgham. They were now deployed on the opposite side of town from the day before. Ruff's infantry, Volstad's tanks and some of Shereen Shah's Afghan soldiers deployed first into a leaguer and then into battle formation to sweep towards Nalgham both on and off the roads. Here the open fields were dry with few crops to be harmed by any cross-country advance.

While they were deploying to advance, a local villager approached the force and gestured that the main road to Nalgham had mines or IEDs planted on it. The attached engineer troop cleared 100 metres of main road while Sgt Sewards turned his mine rollers to start clearing east towards Nalgham itself. Taliban teams tried to stop the advance by firing volleys of RPGs. One of the rockets found its mark and ripped open the front tires on a Bison Maintenance Recovery Vehicle.

All hands around the leaguer deployed to return the fire. LAVs on the south side of the position opened up with their 25 mm cannons on a grape hut and other buildings that were the source of the rockets. A tank and three LAVs rolled south to set up a fire base for dismounted Hotel Company and Afghan infantry who would sweep through the cluster of houses from which the fire was coming. Sgt Sewards's tank crew spotted a four-man Taliban detachment on the roof of a grape hut several hundred metres south of the leaguer. Two were working RPG launchers while a third reloaded them, and a fourth man blazed away with an AK-47 assault rifle. Sewards swung his tank's main gun around and blew off the top off the grape hut, along with all three in the RPG team. The rifleman reappeared when the dust settled but was dispatched with two well-placed bursts of coaxial machine-gun fire. The tanks were quickly proving themselves to be an excellent way to provide precision fire against an enemy that elected to fight in small numbers.

During the fray Lt Ben Rogerson's 5 Platoon was hit by a rocket, but held their own in the fight, accounting for two more Taliban fighters. Hotel Company LAV Capt Dave Nixon remembers that the men of 5 Platoon found the tiny battle "therapeutic"; it helped them overcome the anxiousness of their Easter losses. Volstad's T1A was also once again in the thick of the mini-battle. His tank moved up directly behind the ANA platoons sweeping towards Nalgham and spotted two men bolting. They were carrying an 82mm recoilless rifle, a kind of tripod-mounted bazooka capable of killing a tank or LAV. Taking care to avoid hitting their Afghan comrades only 100 metres in front, Volstad's gunner, Cpl Helliwell, cracked off a main gun round scoring yet another seemingly impossible hit with his massive "sniper rifle." But their large-calibre round "didn't phase the ANA at all!" Indeed the Afghan troops were absolutely delighted to have tank support in this action. A second round caught the recoilless rifle's second crewman. Moments later more Taliban were flushed out and then caught by tank and ANA rifle fire. It was the first successful Afghan-Canadian tank-infantry action since Pashtu soldiers of the British Frontier Force Rifles fought alongside Canadian tankers in Italy in 1944.[8] An even greater sign of things to come was that the Afghan platoons were equally discriminate with their fire as the Canadians, thanks to their own training and to their attached Canadian mentors. In a repeat of the day before, no weapons were fired without a direct target to hit and only then if there was no danger to civilians.

Several more times during the route clearance that morning Taliban RPG teams opened up and were taken out with infantry weapons, LAV 25mm and tank gunfire. Overall, it was another day like the one before. Capt Volstad had deployed cross-country to avoid the IED threat on the main road into Nalgham, and all tankers and infantry including Afghans fought short, sharp engagements against small Taliban RPG teams. The Taliban probably were trying to score a public relations victory by knocking out a tank, but good tank-infantry co-operation never allowed the RPG teams to get close enough to be effective.

Acting battlegroup CO, Maj King concluded that the Taliban were trying to lure the Canadians into a drawn-out fight in the middle of Nalgham–Sangsar where their heavier weapons would smash the village. That would have played perfectly into Taliban Information Operations messaging that ISAF forces were interested only in destroying their enemies at any cost and not in protecting Afghans. Several times during these patrols, Taliban RPG teams had fired rockets and then retreated into buildings obviously occupied by civilians. They were either using them as human shields or trying to create an incident. In at least one case, supporting Dutch Air Force AH-64 Apache helicopter gunships caught them in the act on camera. After firing their rocket, an RPG team fell back into a house with women and children peering from the windows.[9] Ruff's infantry and Volstad's tanks were too well trained to fall for such bait and let them go. The enemy was obviously going to be sticking around Nalgham–Sangsar for a while, so the battlegroup would find them another day, another way. By noon, when the sun was hottest, the latest probe into Nalgham was shut down and the Canadians slipped back out of the Belly of the Beast. Civilians watching could hardly fail to notice that the morning's events meant around a dozen more Taliban fighters were no longer part of the Zharey–Panjwayi garrison. Their deaths had brought no gain to the Taliban cause. Livelihoods and houses were still intact. It might not be war as westerners understand it, but it was a kind of war that made sense to Kandaharis. And the Canadians were winning.[10]

The PRT: Two Steps Forward, One Step Back

The disruption patrols to the edges of Nalgham had the desired effect of keeping the Taliban away from the PRTs main effort. In fact, while Ruff's troops were engaged near Nalgham, WO Bill Hunter ran a PRT patrol right into the heart of neighbouring Kolk and Sangsar to meet with local elders, to follow up on irrigation canal work and check on the status of police checkpoints. Hunter found signs of frustratingly slow progress. A number of irrigation canals lay only partially complete after corrupt contractors had pocketed the last bit of project cash and disappeared. Hunter also found ANP checkpoints low on ammunition and afraid for their safety now that the opium harvest was over. Two steps forward and one step back was the norm in Kandahar in 2007.

What was new for Zharey District was that the PRT members they knew and trusted were there to hear complaints and act on them. And that Hunter showed up to meet with local leaders even as the small battles raged within earshot, only a few kilometres to the west. In Kandahar City itself Taliban forces focused their attention on a British convoy and ignored LCol Bob Chamberlain's team as they went about their city resuscitation work. One of the main projects tackled at that time was getting a raisin factory back up and running to process the coming bumper crop of grapes.[11] So, the plan was working. While Taliban units lashed out at ISAF and Afghan security forces, Kandahar Province continued to regenerate. The Canadians could not be intimidated after all.

TACKLING THE TALIBAN

Back at the battlegroup command post, Major King and the operations and planning staff took stock of Taliban behaviour. Insurgent operations in 2007 were increasingly characterized by lack of coordination and poor planning, which could be attributed to the growing effectiveness of ISAF's Special Operations Forces (SOF). SOF units from all ISAF contributor nations in the south were pooled for the task of arresting known bomb-making cell leaders, drug lords, and senior Taliban commanders. Once enough evidence was massed and a legal case prepared for their arrest, Canadian (and other ISAF) SOF troops would be deployed to apprehend the suspect. As often as not, if the target was a Tier 1 Taliban leader, he would try to shoot his way out, with predictable results. Consequently, Taliban command-and-control capacity in the south in 2007 was less effective than in the previous fall.[12]

But not all Taliban commanders and drug lords were neutralized, and even if disjointed their units and actions were still dangerous. They continued to target international public opinion by inflicting casualties on ISAF troops and drawing them into combat in populated areas, where they would smash property and kill civilians, thus alienating themselves from Kandaharis. That would add to President Karzai's problem of explaining civilian losses to the media and to his own people.

The battlegroup, nonetheless, had to keep up the counter-pressure so that the Taliban could never again assert ownership over Zharey–Panjwayi. But LCol Walker and Maj King would not allow their troops to be sucked into combat on the enemy's terms. A destructive battle to smash the strong Taliban defensive network in Nalgham was not in the cards. Instead, they planned to keep probing and hooking around it, keeping the Taliban constantly guessing where the Canadians would appear next. Meanwhile, intelligence reports indicated that a fresh group of Taliban guerrillas and bomb-makers was moving further east in Zharey to cut Highway 1.

In mid-May, ISAF troops, mostly from the 2RCR Battlegroup, surged into these known Taliban base areas in Zharey to throw off their ambush and bomb-laying plans. Alex Ruff's Hotel Company and supporting tanks moved onto the hill at Ghundey Ghar west of Nalgham while Dave Quick's India Company probed towards Sangsar from the opposite side. They were backed by a new force in ISAF: a Portuguese Commando company, which was placed under Canadian command in May and taken out on joint patrols early in the month to show them around Zharey. The Portuguese were worked into the plan for the next probe into the Belly of the Beast.

The "Battle of Kolk"

The probe started on 16 May when India Company drove to Kolk in their LAVs, dismounted and started poking patrols into the Nalgham–Sangsar area from the east end. Maj Quick, whose back and neck had been injured when his LAV struck an IED, was away on mid-tour leave.[13] But like all the sub-units, India Company had a team of able leaders, so in his absence it was in the good hands of Capt Mark Coté and CSM Steve Jeans. They set up a company command post and observation post on top of the ANP station in the Kolk "Yellow School," while two platoons and a Recce Squadron sniper detachment patrolled westwards, checking out potential tank routes in and out Sangsar for the big Hotel Company surge set for the next day. By late afternoon the situation "smelled wrong." Small groups of women and children scurried out of the area and large numbers of fighting-age males stood in farm fields staring at the India Company riflemen. Coté and Jeans realized they were about to get hit. They pushed 7 Platoon's LAVs closer to where the dismounted patrol was making its way back, so they could cover and extract them if any shooting started. Capt Mark Sheppard's 9 Platoon was probing around to the north of the Yellow School base and making its way back as well.

At 1855 hours, "fighting season" in Sangsar opened. A company-sized force of well-trained Tier 1 Taliban sprang a well-laid ambush. They apparently had watched India Company move from their patrol base, and used wadis and grape mounds to infiltrate between the separated platoons. Suddenly, machine guns and AK-47 rifles opened up from three sides on the patrol. A light machine gun swept the Yellow School roof, sending Coté and Jeans scrambling for their LAVs so they could get their 25mm guns into action.

Taliban fire also lashed into Sheppard's 9 Platoon to the north. Their LAVs were close by, and between their 25mm guns and the rifles and machine guns of the dismounted platoon they put down enough fire to break contact and move back to the patrol base. 7 Platoon and the sniper detachment were not so lucky. They were caught farthest from any direct help and in the middle of the heaviest fire. The lead section under MCpl Gerald Killam, a native of Halifax, was trapped in the middle of a flat, open, killing zone and dove for cover. They were in a jam, cut off from the rest of the platoon and pinned by a vicious crossfire to whatever bits of cover they could find. Killam barked orders and got his section firing back on their attackers. Killam's Medal of Military Valour citation records how he:

> repeatedly exposed himself to immediately direct the fire
> of his entire section to bear on the enemy. He remained in
> full control of the perilous situation, issuing clear target in-
> dications and fire control orders. Through Master Corporal
> Killam's most distinguished leadership, his section fought back
> against the ambush and conducted a successful withdrawal
> under contact that resulted in no casualties to his platoon.

Meanwhile, the rest of the Platoon, under the command of WO Eric Green, responded to the threat, while the commander, Lt Eddy Jun, was away on leave. A wiry and fit Newfoundlander from Carbonear, Green was an experienced old hand with multiple tours of duty under his belt and impossible to fluster. He quickly and calmly deployed 7 Platoon into covered fire positions so they could bring down fire on the force of over 30 Taliban infantry that were among them. The dismounted platoon's heaviest fire-power came from its C-6 belt-fed machine-gun team of Cpl John Williams and Pte Michael MacWhirter. Green ordered them to move forward and put down fire on the flank of the ambush party. Without hesitation, Williams and MacWhirter raced across 40 bullet-lashed metres of open ground to set up their powerful machine gun in the perfect spot to hit one of the Taliban positions. Green then brought the snipers to bear as part of a tactical withdrawal under fire. In a testament to the skill-at-arms infantry training in 2RCR, Green used his other two sections and the snipers to break the enemy's grip on Williams section. They killed an unknown number of énemy troops without suffering a single soldier hurt. After 20 harrowing minutes, 7 Platoon's LAVs finally reached them. By then the surviving Taliban had had enough and left the battlefield. Despite the fact that the numbers involved confirmed intelligence reports that a Taliban light infantry battalion had moved into the area, their ambush had failed miserably.[14] And the locals saw it happen.

Nalgham: Poking the Hornet's Nest

The next day (17 May) Hotel Company, backed by Volstad's tanks with ploughs and rollers and 1 Troop of 41 Engineer Squadron, made yet another run from their base at Ghundey Ghar, probing into Nalgham from the southwest corner. In many respects it was a replay of the Hotel Company battles earlier in the month. The combat team met RPG and machine-gun fire covering the road that was their centre line. Greg Vander Kloet's 4 Platoon dismounted and advanced through fire along that line, with a tank fire base on the north flank and with Volstad and Lt Matt Allen's 6 Platoon leading a breach around the would-be ambushers on the south. After an intensely hot morning's work they drove the Taliban off towards Nalgham.

However, a couple of key developments made this day different. First, the Taliban fired and then pulled back, trying to avoid battle with the powerful combat team. Instead, they tried to suck them deeper into Nalgham, presumably into a prepared killing zone supported with large IEDs. But the Canadians didn't fall for that. The second, more important, new feature was that after the fighting subsided, and the Taliban were driven from the hamlets around the crossroads southwest of Nalgham, the civilians re-emerged. Many had not left, which encouraged Maj Ruff to convene an impromptu *shura* with the hamlet elders. Ruff was quite surprised to learn that these elders were happy to see the Canadians returning regularly to fight the Taliban "foreigners" from outside Kandahar, and that they were not concerned about the small amounts of damage done to fields in the process. Their primary complaint was that the Canadians would not stay with them in the night when the Taliban returned to bully and threaten them. One of the elders asked Ruff through a translator how long the Canadians were going to stay and when they would be back next to chase the Taliban from their villages. To maintain operational security, Ruff did not tell them he planned to come back the next day.[15]

At dawn on 18 May it all started again, this time from the north and feeling along the north edge of Nalgham towards Sangsar. All three of Ruff's rifle platoons dismounted and cleared buildings on either side of the route they were proving with WO John Pudar's roller-equipped tank T11A. The route clearance was just getting warmed up when every Canadian was stopped cold by a deafeningly large blast, the largest of its kind since Easter. When the smoke and dust settled, it showed that anti-tank mines or an IED had left a crater in the road almost a metre deep, into which draped one of the two roller arms which had survived the blast. Manitoba-born Pudar had his driver reverse to pull the rollers out of the hole and was still "good to go." The fact that the rollers had done to IEDs exactly what they were supposed to, giving the combat team some sense of control over that unpredictable weapon, lifted everyone's spirits. That was important, because a short while later a Taliban section opened up with RPGs and rifles, and the battle was on again. Volstad took a Badger and Vander Kloet's platoon on a kilometre-long flanking manoeuvre south, around what looked like a prepared killing zone, while Matt Allen's dismounted platoon took the north side of the road. Ben Rogerson's 5 Platoon came up the middle in reserve.

This time Ruff brought from Ghundey Ghar a reasonably reliable Afghan National Police detachment that could carry out searches of the walled Afghan farm houses along the road. Using the ANP would reduce the need for too many intrusive and embarrassing searches by western "infidels." The process of clearing down roads this way was laboriously slow but critically important to do properly. Simply put, the locals would probably decide which side to support based on what happened to them during such operations. As his sweep teams moved forward, the amiable Alex Ruff talked to locals, and especially elders, constantly repeating that his troops were there to help. They told him that a new IED team, backed by a light infantry platoon, had been busy recently around Nalgham–Sangsar and that the way ahead was very dangerous.

While the clearance patrol went on fighting two small battles against Taliban sections during the morning, their ANP detachment uncovered stocks of weapons, especially RPG rounds, stashed in walled farm houses. By mid-day the heat was once again unbearable. The Canadians had used up all the water they carried and desperately needed more. CSM O'Toole packed LAV 22B full of water and sent it forward along the route cleared by the mine rollers. As it neared its destination, the LAV slipped just inches outside the cleared lane and struck an anti-tank mine. "22B contact, mine strike!" crackled over the net. "This cannot happen again!" Ruff thought to himself. Shortly afterwards came word that, fortunately, no one in the vehicle was seriously injured. But, the hull was cracked and, much worse for the troops in the field, all the water bottles had burst. It was time to wrap up another blisteringly hot work day.

* * *

It would be another week before the Canadians went back to Nalgham. But when they returned they brought more help. In the third week of May, Rob Walker, Dave Quick, and "Boomer" Broomfield were back from leave and ready to plan the next push into Nalgham–Sangsar. Taking advantage of a temporary spike of ISAF troops in Zharey–Panjwayi, Walker's team planned a new massive clearance patrol to push deep into the Belly of the Beast and throw the newly arrived Taliban battalion off balance again. The plan included the entire battlegroup, the Portuguese commando company, and all of LCol Shereen Shah's 2nd Kandak. At the request of Maj Eric Pelicano, Walker's operations officer, the entire battlegroup HQ staff (with all its co-ordination centres to synchronize artillery, engineer, air, supply and medical support) deployed to a forward field CP at Ma'Sum Ghar. There, they could plan and direct this large multi-national brigade-size operation alongside Shereen Shah's Kandak HQ staff and his OMLT mentors. And from the high ground they could see and hear developments unfold.

They planned to push in yet again from a new direction. This time they would change things by patrolling away from the south edge of Nalgham toward the Arghandab River, across Taliban transit routes in and out of their base villages. India Company, Recce Squadron sniper detachments and the Portuguese troops manoeuvred before dawn to set up a hard eastern shoulder. Charles Company 3PPCLI did the same south of the Arghandab, to block to the southern routes in and out of the area. Hotel Company, two troops of Strathcona tanks, and three ANA companies shook out into formation on the north side of the "ring" and started sweeping south. It was a massive demonstration to the people in Nalgham– Sangsar of ISAF capability and resolve, and solidarity with the increasingly popular Afghan troops. On the other hand, the show of force was so massive the Taliban would have been foolhardy to take it on. They did try to pick away at the Portuguese, possibly hoping to test the mettle of these newcomers and doubtlessly to inflict casualties and stir a media event. But they failed to kill any Portuguese soldiers.

Ruff's infanteers and LAVs deployed to the flanks and the Afghans took up the broad front in the middle along with tanks and armoured engineers in Badgers. They planned to avoid roads and instead advance across the major wadis that ran parallel to the river and canalized all movement on the south side of Nalgham. They would breach the wadis using technology first developed for trench crossing in the Great War. Fascines (large bundles of small logs) were dumped into the streams, making an effective temporary bridge that would not interfere with the water flow or cause any damage.

Vehicles and soldiers drove or marched into position to start the sweep. The unstoppable Craig Volstad, whose own tank was always in the middle of a gun-fight, manoeuvred into position on the eastern end of this giant broom. Because—after two weeks of continuous action in the area—Volstad was so familiar with the ground and the new conditions of the fighting season, Boomer left him in tactical command of the tank squadron. But this time

Volstad disappeared in a massive blast that shook the whole area for kilometres. Everyone had known it was only a matter of time before a big IED took out a tank. A triple-stacked anti-tank mine lifted the mighty T1A into the air and fully engulfed it in the blast. But the Leopard tank design did its job. Everyone in Volstad's crew was still alive. At first, it looked like his loader, Trooper Tullis was hurt badly; the blast threw him against the turret floor and knocked him out. Volstad immediately went to his side and after just a few seconds Tullis came-to with only "bumps and bruises." In fact, that was the extent of everyone's injuries. Like cavalry leaders of past, whose horses were shot from under them, Volstad called for a re-placement tank and got back into action.

But that day the Taliban had no intention of fighting the mul-tinational brigade in their midst. The Hotel Company-ANA force successfully crossed the fascines and began advancing on the river, clearing the fields of potential RPG threats so tank rollers could open the roads. Behind the advancing Afghan infantrymen came a section of James Prices's OMLT team, helping co-ordinate the ANA with their supporting tanks and with Hotel Company. The OMLT section spotted an IED in a lane in front of them. When the section commander turned to warn the tank coming up behind him, the IED detonated. The Canadian mentor team commander was only about 10 feet away and was knocked down to the ground, with bits of shrapnel in his face and shoulder and with a finger half blown off but otherwise in good shape. His brave Afghan-Canadian interpreter was wounded but alive. So too was a Portuguese liaison officer. But 25-year-old Cpl Matthew McCully, from Orangeville, Ontario, was on top of the bomb when it exploded. He was killed instantly.

Canadian and Afghan commanders on the ground knew they could not stop. To do so would grant a victory to the Taliban. So as Matt McCully's body was recovered, the wounded were treat-ed, and a medevac helicopter brought in, the rest of the brigade group carried on. There were only a few other minor contacts that day. Villagers in the Nalgham–Sangsar area took it all in. In fact, Canadian patrols later learned from the locals that the Taliban in-fantry unit in Nalgham was holed up and terrified that they were surrounded and cut off by ISAF.[16] But this was not a search and destroy patrol. It was a disruption effort and it worked, although at a price.

PUSHING DEVELOPMENT NORTH

The combat actions in and around Nalgham–Sangsar stood in stark contrast to the rest of the tour for Task Force Afghanistan. With the Taliban fixated on taking the fight to the greenbelt in Zharey District, CIDA officers in other districts in central and eastern Kandahar provided funding to UN and Afghan MRRD project managers to spread the NSP further outwards into the hinterland of the province. Among other things, PRT detachments and CIDA project planners worked the Arghandab and Shah Wali Khot districts, preparing the ground and holding meetings to spread NSP projects into the northern parts of the province. Security and relations with the Afghan government were slightly better there, due to people's loyalty to veteran mujahedeen and tribal leader Mullah Naqib, who brokered an uneasy truce with the Taliban. If tribes and villages in his area were not to be alienated from the provincial government, the next critical step was to expand the NSP and public services there.

The PRT had to deal with the occasional IEDs and ambushes on the major roads in Kandahar City itself, but these were not enough to stop their work. For the most part, Taliban attacks tended to single out under-strength Afghan police posts or patrols that were increasingly effective, thanks to PRT mentoring and an improved flow of American supplies. The ANP were becoming a threat to the Taliban/drug-trafficker alliance. On the south side of the Arghandab River, Chris Henderson's Patricias focused on joint presence patrols with the ANA to continue raising the standard of Afghan police posts in the river peninsula area, by offering examples of how professional security forces ought to behave. It was an uphill struggle with much of the hill left to climb. Overall, Canada's OMLT and PRT and the various UN agencies did not relax the pace of their efforts in May, but to buy them time and space to work, the 2RCR Battlegroup was fully at war.

May was just the beginning. In the next weeks of high summer, the Kandahar ADZ was scheduled to formally expand north. Pushing assistance and government services throughout the province was certainly the main political and reconstruction effort and the best way to defeat the Taliban in this campaign for the public faith. But to do so meant that the area the battlegroup was responsible for securing was about to get even bigger. As if to offer a clue as to what the summer held in store, India Company was preparing to continue the series of disruption patrols in Zharey when a call for help came through the Joint Provincial Co-ordination Centre. An ANP convoy, including civilian contractors, had been ambushed and surrounded up north in Shah Wali Khot. The location was way up the Arghandab River, just a few kilometres below the massive Dhala dam and drought reservoir, ground vital for the long-term economic rehabilitation of Kandahar. Being mobile and closest to the scene, Quick's company got the task. Within minutes they were loaded into their LAVs and roaring north, avoiding IEDs by riding across open desert.

They reached the scene to find the large ANP convoy circled in a bowl at the bottom of a ring of high ground, returning fire on an equally large force of Taliban infantry that had them pinned. One policemen was dead and a large number wounded, including two seriously. Dave Quick ordered his LAV platoons into a firing line to blaze away at the ridge crest with their 25mm guns. Quick, CSM Jeans, and their medic had dismounted to help when volleys of RPGs came thundering down on them, sending them diving for cover. The rock steady, dry-witted sergeant-major leaned over to his friend and company commander, back in his first firefight after his two week rest: "Good to be back off leave, eh sir?"

The cross-country drive north was too much for the drive shaft of E22C, a LAV manned by an attached combat engineer section. Luckily, the mobile combat team had brought along a Royal Canadian Electrical and Mechanical Engineers Mobile Recovery Vehicle. Vehicle technician MCpl Russell Coughlin of Summerside, PEI, leapt out of his vehicle and crawled under the disabled engineer LAV. With RPG rounds and bullets landing all around the circled "wagons," the skilled mechanic put the broken drive shaft back together in 20 minutes. Keeping a fleet of heavy armoured vehicles running in these kinds of conditions took the work of many like Russell Coughlin. That day, he helped save the day. So too did the arrival of 16 LAVs to reinforce and rescue the ANP company. Once the LAV gunners found their targets and ranged on, they quickly turned the balance of firepower against the Taliban, who had no choice but to break contact.[17] But clearly, it was going to be a long hot summer.

May, therefore, was a decisive step forward for Canada and ISAF in Kandahar. A solid joint ISAF and Afghan Army footprint now extended from east to west and covered the most populous and strategically important parts of the province. BGen Tim Grant's Headquarters could now observe and influence the border. Even if sealing off the frontier to the Taliban and drug-traffickers was still a far-off dream, having reliable information about who and what was coming across would be vital in the defence of Kandahar against the spring offensive. In the vital farming districts west of Kandahar City Task Force troops were disrupting that offensive even before it began. And more important, they were doing it without destroying the lives and livelihoods of the population. In return, locals were coming forward with information to help the troops "winkle out" Taliban units. Most critically, this was paving the way for Afghan-led reconstruction and development.

The blazing heat that had stopped most operations in May by mid-day was hard on the Canadian troops, but offered a minor blessing in return. The Canadians had replaced their traditional "boil in a bag" hard rations with the American "Meals Ready to Eat," which includes a chemical heater that can heat the food anywhere, any time: inside a LAV, out in the desert, or even in a tent safely without flame or smoke to give away troops' positions. So, when TF 1-07 deployed into a cool, wet Kandahar winter, the MREs were a godsend. By late spring, however, the heater was superfluous. The sun made the tanks and LAVs so hot that a tinfoil bag meal placed on the armour was cooked perfectly after a minute on each side.

The 45- to 50-degree heat combined with the winter rains were perfect conditions for the newly planted crops of pomegranates, grapes, melons, and wheat. This meant work for many Afghan hands to tend the crops and maintain irrigation from rebuilt and brand-new wadis and *karezes*. For crops to be trucked to new plants and markets in Kandahar City, the roads had to be kept open and the farmers kept free of Taliban interference. A bountiful harvest and a reviving economy, made possible with UN and NATO assistance, could go a long way to persuade unemployed and angry young men that the new Afghanistan offered them a future.

That future would be determined amid the lush fields of Zharey–Panjwayi. Rob Walker and Shereen Shah Khobandi understood that the fight had to be conducted with minimal disruption to Kandahari livelihoods. By June 2007 it seemed that essential condition would be met. Local young men did not appear to answer the Taliban's call in the kind of numbers seen a year earlier. There was plenty of work to be had in the fields and hope was being restored. The population was growing frustrated at the largely foreign Taliban force that came under stealth by night, took much from those who had so little, and gave nothing back except battles to be fought on their farmland.

THE ONGOING FIGHT FOR ZHAREY

By the end of May it was clear that Zharey and Panjwayi districts would not be freed completely of Taliban presence any time soon. Those areas would always be central to the Taliban effort to win allegiance and volunteers for their ultimate aim of retaking Kandahar City. There were not enough International Security Assistance Force (ISAF) troops or trained and professionalized Afghan soldiers and policemen to completely protect those districts, especially as long as hardcore Taliban fighters and drug gangs continued to operate there in the hundreds.

The Canadians' experience in Zharey District that spring had demonstrated that they certainly could sweep the area of Taliban presence temporarily. But they could do so only by advancing deep into the Belly of the Beast and into carefully laid improvised explosive device (IED) kill zones. The Taliban were keenly aware that mass-casualty media events created by spectacular vehicle hits were victories that ate away at the Canadian public's stomach for staying the course in Kandahar. Likewise, smashing the heavily populated agricultural hub and its newly rebuilt irrigation canals with air power and artillery was not an option; it would lead to an equally powerful Taliban media and moral victory.

The Taliban did not get what it wanted. In June the Hotel Company-Strathcona combat team started patrolling into northern Kandahar Province in preparation for expanding the Afghan Development Zone (ADZ). In Zharey, the Taliban were left to fight a far more dangerous enemy: Warrant Officer Bill Hunter of the Provincial Reconstruction Team (PRT). That summer, Hunter ceaselessly roamed the district, meeting with village leaders, surveying completed contract work, and inspecting potential and proposed community projects sites. He proved to people in Zharey that reconstruction and National Solidarity Program (NSP) work would not stop because of fighting season or because of the climate of fear created by the presence of a large Taliban force hunting Canadians.

But under no circumstances could Hunter go alone to his "Key Leader Engagements." For each set of morning and mid-day meetings in June he was accompanied by Major Dave Quick and India Company, a sniper detachment, and by companies of LCol Shereen Shah's now highly capable 2nd Kandak and their Canadian mentors.

Quick's troops were operating on very familiar ground. They did not trip the Taliban early warning system or walk into the most obvious IED traps by driving into village centres in broad daylight. They arrived at night, on foot, and never from the most likely approach. When dawn broke, the Canadians "owned" the town. That set the tone for the meetings that day.

This work carried on without letup after the large operation in Nalgham in late May. A series of India Company-2nd Kandak operations marked the last three days of May. Each of these patrols had the prime purpose of delivering WO Hunter to a meeting with local leaders. But after the gunfight at the Kolk Yellow School, the company never left the gate of their forward operating base (FOB) without a solid plan to meet and defeat the Taliban in a fight—should they decide to pick one.

In fact, that first India Company-Afghan National Army operation went right back into Kolk to figure out how such a large Taliban ambush could get sprung in a village that previously had been so warm to ISAF and the government. The operation centred on getting Hunter into Kolk and nearby Spin Pir to the south for contract and village construction assessments, and on getting LCol Shereen Shah himself to hold a *shura* with his seemingly undecided countrymen. Quick, Hunter, and Shereen Shah found a much cooler reception in those two villages than they were used to. It seemed that locals in the area were fearful and under the direct influence of the Taliban unit now living among them: the same one responsible for the ambush on 7 Platoon two weeks prior. Even so, many were able to get their complaints to Hunter that one particular local leader was levying on farmers taxes of money paid to them by the PRT in cash-for-work projects on nearby irrigation canals. Hunter heard them out and told them he would take the matter up with the accused in front of the District Development Assembly. Taking action against corruption was a proven way to make a deep impression on Kandaharis.

Quick and Shereen Shah were well prepared for any trouble should the enemy show his face again. India Company and an Afghan company patrolled the vicinity for three days from a base set up in the badly damaged but still manned Afghan National Police post in the Yellow School. The location was chosen as a symbol to villagers that ISAF would not be driven out by the Taliban. Late in the afternoon of the second day of the operation, the Taliban company in the area mistakenly tested out the sniper detachment guarding the south-west sector of the patrol area: it cost them a fighter.

Two hours later the main Taliban force struck several kilometres away at the eastern end of the patrol area. They opened up a vicious blaze of machine gun, AK-47 rifle fire, and a volley of rocket-propelled grenades (RPGs) at Lt Sean Wilson's 8 Platoon. Wilson and his 2i/c WO John Blackmore were ready and waiting for this kind repeat performance. They coolly directed their sections to return the favour with a steady and much more accurate stream of fire from their own rifles and machine guns. Lt "Eddy" Jun's 7 Platoon and a Strathcona tank reaction force moved in to help out. From a grape-hut pillbox, a cut-off Taliban section attempted to ambush 7 Platoon's move. That attempt was short-lived after a tank round "put a sudden end to the grape-hut." In a matter of minutes, 8 Platoon won the fire-fight and sent the would-be ambush party scampering off into the dense growth. Pursuing and destroying them was neither feasible nor necessary. Both Taliban attempts to stop the local level diplomacy and reconstruction planning that day had failed. Canadian infantry combat skills had foiled the Taliban with the barest minimum of impact on life and work in Kolk and Spin Pir.

Not long after dawn the next morning, the Taliban company took a swing at what they apparently thought might be an easier target. They went after an ANA company deployed as a blocking anvil on the west end of the patrol area, just north of Sangsar. A flurry of bullets and RPGs flew back and forth between opposing sides. The Operational Mentoring and Liaison Team embedded with the ANA called in the contact details to Quick, who saw that the Taliban were fixed in place and that he had been handed an opportunity to deliver a hard smack to the enemy. His immediate reaction force of tanks and armoured engineer vehicles led by Capt Craig Volstad moved up to establish a flanking cut-off at the end of the firing line, while his attached artillery forward observation officer/air controller, Capt Ryan Sheppard, brought in a flight of US A-10 Thunderbolt ground attack aircraft.

This marked the first time that TF 1-07 had called for close air support, and the decision was not taken lightly. The battlegroup had been contemplating for some time how it could use air strikes with precision to prevent the Taliban from making an easy escape from their increasingly frequent ambush attempts. There had to be consequences for those ambushes. The trick was to lure or drive the Taliban into ground where the air strike could be delivered without harm to civilian lives and minimal property and infrastructure damage. On this day, the Taliban obliged. When they saw Volstad's armoured force manoeuvring to outflank their firing positions facing the Afghan Army company, the Taliban tried to break contact and retreat to cover through an empty field. There they met 30mm cannon fire from two Thunderbolts firing on Ryan Sheppard's directions. At least one Taliban infantryman was hit and a number of others stopped in their tracks by the burst of aircraft fire to their front. The air strike acted like a preparatory barrage for the Afghan Kandak who charged forward and took six of the Taliban prisoner. There was no permanent damage to crops or property or innocent locals. Perhaps most importantly, the whole India Company-Kandak dismounted method backed by air support was now battle-tested.[1] It became a model for operations in June.

Gunfight at Siah Choy

And so every few days for the rest of the month, "Contact" India and 2nd Kandak rolled by LAV into a different part of Zharey, dismounted and walked by night into the heart of villages reported to have Taliban hiding nearby. When the sun rose, the people of Zharey and the Taliban awoke to find Canadian soldiers among them. On 4 June it was Siah Choy close to the Arghandab riverbank opposite Sperwan Ghar. Like the week before, the Afghan Army convened an early morning *shura* with local leaders, this time led by the Afghan company commander. Quick's platoons, the ANA, and a troop of Strathcona tanks set up a series of block positions around Siah Choy for security and support in case of trouble. At the Afghan-led "security" *shura*, visibly nervous locals insisted there were no Taliban in their village. The numbers of women and children around town indicated they were right. When things seemed all-clear, Bill Hunter came forward to hold his own PRT *shura* with community development council (CDC) members to move ever closer towards consensus on their proposed village projects. At the same time, Maj Quick talked individually to village leaders he had come to know in the past months. When the formal and informal meetings ended early that morning, Quick, Hunter, and their inner security detail marched out of town to their vehicle harbour.

A dismounted infantry patrol is perhaps the best way to respond to an insurgent enemy lurking in the middle of dense foliage and high-walled farms. But it is extremely dangerous, requires nerves of steel, and even better infantry skills. Quick's platoons moved out of Siah Choy in a mutually supporting formation. The company HQ group also moved on foot in the middle of the dispersed force, unwittingly right into the path of a Taliban platoon.

Just before 0930, the enemy opened rifle fire on the HQ group as it came to the end of a freshly tilled field and began crossing a mud wall into a narrow lane. Every man dove for cover and tried to locate the enemy riflemen. The front of the tiny column, consisting of India Company's scouts, artillery observer Ryan Sheppard, his radio operator, dismounted engineers, and Dave Quick were pinned down in the walled lane. The two scouts were cut off in a cross-fire at the first corner of the lane. Cut off in the open out in the field were Company Sgt-Maj (CSM) Jeans, the company medic, and two more riflemen. The enemy platoon was close enough to them that the Canadians could hear Taliban battle chanting and changing AK-47 magazines. The morning now had all the makings of a proper disaster.

But every man in the HQ group kept his cool, identified targets, and fought back. Dave Quick stood in the centre of it all, acting as combat team commander—directing infantry, tanks, and supporting arms to converge on the force that had his group surrounded—and leading the immediate fight to bring his cut off elements into a piece of more defensible ground. He asked Sheppard to call in air support and then ordered everyone at the wall to cover the scouts' withdrawal.

The little band of gunners, engineers, and infantrymen all popped their heads up and blazed away with C-8 carbines, C-9 light machine guns, shotguns, grenades, and even an M-72 anti-tank rocket.

The Taliban platoon was only metres away. Quick told Sheppard to give their close air support and the artillery permission to fire "Danger Close." Meanwhile, the company headquarters fell back to a better position under cover of smoke from Maj Dan Bobbitt's 81mm mortars at Sperwan Ghar and a flight of Royal Netherlands Air Force Harrier Jump Jets. The Dutch fighter-bombers made a first pass to get Taliban heads down so Quick and his men could get to safety and then came back to unleash a volley of rockets into the Taliban platoon.

At the same time the rifle platoons set up blocking positions. Dave "Boomer" Broomfield's Strathcona reaction force had planned for trouble too, and when word came that they were needed they dropped fascines into the wadis between them and the trouble. In minutes they were across, had punched holes in the walls barring the way to the ambush site. In less than 30 minutes the deadly jam turned completely around and it was the Taliban who were in peril. It was not overwhelming force that did it, but a carefully laid plan executed by an officer who remained cool as bullets licked at him. When the shooting stopped, four or five Taliban were dead and not one India Company soldier was hurt.

Since regaining local support depended on fighting the Taliban without destroying Siah Choy, Quick and Sheppard set out to assess and repair any damage done in the battle. All heavy fire had been applied carefully to avoid built-up areas and homes. Once again, not one civilian was harmed and crop damage was minimal. For this action and others in which his company intelligently secured Zharey District, Maj David Quick won Canada's Star of Military Valour.[2]

Bur Mohammed and Howz-e-Madad

India Company and the 2nd Kandak companies never paused in June. Every few nights their platoons slipped into villages thought to be Taliban-controlled. When the sun came up, the Taliban would fight or try to run. When they ran, they bumped into blocking forces made up of LAV-mounted India Company platoons, or tanks, or Afghan troops covering all the exits in thick foliage or built-up terrain. On 16 June, a Taliban force was trapped in Bur Mohammed near Route Summit. Most routes out of the village were covered by Canadian or Afghan troops, except for empty fields to the east. Capt Mark Sheppard had those covered with Dragon Battery's 155mm guns. In every direction they went, the Taliban platoon ran into trouble, first from Sheppard's 9 Platoon, then the sniper detachment; 155mm shells finished their day.

As always, every India Company mission was about maintaining the freedom to patrol anywhere in Zharey District and keeping the dialogue open with local leaders. On the morning of 16 June in Bur Mohammed, *shuras* were convened after the Taliban force was defeated and its survivors chased out. Major Quick and the Afghan officers talked to local village and family leaders to reassure them that the Afghan Army and ISAF were not to be deterred.

By this time in the tour, India Company was inflicting a growing death toll on what seemed to be a Taliban infantry battalion in Zharey. That created its own challenges, both for the mental health of the Canadians in regular combat and for the "hearts and minds" campaign. First, Maj Quick ordered that platoons that killed the enemy in a gunfight should not be the same soldiers who had to search and recover the bodies. Secondly, he and CSM Jeans insisted that the troops display at all times respect and dignity for the local people and for the Taliban foe. The latter was essential to persuade the villagers to place their trust in the government and ISAF, and to convince Taliban fighters to lay down weapons and rejoin society.

* * *

On 20 June the action shifted seven kilometres down Highway 1 to Howz-e-Madad. The paved road surface gave the company excellent east-west communications so they could be everywhere in the district. Intelligence reports homed India Company and 2nd Kandak onto a Taliban company operating an IED cell and hitting ANP checkpoints along the highway. Another dismounted night insertion set up an India Company block, while Capt Volstad and a troop of tanks formed up with the ANA in the early morning darkness to sweep south to meet it.

The morning smacked of trouble; the Canadians came across untended fields and found no civilians. The joint Afghan-Canadian force had kicked open yet another enemy nest. Taliban fighters were caught between the Afghan hammer and the India Company anvil. Three Afghan soldiers were wounded in the close-quarter fight to clear through to India's block. Other Taliban sections moved to attack Quick's men from the south. They were met with fire from the sky delivered by American A-10s and Dutch F-16s. Meanwhile, Afghan troops entered the walled farmhouse that was home to the IED cell and found rockets, artillery shells, detonation cord, rifle and machine-gun ammunition, and large food stocks to feed manoeuvring Taliban units. This was not the first time Quick saw Taliban food stockpiles stored among populations that had so little. From what he observed "the Taliban totally controlled access to food in central Zharey; most people had nothing in their houses." But it was a special treat to remove the explosive material before it could be fashioned into the deadly IEDs.

The whole fight was over within a few hours after sun-up when a Taliban rifleman with rare good marksmanship began sniping at 9 Platoon from a grape hut. The Dutch Air Force ended it with one well-placed bomb. Despite all the bullets, rockets, shells, and bombs, no Afghan or Canadian was killed on that day on the northern side of the Arghandab River.[3]

Cat and Mouse: Charles Company in Panjwayi

As the fight north of the river wound down, a huge explosion was heard on the south side, in between outposts manned by Maj Chris Henderson's Charles Company PPCLI. A Gator all-terrain vehicle used to resupply the two outposts had struck a large IED, killing three Patricias instantly: veteran paratrooper Sgt Christos Karigiannis, Cpl Stephen Bouzane, and Pte Joel Wiebe. To those whose only Afghan news was casualty reports, it seemed like Charles Company was now in the fight. But their lonely struggle in Panjwayi District was far more complicated than that.

Since first moving into FOB Sperwan Ghar, Henderson's Patricias hardly stood still. Their presence patrols ranged over the vast expanse of the heavily populated and heavily cultivated northern strip of the district. Charles Company, together with No. 2 Company of 2nd Kandak, were responsible for the great tract of land from Mushan at the end of the Arghandab–Arghestan River Peninsula to the eastern district boundary and beyond into the southern approaches to Kandahar City. The working relationship with No. 2 Company grew strong, not least because it was co-located at Sperwan Ghar with the Patricias, enabling regular joint patrols.

From April onwards, after the arrival of Sgt Pam Hoban's Military Police detachment, Henderson's force turned into a mini-battalion by tightly integrating the Panjwayi District ANP. The two Patricias outposts along the main river road interspersed with the ANP posts created positive and professional examples for the policemen to emulate. Equally important to raising their standards was Sgt Hoban's ANP training program. After only a month, marked signs of improvement were visible among the company-sized force of policemen manning checkpoints around the district and in the district centre in Bazaar-e-Panjwayi. American police supply contractors were also now operating in the area, kitting out and supplying the force, with a net improvement to morale and attentiveness to duty. Every day, Hoban liaised with the police chief and her MPs kept a steady vigil on his officers. She did not have enough staff to be with the police 24/7—that initiative was being worked on at Joint Task Force Headquarters at Kandahar Airfield (KAF), and would be ready to implement during the next roto. Nonetheless, Henderson and Hoban laid the foundation for the first Police Operational Mentoring and Liaison Team (POMLT) in Kandahar Province.

The level of security made possible by this combined ISAF/ANA/ANP team meant that PRT reconstruction work was much further advanced in Panjwayi than north of the river in Zharey. In fact, unlike Zharey where Maj Quick was the main contact with the district *shura*, Maj Henderson came well down the list as a contact with the Panjwayi District *shura*. The primary contacts were civilians, the UN Habitat representative, the NSP director, the PRT members, or the Afghan Ministry of Rural Rehabilitation officials. In Panjwayi, the Taliban threat was simply lower down the priority scale than reaping the benefit of the winter rains to grow and sell bumper crops this summer.

The main task, especially of WO Ken MacLean's PRT detachment, was advancing the NSP and weaning local leaders off of the corruptible American "Quick Impact" cash-for-projects schemes. MacLean operated out of a mini-PRT base or "CIMIC House" on the opposite side of the Ma'Sum Ghar mountain from the district centre and Canadian-Afghan base. It was neutral ground, where locals were free to come to present village project proposals or to complain about landlords skimming funds from cash-for-work projects.

The PRT effort was very frustrating work, but during the spring lull MacLean figured out which people proposing contracts were honest locals looking to achieve a positive community effect and which were city-dwelling absentee landowners looking to make a quick buck. The trustworthy ones were usually willing to meet on the proposed worksite and were not worried about security. Shifty absentee landlords did little more than come to the comparatively safe CIMIC House. But, the process was working. From March to May alone, 97 village projects were approved by the district assembly and were either under construction or finished. They included a number of mosques and schools, but consisted mostly of repairs to irrigation canals and wadis, and the bridges and culverts over them. Eighteen additional projects were on the agenda at the end of May.

During meetings at Ma'Sum Ghar, at the district *shura* and around the countryside, MacLean got welcome positive feedback about LCol Shereen Shah's Afghan soldiers. Reviews on the district police were mixed. But after only a few months of intense work with them, mixed reviews were better than the year before when locals attacked the police. The most disturbing news MacLean received—and that Maj Henderson did not—concerned the arrival of a new force in the neighbourhood. On 5 May an Afghan Special Police Battalion rolled into the west end of the peninsula around Mushan. It was around then that trouble began.

Henderson was still on his mid-tour leave when these strange new "reinforcements" arrived unannounced. Contact reports and attacks against their checkpoints started almost immediately after their arrival. Acting company commander Capt Andrew Vivian met the district police chief to find out what was going on, and also dispatched a joint Patricia/Afghan Army patrol to Mushan to investigate the apparent spike in Taliban activity. The timing was not unusual for a rise in enemy activity. But there was something unusual about the violence in Panjwayi. The only forces coming under attack were the Special Police. When Henderson returned from leave and heard about the new unit in his area, he called a special security meeting with the district *shura*. He was told the same things Capt Vivian was hearing: that the fighting in the west end of the peninsula was a power struggle between two tribal lords, and that the Special Police battalion had been brought in to help wage it.

In June the mood in Panjwayi changed. The sheer number of Canadian and Afghan troops sweeping through Taliban base areas in Zharey, defeating their best ambushes, avoiding their IED traps, and not killing civilians was foiling their plans. So, the Taliban went searching for more fruitful hunting ground. The disruption caused by the local power struggle in north-west Panjwayi seemed to offer a way in to the otherwise stable and secure district. In June, Henderson and his staff of captains Andrew Vivian and Greg Grant pieced together an intelligence picture which showed that two large Taliban IED cells had now set up shop in their area. The Patricias' hunt was on.

The first weeks looking for the IED cell proved frustrating. The Taliban force in Panjwayi avoided a stand-up fight with Charles Company and No. 2 Company, no doubt because they knew they could only lose. Instead they planted IEDs, hit isolated police posts, and occasionally fired a rocket into Ma'Sum Ghar. Some of these IEDs struck Special Police trucks in west Panjwayi. Others, especially on the river road where Charles Company worked closely with the ANP, were located before they could explode. In some cases the ANP called the Patricias for help and promptly got Explosive Ordnance Disposal (EOD) teams from KAF to remove them. In another case, a Charles Company patrol surprised a Taliban cell before they completed planting a heavy 120mm mortar bomb in the river road. A day later, members of another IED cell on the other end of the district became victims by their own hand when the device they were planting in a road culvert detonated prematurely, killing two and wounding another.

Capt Craig Volstad (left), "A" Squadron 2i/c and the crew of T1A, drenched in sweat after dismounting from their tank, before the arrival of the crew cooling vests. Volstad and his crew frequently "breached" mud walls and wadis into adjacent fields to outflank Taliban ambushes set up on roads. *Photo: Capt Eric Angel, LSH*

The Force Protection Company from the Royal 22e Régiment provided security for PRT detachments and Canadian civilian government officials. Here they stand watch during a meeting at the Arghandab District ANP Headquarters. *Photo: Sgt Craig Fiander DND/Combat Camera*

Vandoo Force Protection Company soldiers from the PRT secure a job site for an irrigation canal restoration project in Kalacheh south of Kandahar City. Restoring the badly damaged and neglected millennium-old irrigation system was the priority for rebuilding Kandahar and breaking the opium dependence of tenant farmers. *Photo: Sgt Roxanne Clowe, DND/Combat Camera*

Technicians load a pallet of 155mm artillery rounds onto a transport truck at Patrol Base Wilson. Supplying and maintaining the Task Force in the field took hundreds of specialized Combat Service Support soldiers grouped together as the National Support Element. *Photo: DND/Combat Camera*

Maj David Quick (right), commander of India Company. His company's highly successful disruption campaign against Taliban bomb-cells and ambush teams in Zharey and personal bravery under fire earned him Canada's Star of Military Valour. *Photo: MCpl Kevin Paul, DND/Combat Camera*

India Company C-9 gunner stands watch in Asheqeh in east Zharey at dawn. TF 1-07 took the night away from the Taliban during their tour. *Photo: Sgt Craig Fiander DND/Combat Camera*

SPERWER or "Skidoo" Tactical Unmanned Aerial Vehicle (TUAV) being launched from Kandahar Airfield. These devices provided life-saving observation of Taliban activity often hidden by high mud walls and vegetation. *Photo: DND/Combat Camera*

Sweat-soaked C-6 machine-gunner from India Company on high ground in Zharey providing cover for his platoon patrolling the village below. Kandahar's varied terrain and extreme heat demanded the highest fitness standards from Canadian troops. *Photo: Sgt Craig Fiander DND/Combat Camera*

Afghan National Army soldiers from 2nd Kandak/1/205 Corps in action with India Company near Howz-e Madad. This unit reached a high standard of professionalism and tactical skill by tour's end. *Photo: Sgt Craig Fiander DND/Combat Camera*

M777 155mm howitzer of Dragon Battery, 2nd Royal Canadian Horse Artillery at FOB Sperwan Ghar. Maj Dan Bobbitt's "guns" fired only with careful precision to avoid harming the civilian population that was returning to Zharey–Panjwayi in early 2007. *Photo: MCpl Kevin Paul, DND/Combat Camera*

Corp John Williams takes up a defensive position following an India Company dawn skirmish with the Taliban. Williams, and his loader, Pte Richard MacWhirter, raced through enemy fire to cover their platoon mates with their C-6 medium machine gun after being ambushed near Kolk on 16 May 2007, earning them both a Mention-in-Dispatches (MID). *Photo: MCpl Kevin Paul, DND/Combat Camera*

India Company's 7 Platoon Leader, Lt Ed Jun, and one of his section commanders, Sgt Brian Durelle, liaise with supporting Strathcona tanks during the action near Howz-e Madad north of the Arghandab River on 20 June. *Photo: MCpl Kevin Paul, DND/Combat Camera*

Maj Chris Henderson, commanding Charles Company, 3PPCLI, and his Company Sgt-Maj, MWO Craig Green, in the early morning heat of western Panjwayi District. *Photo: Charles Coy, 3PPCLI*

C-9 gunner directed onto a potential target by his section 2i/c covering a Charles Company patrol in Panjwayi. This photo captures the subtle differences in regimental character between the western-based PPCLI and the eastern based *RCR*. *Photo: Charles Coy, 3PPCLI*

"A" Squadron/-Hotel Company Combat Team heading north through "Middle Earth" to reinforce US Special Forces and Afghan units in Khakrez District. These operations protected the northern expansion of the Kandahar Afghan Development Zone. *Photo: DND/Combat Camera*

Convoy leaguered up in the northern Kandahar barrens en route to resupply the joint US Special Forces-Afghan force at Khakrez, which was backed by artillery from Dragon Battery. *Photo: DND/Combat Camera*

PRT commander LCol Bob Chamberlain accompanies then Governor Khalid to a meeting to reassure local police and the Ghorak District Leader, shortly after the District Centre was recaptured from the Taliban in late June 2007. *Photo: Cpl Dan Pop, PRT*

Capt Mark Sheppard, 9 Platoon Leader in India Company, holding an impromptu *shura* with tribal elders near Asheqeh after one of the company's successful night operations to flush Taliban units out of villages in Zharey District. *Photo: Sgt Craig Fiander, DND/Combat Camera*

PRT Capt Clayton Ereaut (right), Royal Canadian Mounted Poice Cpl Barry Pitcher (centre left), and other members of the PRT Civilian Police Section negotiate the location of a new Afghan National Police checkpoint with residents of Arghandab District. Canada's Provincial Reconstruction Team improved ANP professionalism inside Kandahar City in 2006-07. Police in the rural districts remained a work in progress. *Photo: Cpl Dan Pop, PRT/DND*

Canadian lessons from Bosnia. Kandahar City school children attend a mine and IED awareness session. Teaching civilians about the threa around them empowersed them to call in help when they found explosives and restored their freedom to move, farm, shop, and get goods to market and children to school. *Photo: Capt Dave Mualt, PRT/Combat Camera*

Typical Afghan jingle truck making its way down Highway 4 past an Afghan National Police checkpoint. Drivers adorned their vehicles with personalized local folk art, not unlike North American truckers. As a road junction between continents, the truck transport industry was a key to rebuilding Afghanistan. *Photo: DND/Combat Camera*

3rd Troop, "A" Squadron, LSH pose on one of their steel "horses" and their life-size cut out of sports icon Don Cherry at FOB Ma'Sum Ghar. Hockey and other reminders of home kept spirits up in trying times. *Photo: Sylvia Pecota*

LCol Shereen Shah Khohbandi presents LCol Rob Walker with a letter of thanks during the handover ceremony with the next rotation. During the TF 1-07's tour, Shereen Shah rose from commanding an Afghan unit-in-training to being a full partner and equal to Walker. *Photo: Cpl Simon Duchesne, DND/Combat Camera*

Maj Joe Hartson (centre) commanded the Task Force Rear Party and coordinated the return of TF 1-07's wounded and dead. Here he performs the joyous task of welcoming home safely returning soldiers in August 2007. A year later, Hartson led 2RCR's Golf Company to Afghanistan as part of TF 3-08's PRT. *Photo: 2RCR*

After marching into 2RCR's Ortona Building in CFB Gagetown behind a piper, chalk of returning TF 1-07 soldiers is about to be dismissed to their anxiously waiting families and friends. *Photo: 2RCR*

Maj Chris Henderson at the front of the regular force Patricias and western reservists who made up Charles Company receiving their Afghanistan Campaign Star at CFB Edmonton. *Photo: Charles Coy, 3PPCLI*

MCpl Chris Lawrence, an Electrical and Mechanical Engineer (EME) with the Task Force, holds his three-week-old son, Aiden. Beside him is his wife Ashley White, at CFB Gagetown, August 2007. *Photo: courtesy of Meghan Cumby, Saint John Telegraph Journal*

Melissa Hunt welcome's home Pte Andrew Ward as another chalk of 2RCR soldiers arrives back in New Brunswick.

Photo: courtesy of Dave Smith, Fredericton Daily Gleaner

Henderson and his company were well aware of the threat in their area. They continued to play tag and gather intelligence on the bomb cells. Several times in early June, Henderson's patrols got the drop on cells in the act of planting very specialized remote-controlled devices as well as pressure-plated IEDs. A 1 Platoon patrol bumped into what they figured was an IED cell while hunting on the night of 10-11 June, but the Taliban avoided contact. Henderson called for the Sperwer Tactical Unmanned Aerial Vehicle (TUAV)—or "Skidoo" as it is affectionately dubbed (for the engine that powers it)—to fly over, and its surveillance gear picked up the contact. Henderson then had a Dutch Harrier buzz them at 250 feet, but in the dark it could not be confirmed that they were Taliban or were actually the IED team. The effort was not wasted, though, because a few hours later the patrol found a propane tank-based IED that the cell had been planting when it was surprised and abandoned the site.

However, that was not the only bomb they planted that night. Early in the daylight hours, as the patrol headed back to Sperwan Ghar, the lead RG-31 Nyala triggered one on the river road. The Nyala performed as designed: wheels and suspension parts sheered off while protecting the crew from everything but minor bruises. Still, the IED team had been very busy on the river road during the night. An Engineer LAV moving to the first blast site struck a second IED. Tires and suspension parts took the blast. Two sappers were hurt, but not seriously. Other IED teams were obviously working in tandem, for when an Electrical and Mechanical Engineer Wrecker moved out to recover the damaged vehicles it too was blown, setting the vehicle on fire and cooking off the ammunition inside. Again, luckily, no one was hurt. But it was abundantly clear the Taliban were now deliberately targeting Canadian patrols and convoys in Panjwayi. The hunt for those IED teams now became even more intense. Joint Canadian-Afghan dismounted patrols hiked around the district. On 18 June they moved into lower Zangabad (or Zangabad 2 as it is known), one of a handful of small villages strung out in a line a few kilometres south of the river road. One of them had to be the IED cell's base.

The cat-and-mouse game only got hotter as the Patricias and Taliban hunted each other. That night the Taliban infiltrated between

Charles Company's two river checkpoints, planting an anti-personnel mine on a road well used by local residents. Fortunately, the mine was discovered before anyone stepped on it. But Henderson ordered his platoon manning the two outposts to tighten security and change their pattern of movement, as the Taliban obviously were watching. Local villagers were passing along plenty of information about locations and planned attacks on the outposts. Charles Company's attached engineer troop spent 19 June clearing all of the roads around the outposts, just to be sure.

Very early the next morning, not long after sunrise, while Maj Quick's India Company was in the midst of its gunfight north of the river, Charles Company's 2 Platoon sent out its Gator with a load of essential supplies for the smaller Check Point 10. To be on the safe side, they were not to use their usual route to the nearby post. Minutes after they left, a tremendous explosion echoed all around Zharey and Panjwayi districts. 2 Platoon reported immediately that their Gator had left the larger outpost; it had to be them. From his position on the north side of the Arghandab, where he was supporting the morning battle south of Howz-e-Madad, LCol Walker could see a cloud of smoke rising from Panjwayi.

Henderson ordered one of 2 Platoon's sections to check out the source of the blast. That section came upon a horrific scene. The Gator had been blown into a thousand pieces. The only comfort to be had was that it was clear the veteran Sgt Karigiannis, along with young Bouzane and Wiebe, were killed instantly in a blast so powerful that it completely disintegrated the C-9 light machine gun the team carried. The first 2 Platoon soldiers on the scene immediately called for engineer and medical assistance, and for the specialized engineers from KAF to come search the site for clues as to who the bomb-makers were and where the Patricias could find them. Sgt Sean Connors, Engineer Field Section commander at Sperwan Ghar, dashed down to the scene with the Charles Company Quick Reaction Force. As lead engineer on the ground, Connors calmly secured the scene and began the horrible process of rendering it safe for the special investigators from KAF. After completing their grisly task in the baking June sun, a 2 Platoon Nyala hit a second IED on the run back to Sperwan Ghar. Connors and his sappers worked a long day and it was with great relief towards last light after clearing and investigating the second blast site that the engineers returned to the safety of the FOB for a hot meal and, no doubt, a fitful sleep.[4]

The irony is that on this horrific day, one major IED cell was taken down in Zharey, but another achieved its gruesome goal in Panjwayi. It is safe to say that the bomb-makers hoped for a bigger Canadian vehicle than the lightweight Gator that actually struck it. But the effect was the same. The blast meant more dead Canadians, another ramp ceremony, and more media coverage of a difficult mission. To put a finer point on the issue, the successful takedown of the IED cell near Howz-e-Madad, the successful location and disarming with local help of large numbers of bombs on the south side before they could do harm, never made it to the papers. In this case, the media missed the most important part of the story: that the Taliban were expending most of their resources and energy attacking the battlegroup and the ANP, while PRT teams, NGOs, the UN, and local Afghans themselves were rebuilding Panjwayi District together as part of the Afghan solution, wrestling it ever further away from Taliban control. The Taliban were gravitating to the warriors like mosquitoes to bug lamp. In the meantime, Afghan government departments, with CIDA, NGO and UN support, were filling the void in other quiet areas outside of Zharey and Panjwayi—letting the tentacles of new commerce and governance spread quietly under the very noses of the Taliban.

INTO THE "LAND OF MORDOR"

The 20 June strike was actually the second fatal IED attack that month. The first came in an area Canadians back home had heard precious little about. The northern districts of Khakrez and Shah Wali Khot are sparsely populated and desolate, yet ruggedly beautiful. And they are important to the larger ISAF and UN mission in southern Afghanistan for a number of reasons. The main hard-packed road runs north through it from Kandahar to the Dutch-Australian PRT and base in Uruzgan Province. Its east-west passes across the southern fringes of Afghanistan's central mountain range serve as important Taliban-drug trafficker "rat-lines" between Pakistan and the opium and battle fields in Helmand Province.

For some time plans had been on the table to push ISAF troops to the north as part of the next phase of expanding the Kandahar ADZ. It began in June 2007. Canadian newspapers reported that this northern drive was part of an effort to hunt down Taliban fighters and drive them from safe havens in remote mountain villages in Shah Wali Khot, Khakrez and Ghorak districts. That was true, but there was much more to it than that. This military offensive deep into enemy-held territory had it its heart a development project of almost epic proportions.

This remote and rugged area contained a watershed vital to southern Afghanistan's long-term economic sustainability. On the upper reaches of the Arghandab River lies the massive Dhala dam that controls flooding down river; its giant basin catches the runoff from the winter rains. A number of similar smaller dams can be found all along the northern foothills. Damage from the Soviet war and lack of maintenance during the Taliban years had rendered the Dhala dam inoperable. Silt had clogged up the sluice gates, because the forests that normally prevented the hillsides from eroding into the basin had been cut for fuel or construction during drought years. Nonetheless, a major restoration effort promised to bring the Dhala dam back to full capacity and beyond, so that when full, the basin could hold a two-year water reserve to feed the greenbelt around Kandahar City. This would ensure that tenant farmers would have enough water to keep most of their fields open to a variety of crops. Crop diversity and high yield were key to breaking the cycle of opium dependence. If the area around the dam could be protected from Taliban units and drug-trafficking opium convoys, then Afghan engineers and labourers could be trained and employed to carry out the work. The project would be massive and ambitious; it would take time and patience to hold local *shuras* around the districts to get support and labour, and more time for engineering surveys and to secure donor funding. The rebuilding itself will take years. But it is just the kind of long-term project that CIDA does best.[5]

The mission started with US Special Forces teams and an Afghan Kandak sweeping northwards in Khakrez District to find a Taliban force mustering there, possibly for a drive south to Kandahar or at least to cut the Kandahar–Uruzgan road. Dan Bobbitt detached

Capt Jaime Phillips' 3 Troop from Dragon Battery to support them. They were lifted by air into the new FOB Khakrez at the tiny district centre. Along with the ANA Kandak, they provided the first visible signs to people in remote northern villages that they were important to the larger national Afghan picture. As usual, the military push ran together with standing up new CDCs and improving Afghan police standards. Ruff's Hotel Company and Boomer's tanks also started running patrols in the area to map out new potential access routes and to meet with local leaders.

The first weeks of June in the north were mainly about the Green Beret and ANA fight against a large Taliban force, which was very unhappy about this intrusion into their turf. The 3 Troop guns fired hundreds of shells in support of the tiny US-Afghan teams scouring mountaintops and driving Taliban cells into the open on low ground. The barren landscape was a Canadian gunner's dream, as there was hardly anything which could suffer collateral damage. Even so, Capt Phillips understood that her mission and intent was to fight the Taliban without harming the people. Thus she refused several fire missions requested by the Americans that risked bringing shells in on tiny farm hamlets not entirely clear of civilians. It only took a few such refusals for the Canadians and Americans to understand each other's requirements. The Green Berets came to respect her need to verify targets, and went out of their way afterwards to make sure her shells killed the enemy and not the people of Khakrez.

Overall, the Canadian area of responsibility in Kandahar Province was growing. That was great news for the provincial government and the UN, as it meant they could expand the reach of their programs. But for the Canadians it also meant that the supply convoys, called Combat Logistics Patrols (CLPs), had to travel many more kilometres to keep the "bombs, bullets, and beans" flowing to far-flung outposts. Back at Kandahar Airfield, mechanic and maintenance troops of the National Support Element (NSE) worked long and frequently dangerous hours putting back together vehicles broken by endless hard driving on poor roads, open desert, and rocky wadi bottoms. They were the unsung heroes of this operation.

On 11 June, one of those CLPs was heading north with a load of water, fuel, food, 155mm shells, and mail for FOB Khakrez.

One troop of Recce Squadron's Coyotes had been assigned to escort the convoy. As the convoy moved off tension was thick in the battlegroup command post, still deployed forward at Ma'Sum Ghar. The command staff was coordinating patrols in Zharey, the recoveries from three powerful IED strikes on the Patricias in Panjwayi, as well as the resupply runs to isolated recce troops and gunners at the far corners of the province. The morning was nearly over, with only minor injuries sustained, when the call came in from Recce Squadron's 1 Troop. The lead Coyote escorting the FOB Khakrez convoy had hit an anti-tank mine-based IED. For the third time on this tour, Cpl Dave Gionet raced out of his own vehicle to be the first man on the scene. The front of the vehicle around the driver's compartment was smashed. Gionet climbed on anyway to check on his friend and barracks-mate, Tpr Darryl Caswell from Bowmanville, Ont. But Caswell was already dead.[6]

BATTLE FOR THE BELLY BUTTON

In mid-June the Taliban summer offensive was in full swing, but was not going as the Taliban had hoped. Taliban Tier 1 units in Zharey, in Panjwayi and now in Khakrez had little luck recruiting local fighters. The locals, it seemed, had better things to do. So, the Taliban went from hunting ISAF and Afghan soldiers to being hunted themselves. Their latest manoeuvre force, committed to a thrust into Kandahar City from Khakrez, now had US, ANA troops, and Canadian artillery chasing their every step. In fact, so many Taliban were identified surrounding the great round bowl of land, known affectionately to TF1-07 as the "Belly Button," that the Americans asked for and received Broomfield's tanks. In the third week of June a column of Strathcona armour, backed by two LAV platoons under Hotel Company's 2i/c Capt Mike Archibald, rode north to add serious firepower to the Battle for Khakrez.

The armoured drive was spooled up just as the Taliban searched for more vulnerable and unsuspecting targets to achieve some kind of public relations victory in the midst of a string of defeats. Remote district centres in the far north, lightly defended by small, forlorn bands of new, young ANP recruits offered an ideal target. On 18 and 19 June, Taliban infantry stormed the small ANP garrisons at

the district centres in Ghorak and Mianashin. In the greater scheme
of decisive actions taking place in the more populous areas of province that summer, losing the northern posts meant little. But the
Taliban crowed that they had won a great victory over an Afghan
government powerless to stop them, and that they could take any
district centre they chose. Because the "armed election campaign"
was now on in those northern communities that were an important
piece of national development strategy, that Taliban message had to
be countered.

Taliban dispositions in the north suggested that their plan was
to divert US Special Forces and ANA attention away from the Belly
Button stronghold at the town of Padah in Khakrez, and to ambush
whatever weak ANP relief columns attempted to re-take the nearby
district centres. The insurgents ordered villagers in Padah, Ghorak,
and Mianashin to leave their homes, possibly expecting US-directed
air strikes. It is probably safe to say the Taliban did not anticipate the
kind of response that came instead.

On 22 June most of Broomfield's tanks formed up with Hotel
Company near Padah in the centre of the Taliban storm. Far over on
the Canadian left, Strathcona Squadron Battle Capt Eric Angel drove
a combat team consisting of a tank troop, armoured engineer troop,
Mark Sheppard's 9 Platoon from India Company, and a recce/sniper
detachment to re-capture the Ghorak District Centre. On the right
flank of the great push, the LAV-equipped PRT Force Protection
Company from the Vandoos drove on the Mianashin District Centre,
backing an ANP platoon.

LCol Walker and his roving tactical command group led
Broomfield's centre column onto its start line, and that is where the
fight began. The armoured force drove into the midst of a heavily
defended Taliban company position, which they apparently planned
to defend. The L-shaped position included the houses of Padah itself,
along with fire trenches and earthen bunkers concealed by foliage
surrounding the wadi-side of the village. In all other actions the TF
1-07 battlegroup fought, small Taliban sections peeled back when faced
with annihilation. But this force was intent on holding their ground.
And this time, all civilians were gone. It was an empty battlefield,
not unlike that which 1RCR found almost a year before.

The first RPGs came out to meet the Canadian force just before 0900. Tank and LAV gunners tracked onto targets with 25mm cannons, coaxial machine guns, and 105mm main guns, picking them off with precision both at close quarters and at ranges of 2,000 metres. Broomfield and his attached artillery observer also called in shoots from Capt Phillips's 155mm guns. It was a conventional stand-up battle that proved the value of pre-deployment training time spent on these fundamentals. Boomer's tank-infantry force fought into the midst of the Taliban position, fixing the enemy to a wild gunfight to their front. That was when US Army Blackhawk helicopters swept in to land the Special Forces teams behind the enemy to prevent their escape. In two hours, 40 Tier 1 Taliban fighters were dead. The Green Berets accounted for 10, Phillips's artillery another 10, but most succumbed to the "A" Squadron Combat Team. The battle went on for a week. The combined conventional and Special Operations Force (SOF) battlegroup swept around the Belly Button with the tanks and LAVs on the low ground, while the Green Berets cleared the high ridges. The Americans were overjoyed with their heavy fire support.

Supplying and maintaining this mechanized juggernaut in such rugged country so far from its base was a testament to SSM Crabb's echelon, the attached maintenance section and the Canadian Air Force. Their C-130 Hercules out of Kandahar Airfield delivered ammunition, food, and fuel to the thirsty force by Low Altitude Parachute Extraction System (LAPES). Even so, the tired old Leopard C1 tanks were at the end of their lifespan and gave no end of stress and strain to Broomfield and his Strathconas. They all had heard the news that Canada was purchasing Leopard 2s. Unfortunately for these tired tankers, the new vehicles would reach Kandahar only at the end of this tour.

The operation up north was another "unique change for Hotel Company and Strathcona Square Combat Team," recalls Capt Archibald. "We were always getting shifted to do something different, like the Task Force fire brigade." When it was over they had cleared the giant drainage basin all the way to Gumbad, site of a Canadian patrol base back in early 2006. Archibald got a sense from talking to the few civilians they did encounter that they were accustomed to Taliban units moving through their villages but not staying. They seemed to hope that everyone would just leave them be in their remote mountain hideaway.[7]

The slightly more populous villages of Ghorak to the west and Mianashin to the north-east were a different story. There Taliban units had tried using fear to assert control. The PRT's Vandoo Company joined the fairly effective ANP force they were escorting in a small attack to drive the Taliban out and retake the Mianashin District Centre. The Vandoos then made the new centre defensible. At Ghorak, Eric Angel's rescue force found that most of the original police garrison had fled the scene when villagers warned them about the large Taliban force marching in to destroy them. This did not instil confidence in the new ANP detachment, moved up to re-establish government presence and take over from Angel in the last days of June. Locals warned that the Taliban had not gone far and would be back as soon as the Canadians were gone. A stronger, more lasting presence was needed in this far-off village on the east-west smuggling route. Given the military nature of the task of holding that ground, it was not a job for police alone. What was needed was the Afghan National Army.

It just so happened that in the early summer, LCol Wayne Eyre's Operational Mentoring and Liaison Team grew in size and took responsibility for the training and staff professional development of the ANA's 1 Brigade of 205th Corps. The whole brigade would not arrive until fall, and it would take months after that to train them to the same standard displayed by 2nd Kandak. In any case, during the first half of 2007 the Canadian OMLT staff did not have enough mentors on hand to train all of 1 Brigade. That would not occur until the next rotation. But considerable progress had been made in a short time with the 4th, or Combat Support, Kandak, including its artillery company at Sperwan Ghar and the Recce Company at Spin Boldak. The newest addition to 1 Brigade was 3rd Kandak. The OMLT assigned to them was made up of Canadian soldiers and Royal Netherlands Marines. The 3rd was nearing the end of its training and ready to start running limited operations as on-the-job training when the call came to mount up in Dutch Air Force Chinook helicopters for a ride to Ghorak.

By the time this was all organized, the new ANP detachment in the Ghorak district centre was under siege by a large Taliban force. The detachment had reportedly already fought off one Taliban attempt to storm its defences. An ANP convoy sent up to re-supply and reinforce them was ambushed and destroyed, its survivors beheaded. It was only a matter of time before the besieged ANP force was also massacred. No matter how tiny was the population up north and no matter how intense was the campaign for support closer to Kandahar City, Governor Khalid and President Karzai felt they could not afford to lose that campaign in any district. Ghorak needed an ANA garrison.

As a consequence, Alex Ruff's Hotel Company "fire brigade" got the call to make the long, dangerous drive back up north to relieve the beleaguered policemen. Along with them went 1st Company from 3rd Kandak. The formation arrived on 8 July to find the jittery ANP platoon ecstatic to see them and equally keen to leave now that soldiers had arrived to protect the post. A day later all of the policemen were gone.

It did not take long for Ruff to figure out why. A local Ghorak boy, 10 years of age, had worked as a cook at the police station. While the policemen were besieged inside their post, the Taliban had seized the boy and cut off his head. When his father attempted to intervene, the child was hanged in the centre of the village and his body left there to warn the citizens of Ghorak that the Taliban were the authority. To reinforce the message, the Taliban also put the boy's severed head on display. The incident left a deep impression on the Hotel Company soldiers and Strathcona tankers. Although the end of their tour in Afghanistan was only weeks away, the act of brutality renewed their sense of purpose and resolve to prevent the Taliban from ever regaining power over the Afghans.

Ruff's troops and the Afghan infantrymen set to work clearing out the smashed-up district centre and turning it into a proper, defensible FOB. A week later, the Dutch Chinooks brought the new garrison for Ghorak: 2nd Company of the 3rd Kandak and its all-Canadian OMLT led by Capt Chris Blencowe. Governor Khalid personally flew to Ghorak and Mianashin for *shuras* with local leaders to re-assure them of government willingness to protect them and to fight the Taliban.

The demonstrations sent a powerful message. No one in Ghorak had ever seen the governor, or a NATO heavy armoured force before the events of the previous weeks. Nor had they seen professional, disciplined soldiers from their own army with the training, weapons, and resolve to protect them.

Throughout this entire display, the Taliban stood back and watched from nearby hilltops. They could not win a stand-up fight against this Canadian-Afghan force on the wide-open terrain of the valley floor in which Ghorak sat. They patiently waited for Ruff's combat team to withdraw leaving behind 80 soldiers of 2nd Company 3rd Kandak, Blencowe's OMLT, and their forward artillery observer and air controller to provide air support.

The story of what happened after the heavy armour rolled back south to Kandahar City is a microcosm of how Afghanistan will stand on its own. Within days, Blencowe and 2nd Company were patrolling on foot in and around the village, re-asserting government control and sending a visible message to locals hiding in the hills and to the Taliban. At one point Blencowe leaned over to the Afghan company commander offering a suggestion for how to enter the village safely. His Afghan counterpart told him to look up. Like Canadian infantry in Ortona, Italy in 1943, the Afghans took control of the village high ground by entering via rooftops. There could be no ambush from behind mud walls. Blencowe realized he had as much to learn from his Afghan colleagues about counter-insurgency warfare as he had to teach them about staff planning and military professionalism.

The ANA's demonstration of will and resolve made villagers feel safe enough to return. The 40 families, totalling about 100 people in all, returned to their hamlets. In a few days Blencowe was summoned to a *shura* with village elders in the Mosque. "All they wanted was for someone, somewhere to keep a single promise previously made to help them. All I could do was promise I would listen. They clearly wanted nothing to do with the Taliban, were desperate for security and wanted water. I later showed up in their villages at dawn to prove I was providing security as they awoke and watched the ANA buy rice and tobacco with cash. I don't think the Taliban pay cash for supplies and give candy to the kids!"

The Taliban force in the area fired a few rockets into the new FOB without effect. They ultimately realized that for now, they had lost control of Ghorak. In the coming weeks the new-found stability provided by the ANA garrison and the Taliban defeat allowed UN and Afghan government officials to come north to set up CDCs in Ghorak and Khakrez. Promises of water were honoured.[8] The Afghan Army and police and the international development agencies would stay in this struggle till it ends.

THE BORDER, REVISITED

In June, down on the border with Pakistan in Spin Boldak District, reports were received that the Taliban had launched a small backlash against reconstruction activity in May. Early in the month, a prominent member of the district *shura* was dragged from his home and into a ditch by a Taliban gang. There they pummelled his body from head to toe for six hours before leaving him a bruised and broken mess as a warning to those who worked with the government and ISAF.

Days later, Major Steve Graham's Recce Squadron and 4/1/205 Afghan Recce Company patrols ranging across the barren countryside learned that the Taliban had shut down the new clinic in the town of Loi Karez by threatening the kill the staff. They had done the same at the town's two schools months before. From other border region villages came reports of Taliban cells transiting through from Pakistan en route to the battlegrounds of the Arghandab and Helmand valleys. These units demanded food and water from already scant village supplies and warned that they would kill any villager who chose to work for the government or ISAF. In the twin towns of Spin Boldak-Wes, Afghans living in the displaced persons camp and hired to work at the Canadian-Afghan FOB received dreaded Night Letters, telling them to cease their work.

This wave of violence and intimidation ran counter to the live-and-let-live kind of truce that had held in the district up to that point. The Taliban-drug trafficker alliance was clearly worried that an effective Afghan government and international aid effort was replacing the lawless chaos along their critical supply route. Nor were they happy with Recce Squadron and Foreign Affairs efforts to halt what amounted to a turf war between the Afghan police forces and their associated tribes. A new spirit of co-operation emerged, albeit painfully slowly, between the largely Achekzai Afghan National Border Police (ANBP) and the mainly Noorzai ANP. Steve Graham and Capt Francis Conliffe liaised between the US-mentored ANBP and a fairly new local ANP chief keen to turn things around in the district. In 2007, ANP reform efforts in the district got a much needed shot in the arm of American assistance with organization, pay, and equipment. The highly corrupt Afghan Highway Police in the district were more of a challenge. Orders to shut down their posts and merge with the improving ANP went unheeded. It would take more work to bring them in line.

Just as Major Graham had encountered earlier in Zharey District, it took a few months of steady Canadian patrolling, honoured promises of return patrol visits, and visible signs of government and police improvement for local Afghans to want to be part of the solution. In the summer of 2007 they poured into Graham's command post, offering information and complaining about how the corruption worked and how the Taliban-drug trafficker forces moved across the border.[9]

On the international front, Canadian diplomats and US Customs and Immigration officials were inching closer to a deal between Kabul and Islamabad. The deal included counter-smuggling police efforts and a new streamlined border crossing station instead of the separated and inconsistent posts then in operation on both sides of the International Arch.

Taliban IED cells tried repeatedly to hit Graham's patrols, but without success. Likewise, the open terrain did not favour ambush tactics. They tried several against NSE CLPs running the 100km gauntlet down Highway 4, but were shot up by the security escorts. Soldiers from the Royal New Brunswick Regiment, the Princess Louise Fusiliers, the Royal Newfoundland Regiment, the Nova Scotia Highlanders, the West Nova Scotia Regiment and many other eastern Canadian units riding in the RG-31 Nyala armoured trucks earned their spurs in running gun battles, while protecting dangerous loads of fuel and ammunition and precious food and water from Taliban RPGs and bullets.

Despite their best efforts, the Taliban could not kill another Canadian soldier down on the border. Instead, they resorted to assassination attempts, IEDs, and suicide bomb strikes against the police inside Spin Boldak town itself.[10] But even these were limited, doubtlessly because most Taliban forces and supplies for the 2007 fighting season were already committed to Zharey and Panjwayi and the Taliban's unwavering main goal of re-taking Kandahar City. In the meantime, for TF 1-07, there were only a few weeks to go.

THE TAJMOHAMMAD TRAP

Taliban fighters in Zharey–Panjwayi were fugitives in July 2007. The Canadians now owned the night. Before the sun rose on 3 July, India Company infiltrated into the midst of a Taliban infantry company hiding out in Tajmohammad, on the north side of the Nalgham–Sangsar egg. The insurgents were laying in wait there to launch ambushes on Highway 1, but instead found themselves in a snare. When they realized there were Canadians among them at first light, a Taliban section opened up on Capt Mark Sheppard's 9 Platoon to cover the withdrawal of the rest of their force before making a break for it themselves.

At Sperwan Ghar, Dragon Battery's guns waited for word from their eyes on the ground, in the form of Capt Ryan Sheppard, and from their eyes in the sky: the Sperwer Tactical Unmanned Aerial Vehicle (TUAV). Two Taliban columns bolted from town to escape a gunfight they knew they would lose. But in every direction they turned, they found Canadians and Afghan National Army (ANA) troops waiting for them. One Taliban platoon ran north into an empty field and received a tightly grouped concentration of 155mm high-explosive shells. Another bolted out of the village to the south-east—and straight into a Dutch air strike. Three were hit. The survivors then ran into Lt "Eddy" Jun's 7 Platoon blocking line, losing one more. Jun moved forward to check on a Taliban infantryman apparently wounded in the short fire-fight, when a number of men popped up from behind a wall to his front and ran away. He and his lead section could have mowed them down, except that the men running from them carried no weapons.

The unarmed group turned out to be a fugitive Taliban section attempting to blend into the village when they bumped into 7 Platoon. Apparently the group retrieved their weapons from a grape hut and opened fire. Their first volley caught Jun by surprise and nearly cut him and the lead section down. But the enemy soon lost the advantage of surprise. Eddy Jun and WO Eric Green called out fire orders—C-8 carbines barked, C-9 light machine-guns (LMGs) spat, M203 rifle grenades thumped, and the Taliban were driven from the field.

That said, most of the Taliban force escaped Tajmohammad. But then the goal of the operation, and indeed of ISAF's presence in Afghanistan, was not to wipe out every Taliban who showed his face. The purpose in this case was to disrupt an enemy ambush before it started and to show villagers that the Taliban did not own Tajmohammad or even Nalgham–Sangsar. India Company and 2nd Kandak did this by fighting the Afghan way, on foot and close to villages without laying waste to them. Women and children moved out of the way of the immediate fight into houses next door, but not out of their villages. Artillery and airstrikes landed with precision, in small quantities, and were immediately followed up with damage assessments to make sure that any damaged civilian property was repaired or compensated for. No civilian was harmed and not one Canadian or Afghan soldier killed. And once again, Major Quick and the Afghan company commanders held *shuras* with village elders in the aftermath of a battle that saw the Taliban leave the field. They were losing their grip in Zharey.[1]

The Taliban attempt to regain presence and win over the people of Panjwayi also faltered. The pace of improvised explosive device cells slowed, but could not stop, while efforts by Ken MacLean's Provincial Reconstruction Team detachment, UN agencies, and the Afghan government increased, to rebuild mosques, schools, and the irrigation systems, so farmers could break their opium dependence and life could return to normal. Taliban units in the area, unwilling to stand and fight the Patricias, attacked and killed policemen instead. But their attacks were unable to halt the professionalization of Panjwayi District Afghan National Police (ANP). In fact, at the end of June, Sgt Pam Hoban's Military Police (MP) Detachment evolved into Mobile Mentoring Team "A"—Canada's first Police Operational Mentoring and Liaison Team (POMLT). Even as critics back home were demanding that the Canadian mission in Kandahar be changed to focus more on development, that transition was already underway in the croplands of Zharey and Panjwayi.

TRAGEDY AT ZALAKHAN

All the while, Henderson's company and his partnered Afghan 2nd Company closed in on the IED cells that had claimed three of their own two weeks before. Hours after India Company finished up in Tajmohammad, a Charles Company Combat Team surrounded a bomb cell in Zalakhan.

The operation at Zalakhan came after reports from a range of sources yielded an intelligence picture of a different kind of IED unit taking up residence in the vicinity. The information that Company "Ops" Captain Gregg Grant pieced together suggested that this was not a clumsy group of Madrassa-trained amateurs, but a far more dangerous group of experienced foreign bomb-making specialists. In the early morning darkness of 4 July, the cell was surrounded. Recce Squadron Coyotes and an artillery forward observation team held the nearby mountaintop. 9 Platoon and the company sniper section marched by foot to quietly block the escape from the village's north edge. The cut-off teams were in place when an Afghan-Canadian mechanized combat team deliberately thundered down the only and thus obvious road into town, kicking up dust and hoping to flush the enemy.

At the head of the column, Eric Angel led a combined troop of tanks with rollers and ploughs and a Badger to clear the route. Behind them came the ANA infantry of 2nd Company and their Canadian Operational Mentoring and Liaison Team led by WO Dave Hood. They rode together with Capt Matt Dawe's 8 Platoon and 2 Troop engineers. Capt Jeff Francis, the artillery observer detachment commander, rode with Dawe to provide "danger close" fire support in case of a fight. Sgt Hoban's MPs completed the force, riding along as mentors to an ANP detachment that would carry out searches of any suspect buildings. In all, there were three Afghan soldiers or policemen entering the village for every Canadian. The training of the Afghans had come a long way since the beginning of the tour.

On arrival at Zalakhan, 2 Troop engineers and LAVs set up another cut-off east of town while the Afghan company and Dawe's platoon walked in fully expecting to meet the enemy. All on the scene could smell trouble. Reports from locals suggested the enemy aimed to spring a trap. But the Taliban remained quiet, avoiding a gunfight they would most certainly lose. Tension was high, but the force remained professional in its conduct of the village patrol. In the end, the best intelligence and the clearest hunches were not grounds to open fire, or even kick-in doors, in an apparently quiet and friendly community. Despite certainty that the enemy was present, if the Taliban chose not to show themselves, then it was over for the day.

At least the Patricia-Afghan combat team took comfort in the fact that they demonstrated to the people of Zalakhan that ISAF and the ANA were concerned about the villagers and their welfare. They could have battered down all the doors and searched every home to hunt for the Taliban, but that kind of behaviour would not win the trust of the people of Zalakhan. Dismounted Afghan and Canadian foot patrols, showing respect for people and property in a known Taliban stronghold, while the frightened enemy hides, was far more effective. If the Taliban chose not to stand and fight, then they would be found another day.

By mid-morning, after *shuras* finished, the presence patrol had served its purpose. The force mounted up and headed back to Sperwan Ghar with tanks and mine-rollers in the lead. The tanks and MPs had been watching the route the whole time the Patricias and Afghan soldiers patrolled the village, so IED concerns were not high. Nor was there a real fear that two infantry companies and a tank troop would be ambushed in comparatively open and empty terrain.

The Taliban bomb cell in Zalakhan had waited a long time for this moment, probably months. Buried deep beneath the main gravelled east-west road that connects Panjwayi to Kandahar City was a powerful package of anti-tank mines and old Soviet heavy artillery shells. The IED had been buried so deep and for so long that the road showed no tampering. A Taliban observer team, watching the convoy from a grape hut some distance away, let the tanks roll past unharmed. They were waiting for the RG-31 Nyalas. When the third RG in the column was directly over the device, the observer team connected the wire.

No one was prepared for the massive size and power of the explosion that tore through the hot morning air and over the radio net. The target was Matt Dawe's platoon headquarters carrier. The moment after the blast, Patricias in the first RG-31 looked back into the dust-filled blast area. Dawe's RG had vanished. They were horrified to imagine that it had been blown to dust. And even more horrified when it fell from the sky and slammed into the road behind them. Tankers and engineers behind Dawe's RG saw it hurled high into the air. Some reports say 20 feet, others say 80. It doesn't matter.

The vehicle behaved exactly as it was supposed to. The suspension and wheels sheared off and the engine compartment separated, leaving the crew compartment as an independent pod. The RG is meant to defend against mines, but heavy artillery shells buried in that road had such massive explosive power that they blew a crater in the hard-packed gravel road ten feet across and a full six feet deep. The only saving grace was that none of the seven good men inside felt the end. Capt Matthew Dawe, MCpl Colin Bason, Cpl Jordan Anderson, Cpl Cole Bartsch, Pte Lane Watkins, and artillery observation officer Capt Jeff Francis were all gone, together with the platoon's Afghan interpreter, whose name is protected for his family's sake. Some day he too will be honoured.

Capt W.M. Dixon's 2 Troop, 41 Field Squadron sappers were riding immediately behind. They leapt out to secure yet another IED site for the "CSI" team from Kandahar Airfield. As the engineers responsible for Panjwayi and for protecting the combat team against mine threats, 2 Troop was very keen to find the perpetrators. They took to their investigative task with special rigour, none more so than 2 Troop MCpl Jason Francis; Jeff Francis was his cousin. They found the grape hut where the Taliban observer team had been hiding, hundreds of yards away. The feces and food found inside indicated they had laid there for days. More clues turned up. 2 Troop and Charles Company would get them, very soon.

The 4 July IED caused exactly the kind of media effect that Taliban commanders sought. Back in Canada there were more questions about vehicle safety and whether or not the Afghan mission was succeeding. The questions were understandable. But those raising them seemed to have only one measure of mission success or failure: the Canadian body count. They paid little attention to the fact that Panjwayi's ir-rigation system had improved and was yielding bumper crops. Or the fact that a better crop yield undermined drug trafficker control and improved quality of life of the people. Nor did they take note of the fact that Afghan soldiers and police were assuming much more of the security burden.

In fact, despite the attack on 4 July the pace of rebuilding Kandahar Province never slowed. While Taliban bomb-makers fixated on the battlegroup and Afghan security forces, WO MacLean surveyed an Afghan Ministry of Agriculture canal restoration project. In Kandahar City, Drew Gilmour's Development Works mills and bakeries were ready to buy-up and process the wheat harvest of Ghundey Ghar. Battlegroup and ANA patrols to divert the Taliban from Kandahar's regeneration did not stop now that crops had to get to market. Yet, most of these achievements, what Matt Dawe and his team had worked and died for, went unmentioned.

Turning the Tables at Makuan

Evidence gathered at the 4 July IED site and other intelligence col-lected that month led back to two IED storage and manufacturing sites in Panjwayi and a Taliban infantry force in eastern Zharey. To deal with the latter problem India Company continued to slip into Taliban strongholds by night and flush them out into ANA cut-off teams. But there was one notable difference. LCol Shereen Shah's 2nd Kandak had made great strides since February, when they first sent out single platoons to hold ground while the Canadians manoeuvred around them. By July the colonel and his staff were running the operational planning process. And the soldier-level skills and junior leadership in his companies had risen to meet his own professionalism. The most telling example came in the early morning of 17 July, when Afghan soldiers navigated silently in the darkness into the hamlet of Makuan alongside Maj Quick's India Company. The Taliban platoon there was heavily armed with machine guns, rocket-propelled grenades (RPGs), and even a mortar and an 82mm recoilless rifle. But they were trapped by the Afghan-Canadian force that crept into the nar-row strip between Highway 1 and the Arghandab River. The Taliban tried shooting their way out. At dawn on 17 July, Royal Netherlands

Air Force strikes and Dragon Battery shells added to the din of small arms fire poured into the Taliban ambush team by Afghan and Canadian infantry. Sixteen Taliban fighters were killed and the survivors arrested by the Afghan Police in full view of Makuan's residents. To Dave Quick the operation "was the perfect way to wrap up the tour. It was a culmination of our all our efforts to turn the Afghan Army and Police into something."

The Zangabad Sting

That afternoon in Panjwayi, most of Charles Company and the ANA 2nd Company mounted RG-31s and trucks and headed for the 1,000-metre-high mountain wall due south from Sperwan Ghar and five kilometres east of Zangabad 2 or upper Zangabad. There they dismounted for what looked like a joint live-fire exercise, blasting away with all weapons at the mountainside generating a tremendous amount of noise and commotion for the remaining daylight hours. It was an elaborate ruse. Missing from the unit were the surviving members of 8 Platoon and the company sniper section. At last light they set out from Sperwan Ghar under command of Platoon WO Ian Long. They marched 10 kilometres west and quietly took up positions covering a farm complex between Zangabad 1 and Zangabad 2. Inside was an IED factory. Just before dusk the "exercise force" at the mountain loaded up and headed back to Sperwan Ghar. Partway back to the forward operating base, the convoy stopped. Canadian and Afghan infantrymen quickly and quietly jumped from their vehicles and set off in the darkness towards Zangabad.

The ruse and the stealthy night march worked. 7 Platoon and the Afghan company crept through grape fields approaching the compound from the southeast. 800 metres out, the Patricia vanguard nearly walked on top of a sleeping Taliban sentry post. The sentry broke the night's stillness with a burst of machine-gun fire, stopping the platoon in its tracks. Every man dropped to one knee, kept still and calmly raised weapons to shoulders. The moment the Taliban machine gunner fired his next burst he was dead. It was almost dawn. The Patricias moved quickly but with practiced cover and movement to close the distance now that the Taliban were alerted to their arrival. They reached the compound in the first wisps of daylight to see one of the Taliban IED cell members peeling out of the compound on a motorbike with an RPG on his back. A well-aimed M203 rifle grenade knocked him off the bike. On the north side of town another part of the cell opened up with RPGs, trying to shoot their way through 8 Platoon's block. The attempt failed in a blaze of Patricia rifle and C-9 LMG fire. Charles Company closed in to surround the compound. When the sun was full up, Afghan soldiers and police swept inside, seized bomb materials and arrested the suspected cell leader. It was all over by mid-morning.

Two days later, back in Sperwan Ghar, Sgt-Maj Green, who had just come from a meeting with the Physicians Assistant, sat down to talk to Major Henderson about the mental health of the company, which had been badly strained by the months-long, nerve-rattling test of wills with the IEDs. The two leaders agreed that the Company and their attached engineers were in much better form now that the IED cell that had taken so many Canadian and Afghan lives was finished.[2]

Exactly one week later, Charles Company formed up with almost the entire 2 RCR Battlegroup, all of 2nd Kandak and three detachments of ANP. LCol Alain Gauthier's 3rd Battalion, Royal 22e Régiment battlegroup from TF 3-07 would begin taking over TF 1-07's duties in six days. So it was the time in the rotation when leaders at all levels had to summon all their energy reserves to inspire and encourage their troops, and when the soldiers themselves had to exercise the utmost self-discipline to carry on as professionals to the very end, fighting their own natural human reaction to want to take it easy and survive. Fortunately, the 2RCR Battlegroup had no shortage of inspiring leaders and disciplined soldiers.

CORDON AND SEARCH IN NAKHONAY

LCol Walker's team was determined not to relax their pressure on the Taliban. The force set up a cordon around Nakhonay, sister town to Zalakhan, along the main Panjwayi road to Kandahar, within view of the 4 July IED strike site. *Operation Porter*, therefore, was a fitting end to TF 1-07's tour of duty. It was actually a Panjwayi District ANP mission to search for and seize terrorist materials. Intelligence gathered in the past weeks suggested that the elite Taliban foreign

IED responsible for 4 July had moved their bomb lab from Zalakhan to neighbouring Nakhonay. Walker pushed his command post (CP) out of KAF once more to Ma'Sum Ghar to co-ordinate personally with Shereen Shah's staff. The battlegroup and 2nd Kandak worked as equal partners to throw a solid cordon around the town.

Their common plan called for Dave Broomfield's tank squadron to set up a ring of steel on routes in and out. A tank and engineer breaching team blew holes in walls and ploughed safe lanes to the edge of town. Dan Bobbitt's artillery was on call, and his forward observers moved to vantage points all around the village. Jake Galuga's engineers made ready to clear all positions in the cordon for mines and IEDs. No one was taking any chances. Henderson's and Quick's companies, the engineers, and the Afghan soldiers filed through the breaches in the morning dark of 26 July. The overwhelming display of ISAF and ANA combat power convinced the Taliban not to fight, but they did not escape with their deadly supplies.

The Panjwayi District ANP turned up with 80 officers, two-thirds of whom were in uniform. That might sound pitiful, but compared to the mess that Sgt Hoban found when she first came to Panjwayi it was actually rather impressive. In fact, the Panjwayi chief of police and his staff were part of the planning process, acting on leads and tips about the bomb-makers.

The policemen behaved as law-enforcement officers empowered with warrants to search homes under Afghan law. There were no home intrusions by Canadian "infidels." They unearthed ten RPG rockets, five anti-personnel mines, two grenades, a box of mortar fuses for detonators, as well as more sophisticated detonator devices, four boxes of ammunition, a package of plastic explosive, rolls of wire, and to top if all off, a "night letter" for terrorizing locals. Seven men were arrested, including two known suspects on the provincial "wanted list." When it was all over, the force filed out of town with not one soul injured or killed.

Of course the Taliban were not defeated in Kandahar. More battles would be fought there. Toward the end of the handover to TF 3-07 Broomfield's tanks, the last TF 1-07 unit to depart fought alongside the Vandoos at Ghundey Ghar. The fall of 2007 saw a major action in Arghandab District, repeated in the summer of 2008, in which Afghan soldiers took the lead. Zharey and Panjwayi were by no means swept clean of insurgents, nor would they be until the ruined state that spawned the Taliban-drug trafficker alliance was fixed. That process had come a long way since Canadians first showed up in Kandahar in 2005. But it is still too soon to say with certainty how it will all turn out and whether the effort of TF 1-07 contributed to a functioning and healthy Afghanistan. Whatever the final outcome, their sacrifices were noble and their efforts made a difference in the lives of Kandaharis. Now they could turn their attention with honour to getting home.

TO KANDAHAR AND BACK

One of the most important lessons learned from the Bosnia experience was that a soldier must not be plucked from the midst of a war, put on a plane and—in less than 24 hours—find themselves in their own quiet living room. After TF 1-07 had handed over to the Vandoos and left Afghanistan, they stopped over in Cyprus for four or five days for what is called Third Location Decompression (TLD). There they had an opportunity to relax and "come down" from the mission in a very casual setting among their comrades before arriving back in Canada. A team of mental health care workers, including psychologists and social workers, padres, and Operational Stress Injury Social Support (OSISS) representatives, were on hand to discuss any problems or concerns with the troops, as well as provide mental health briefings on such subjects as stress and anger management. For master corporals and above there was training on how to recognize stress among their soldiers. The briefings included "Battle Mind" presentations, an American program that featured vignettes depicting various scenarios about returning home that the soldiers watched and then discussed. Attendance at these briefings was mandatory. The troops also joined in various recreational and tourist activities. Although the troops were anxious to get home, many came to see the value of the decompression program. Given the size of the task force, it took five weeks to rotate them all through the TLD process.[3]

The troops began returning to Canada in early August, receiving a well-deserved homecoming at their various bases. At CFB Gagetown a bagpiper led them into the reception area where they were met by families, some coming from Ontario and Newfoundland. Members of the community held red balloons, yellow ribbons, and "Thank You" banners. Shelly Hillier from the Georgetown Military Family Resource Centre, who attended most of the arrivals, remarked, "these were evenings that I will never forget for the rest of my life."[4] Groups of soldiers continued to arrive at two-day intervals until early September. They were then granted leave, during which time they could begin the reintegration process. This could be a difficult period, when troops still needed support but were separated from the embrace of the task force. To prevent them from becoming isolated, many of the Regular Force personnel were retained within their mission sub-units for a time so they could continue to draw support from among their comrades. Troops also received briefings on recognizing the signs of stress, and what to do about it.

Reservists who returned to their local units and sometimes smaller communities, far removed from facilities and services provided at larger centres like Base Gagetown, were of particular concern. In the case of TF 1-07, the number of reservists who had served was substantial. In the past, many reservists had returned to their civilian jobs and little follow-up took place. Under an initiative introduced by the Vice Chief of the Defence Staff, base personnel received the names of returning reservists throughout their area of responsibility (for example, Gagetown was responsible for reservists in New Brunswick and Prince Edward Island). They then connected with the soldier's unit who in turn contacted the reservist to make sure the post-deployment screening took place, usually at a base like Gagetown. Units assisted in this process by, among other things, arranging transportation and covering costs. If the screening and subsequent interview indicated that treatment was needed, it took place at a base when convenient, or if distance was a problem they were referred to a health care specialist within the member's own locale. Six weeks after the post-deployment interview occurred, base personnel followed up with the member to ensure that the recommendations for treatment were being implemented. Another longstanding problem was also resolved, whereby reservists reverting from their Class B contract status following their tour remained eligible for services for any injuries incurred during their operational tours.[5]

Various services were available to soldiers having problems re-adjusting to their return home, or showing signs of operational stress injuries (OSI), including post-traumatic stress disorder. Counselling services were available through the base mental health services or within the public and private health care systems, while OSISS offered peer support for the troops and their families. Fred Doucette, himself an OSI "survivor" from his tour in Bosnia, stated that between September 2007 and June 2008 he had talked with over 80 personnel from New Brunswick and Prince Edward Island experiencing some form of distress.[6]

The Gagetown Military Family Resource Centre (GMFRC) and Deployment Support Centre (DSC) also continued to provide support to military families throughout the post-deployment period. The GMFRC delivered re-integration briefings throughout their region that helped families with deployed members deal with reunion, which brought with it its own set of stressors. Initially, things were quiet at the GMFRC during what Shelly Hillier called the "honeymoon phase" of the return, when troops were at home on vacation. In time they did receive some requests for referrals to outside agencies from families whose re-integration was not going as well as it might. The Tuesday night coffee meetings also continued at the GMFRC so that spouses could keep their "bond" intact.[7] The DSC provided briefings on re-integration and referrals to those needing assistance.

Community organizations continued to show support for the troops and their families during the post-deployment period. The Neighbours for Peace (now Neighbours in Prayer) meetings held by local clergy continued into the fall. So too did community rallies. On 28 September 2007, a large Red Friday rally was held in Saint John to thank the troops for their efforts and show ongoing support for their families. Among the thousands who marched through the downtown were students from local schools, members of the Royal Canadian Legion, police and firefighters, and the public. Local businesses contributed funds to defer costs. Proceeds from the rally went toward a bursary named for Pte David Greenslade of Saint John who was killed on Easter Sunday. The bursary was to benefit any young cadet or military personnel who planned to further their education beyond high school.[8] In return, units from the battlegroup took the opportunity to thank members of the community for their support during the deployment, presenting them with plaques and other symbols of appreciation.

Other new initiatives began once the troops returned from Afghanistan. These included a project on the North Shore of New Brunswick to collect used textbooks and other reference material for schools in Afghanistan. It was initiated by task force veteran MCpl Dan Wiese of Dalhousie, who had been asked by an Afghan interpreter to help acquire books for distribution in Afghan schools. Several local schools within the district collaborated on the project.[9]

The official welcome home took place at Gagetown on 12 October 2007 with the Minister of National Defence, the Hon Peter McKay, and the Chief of the Land Staff, LGen Andrew Leslie, among others, in attendance. Assembled for the last time were more than 400 members of the 2RCR, 41 Field Engineer Squadron and hundreds of other Gagetown-based supporting arms soldiers from the National Support Element. They received the Afghanistan Campaign Star, a symbol of the country's gratitude for their service.

By then, a number of the key leaders had been posted to new assignments in other parts of Canada. Among those who could make the trip to be with the 2RCR family for this symbolic day was LCol Rob Walker, back from his new post at the Land Forces Command and Staff College in Kingston to take command of the parade. Maj David Quick returned from a new job at National Defence HQ in Ottawa to fall in for one last time at the head of India Company. Within 2RCR, Maj Alex Ruff moved upwards to a new staff position, but on that day he too took position for the final time in front of his Hotel Company. 2RCR's pipes and drums played and the Minister personally decorated each soldier on parade with their medal. For the cynical that might be no big deal, but for many a soldier, receiving it from a federal cabinet minister on this grand day with television cameras and flashbulbs, meant that their service was important. It gave some sense of closure for their hard months of preparation and a difficult rotation.

"TRANSITION ROTO"

Canadian Foreign Service Officer Gavin Buchan refers to TF 1-07's tour in Kandahar as the "transition roto." So does CIDA's Michael Callan. After the huge job of patrolling all of southern Afghanistan in the early days, followed by the concentrated conventional battles of 2006, the mid-2007 handover from TF 1-07 to 3-07 was the first time in Kandahar that the incoming Task Force carried on with the same tasks in the same places in the same fashion as their predecessors. The initiative was no longer with the Taliban, and reconstruction was at last the main effort, just as so many Canadians wished.

At the beginning of TF 1-07's tour, the Afghan National Army presence was small and unproven, while the police were among the greatest dangers to Kandahar. By tour's end, thanks to the Operational Mentoring and Liaison Team concept and Afghan will, the ANA presence had tripled in numbers and reached levels of professional ability that saw it take the lead on military operations. That growth was always part of the ISAF and UN plan. It just materialized during the first half of 2007. Similarly, by the end of the tour that model had been expanded to Afghanistan's police services, attacking head on that Achilles' Heel of corruption in Kandahar.

During the first half of 2007, Canada's Provincial Reconstruction Team could finally work at full capacity to become a platform for projecting the mentoring support and financial aid of a half dozen Canadian government departments. After two years of laying foundations, Foreign Affairs and CIDA projects to rebuild Kandahar took off at great speed. The joint effort to reform Kandahar's justice system by Foreign Affairs, the RCMP and Corrections Canada began in earnest. Two years of PRT trial and error experimentation in Kandahar was transformed into a sophisticated long-term rehabilitation plan for the province.

The problem of the troubled border area is not over, but building on the Recce Squadron deployment to Spin Boldak, it is now a focus of effort for all Canadian mission elements of defence, diplomacy, and development.

Among the most important Canadian reinforcements that arrived in Kandahar during TF 1-07's tour was BGen Tim Grant's Joint Task Force Afghanistan Headquarters. This was a new kind of command machine for a new kind of operation. In early 2007 it became the synchronizing headquarters to manage the complex array of security, mentoring, and rebuilding jobs that needed to be done in Kandahar. BGen Grant and his staff enabled all the moving parts of the Canadian battlegroup, the PRT, and the OMLT to mesh with Afghan counterparts and NATO allies to manage operations all the way from the Maywand in the west to the Pakistan border in the east and north beyond the great Dhala Dam to Khakrez.

During TF 1-07's time, the Taliban dropped dramatically in size and influence in Kandahar Province and abandoned attempts to take on Canadians in combat. The Tier 2 recruiting drive among Kandaharis failed and only small Tier 1 units materialized. The size and nature of battles against those Tier 1 units changed to short, sharp clashes between small groups, with little disruption to the pattern of life in Kandahar. Indeed, the comparisons with 2006 are striking. During *Operation Medusa* in 2006, almost 9,000 rounds of artillery ammunition blasted Pashmul alone. In the whole TF 1-07 tour, Dragon Battery fired less than 2,500 rounds across all southern Afghanistan, most of those falling in remote Helmand and Khakrez. At the end of the tour, Taliban attacks turned to symbolic Afghan government targets, such as the police. The result was high ANP casualties and occasional IED strikes on Canadians. But that Taliban focus allowed life in Kandahar City and reconstruction and governance reform to proceed comparatively unmolested.

Perhaps the most remarkable development during TF 1-07's stay was how much rebuilding went on in Zharey–Panjwayi in the midst of security operations. This work was thanks in part to people like the National Solidarity Program Director for Zharey District. An Afghan-Canadian who answered the country's call for expatriates with skills to return and re-build, he was doing just that.[10] If the greater mission succeeds in the end his name will be revealed and honoured. If the mission fails, people like him will pay the price.

Endnotes

CHAPTER 1

1 *9/11 Commission Report* (2004), pp. 1–14.

2 *The Economist* (2001), cover page and lead editorial.

3 Privy Council Office official (2002).

4 Walker to Charters (2006).

5 Dupree (1973) remains the authoritative English language source on Afghanistan history and anthropology prior to the Soviet occupation.

6 Jalali (2006); Alexander (2006).

7 Blood (2001). Statistics estimated as of 1996; Shah (2007).

8 Goodson (2001), p. 107, pp. 110–11.

9 Goodson (2001), pp. 49–52; Bradsher (1983), pp. 43–44, p. 51; Roy (1986), p. 71; Ghaus (1988), pp. 159–82, pp. 187–200.

10 Goodson (2001), pp. 55–56; Bradsher (1983), p. 74, pp. 77–78, pp. 86–96; Roy (1986), pp. 84–95; Arnold (1983), pp. 73–76.

11 *Cold War International History Bulletin* (1996/1997), pp. 128–61; Coll (2004), pp. 40–50; Collins (1986), pp. 65–66, pp. 77–79; Roy (1986), pp. 95–97, pp. 99–102, pp. 106–8; Jukes (1989), p. 83; Grau (1998), p. xiv.

12 Goodson (2001), pp. 60–61, p. 90, pp. 92–97.

13 Goodson (2001), p. 61, pp. 143–46; Coll (2004); Crile (2003); Cuthbertson (2005).

14 Goodson (2001), pp. 145–46; Roy (1986), p. 208; Coll (2004), p. 65, p. 67, p. 72, pp. 81–84, p. 134, pp. 145–46, pp. 154–57, p. 165, p. 201; Cooley (1999), p. 112; Wright (2006), pp. 105–8, pp. 129–30.

15 Wright (2006), pp. 3–6; Coll (2004), p. 85, pp. 87–88, pp. 153–58, pp. 199–204.

16 Goodson (2001), pp. 70–76.

17 Goodson (2001), pp. 104–8; Coll (2004), pp. 282–92; Rashid (2001), pp. 25–29.

18 Goodson (2001), pp. 77–86.

19 Goodson (2001), pp. 110–32; Byman (2005), pp. 187–89, pp. 199–218; Rubin (2007), pp. 57–60, pp. 70–71.

20 United Nations Security Council (2000).

21 *9/11 Commission Report* (2004), pp. 47–48, pp. 63–65, pp. 68–70, pp. 115–17.

22 Goodson (2001), pp. 4–5; United Nations Secretary General (2007); Canadian International Development Agency (CIDA) (2007).

23 Thakur (2007).

24 Buchan (2007).

25 CIDA (2007).

26 Stogran (2003); Piggot (2007), pp. 85–86.

27 Olexiuk (2006).

28 Stein and Lang, pp. 55, 67-68, 73-77.

29 Durch (1993).

30 Kaplan (1994).

31 Van Creveld (1991).

32 Kalder (1999), pp. 58–59, 62–63, 113.

33 Windsor (2000).

34 Windsor, p. 28.

35 Krulak (1999).

36 Lizee (1994), pp. 135–36, 139.

37 Morrison (1995), pp. 65–68.

38 Charters "Out of the Closet" (1999), pp. 58–60.

39 Charters (1999), p. 58.

40 MacKenzie (1993), pp. 143, 230–31.

41 Caplan (2005), pp. 34, 36–37, 47–48, 75, 92 133, 164; Talentino (2005), pp. 189, 191–92.

42 Interview with Lieutenant-Colonel Christopher Hand, December 2007.

43 Ibid.

44 Ibid.

45 Interview with Maj Russell King, November 2007.

46 Interview with Shawn Courty.

47 Interview with Renata Pistone, April 2007.

48 Jalali (2006).

49 Levitz (2007); Manley (2008), pp. 14–15.

50 Karzai (2007), 57. In June 2007 HIG leader Gulbuddin Hekmatyar reportedly announced that HIG was withdrawing from the armed struggle, but this was viewed with some uncertainty. Synovitz (2007).

51 Rubin (2007), p. 58; Zabriskie (2003a); Rotberg (2007), pp. 2–3, p. 42; Chayes (2006), p. 160, p. 162, pp. 193–94. These assessments are very similar to those in official sources.

52 Karzai (2007) p. 57; Johnson (2007), pp. 328–32.

53 Chayes (2006), pp. 186–87; Strauss (2002); "U.S. Fights al Qaeda in Pakistan" (2002); Associated Press (2002).

54 Lamb (2003); Johnson (2007), pp. 318–26; Chayes (2006), p. 187, 189.

55 Chayes (2006), p. 190, pp. 233–35.

56 Chayes (2006), pp. 193–94, pp. 232–34, pp. 305–6; Rubin (2007), p. 59; Garcia (2003); Gannon (2003); Reuters (2003); Gall (2003).

57 Larry Goodson, Presentation to OCIGI Afghanistan Conference, December 2006.

58 "Afghanistan: A Chronology of Suicide Attacks Since 2001," (2006).

59 "Taliban Form 'Resistance Force'," (2003); Bone and Hussain (2003); Karzai (2007), p. 65; Johnson (2007), pp. 326–28.

60 Zabriskie (2003a and 2003b).

61 Radio Free Europe/Radio Liberty (2004); Gall (2004); Salahuddin (2004). The UNHCR made its announcement on 6 August.

62 Lobjakis (2004); Lobjakis (2005).

63 Reuters/Agence France Presse (2005); Esfandiari (2005); Chayes (2006), pp. 1–7, 343–58, believes that the murder of police chief Akrem in 2005 was instigated by Pakistan with the co-operation of then Kandahar governor Gul Agha Shirzai.

64 "Afghan Election Results Finalized," (2005) The election was marred by fraud, but was validated.

65 Charters (1989); Rubin (2007), p. 60; Karzai (2007), p. 73.

66 Karzai (2007), pp. 63–68. Exact undisputed figures on the size of the Taliban are not available. Official estimates suggest perhaps 2,000 full-time and 6–8,000 part-time fighters, which are not dramatically different from the Taliban's own claims of about 10,000 fighters in all. But they are unable to deploy and support all of these inside Afghanistan at any one time.

67 Rotberg (2007), p. 2.

68 Robinson (2007).

69 See polling data cited in Manley Report, p. 93.

CHAPTER 2

1 UN Secretary General's Security Council Report on the Situation in Afghanistan, 21 September, 2007.

2 Interview with Col Mike Capstick, May 2007.

3 Ali A. Jalali, Address to CIGI Conference on Afghanistan, Dec 2006.

4 Stein and Lang, p. 181.

5 Interview with Richard Arbieter, Deputy Director, Policy and Advocacy Division, Afghanistan Task Force, Department of Foreign Affairs and International Trade, November 2007.

6 Stein and Lang, p. 181.

7 Interview with Gavin Buchan, November 2007.

8 Rotberg, pp. 2–3.

9 Paul Gallis, *NATO in Afghanistan: A Test of the Trans-Atlantic Alliance. Congressional Research Service Report*, 23 October 2007 p. 13.

10 Interview with Brian MacDonald, Former British Army Counter-Narcotics Liaison Officer at UK Embassy in Kabul, February 2007.

11 Chayes, pp. 77–83.

12 Interviews with Michael Callan, Manager of CIDA Kandahar Unit in Afghanistan Task Force, Dec 2006, Nov 2007.

13 Interviews with Maj Shawn Courty and WO D. MacLean, KPRT CIMIC TF 1–07 Team, Dec 2007.

14 Interview with Col Stephen Bowes, CO, KPRT Roto 0, Oct 2007.

15 War Diary, Task Force Orion, 3 August 2006. Christie Blatchford, *Fifteen Days: Stories of Bravery, Friendship, Life and Death from Inside the New Canadian Army*. Toronto: Double Day, 2007.

16 Mike Capstick, Presentation to Gregg Centre Conference, October 2007.

17 Rubin, "Saving Afghanistan," pp. 67–69.

18 Jalali, "The Legacy of War," pp. 41–42; David Rohde, "Afghan Symbol for Change Becomes Symbol of Failure," *New York Times*, 5 September 2006, www.nytimes.com, accessed 5 September 2006.

19 Larry Goodson, Presentation to CIGI Afghanistan Conference, December 2006.

20 Chris Alexander, Presentation to Centre for International Governance Innovation, Waterloo Ontario, December 2006.

21 Alexander (2006).

22 War Diary, 1RCR, End Tour Report.

23 Interview with BGen David Fraser, Dec 2007.

24 Interview with Maj Mark Gasparatto, December 2007.

25 Interviews with Gavin Buchan November 2007, MGen Tim Grant, December 2007.

26 Rubin, "Saving Afghanistan," p. 57; Graeme Smith, "Insurgents Melt Away From Battle, *Globe and Mail*, 12 September 2006; "Canadian-led Offensive May Have Killed 1,500 Taliban Fighters," *CBC News*, 20 September 2006. *Note*: estimates of casualty figures were never confirmed. See also: Bill Curry, "Time to Bring Troops Home, NDP Says," *Globe and Mail*, 11 September 2006; Canadian Press, "Military Worried About Tory failure to Defend Afghan Mission," *Globe and Mail*, 1 October 2006.

27 Stewart Bell, "Al-Qaeda Warns Canada," *National Post*, 28 October 2006; "Analysts Expect Spring Assault on NATO Troops," *CBC News*, 21 December 2006, www.cbc.ca/world/story/2006/12/21, accessed 30 January 2008. The dire predictions seem to have been based on threats in December 2006 from Mullah Omar that blood would flow and claims of Taliban commanders that they had thousands of fighters ready: "Afghanistan's War: A Double Spring Offensive," *The Economist*, 22 February 2007, www.economist.com, accessed 30 January 2008.

CHAPTER 3

1 Telephone Interview with Serge Boudreau, 25 January 2008.

2 Telephone Interview with Capt. Virginia Thomson, 26 February 2008.

3 Alexandra Heber, Stephane Grenier, Donald Richardson, and Kathy Darte, "Combining Clinical Treatment and Peer Support: A Unique Approach to Overcoming Stigma and Delivering Care," in *Human Dimensions in Military Operations—Military Leaders' Strategies for Addressing Stress and Psychological Support*, Meeting Proceedings, (2006), pp. 23–1–23–14, available at http://www.rto.nato.int/abstracts.asp.

4 Interview with Fred Doucette 10 June 2008.

5 Interview with Shelly Hillier, 10 June 2008.

6 Telephone Interview with LCol Chris Hand, 16 January 2008; Maj Dyrald Cross, e-mail correspondence, 17 March 2008.

7 National Defence and Canadian Forces Ombudsman, "From tents to sheets: An analysis of the CF Experience with Third Location Decompression after Deployment," (Ottawa: Department of National Defence, September 2004); Telephone interview with Serge Boudreau, 25 January 2008.

8 Mark A. Zamorski, "Evaluation of an Enhanced Post-deployment Health Screening Program for Canadian Forces Members Deployed on Operation APOLLO (Afghanistan/SW Asia), Preliminary Findings and Action Plan," (Ottawa: Department of National Defence, 1 June 2003).

9 Perhaps the best-known spokesman has been LGen (retd) Romeo Dallaire who chronicled his experience with PTSD in *Shake Hands with the Devil* (Toronto: Random House Canada, 2003). Doucette told the story of his own injury in *Empty Casing: A Soldier's Memoir of Sarajevo under Siege* (Toronto: Douglas and McIntyre, 2008).

10 Interview with Fred Doucette, 10 June 2008.

CHAPTER 4

1 Interview With LCol Rob Walker, December 2007.

2 War Diary (W.D.), 2RCR Battlegroup. Operations Order, 14 Feb 2007.

3 W.D. 2RCR Battlegroup, Winter Operational Plan, Feb 2007.

4 Interview with Maj David Quick, April 2007.

5 Interview with MWO Stephan Jeans, November 2007.

6 Interview with Capt A.J. Gimby, November 2007.

7 Interview with LCol R. Walker, April 2007.

8 W.D. 2 RCR, Weekly Assessment Report, 2 March 2007; Interviews with Alex Ruff and David Nixon, November 2007.

9 Presentation by Col (Ret'd) Michael Capstick to Gregg Centre Fall Conference, Oct 2007.

10 Interview with Maj Shawn Courty and WO C. Maclean, November 2007.

11 The word has been part of the Canadian Army's vocabulary since the South African War of 1899–1902. Derived from the Boer term "laager," it refers to a wagon and horse-drawn column circled in for the night on open terrain to defend itself, and was adapted for use by armour.

12 Interview with MCpl Tracy Price, 28 November 2007.

13 W.D. 2RCR BG, Weekly Assessment Report 23 March 2007; Interview with Steve Graham, Interview with Sgt. David Camp, April 2007.

CHAPTER 5

1 Interview with Louise Garwood-Filbert, April 2007.

2 W.D. 2RCR BG, Weekly Assessment Report, 6 Apr 07.

3 W.D. 2RCR BG, Recce Squadron After Action Report, 2 April 07; Interview with Maj Steve Graham, Apr 07.

4 Interviews with Michael Callan and Kevin Rex, November 2007.

5 W.D. 2RCR BG, Witness Statements, After Action Narratives and Consolidated Situation Report, 8 Apr 07, Interviews with Alex Ruff, Ben Rogerson, Wayne O'Toole, Apr and Nov 07.

6 Interviews with Maj David Quick, and WO William Hunter, April 2007.

7 This event reconstructed Post-operation Witness Statements, medal recommendations, After Action Reports from the War Diary, 2RCR BG and the personal observations of the author, present during the events.

8 W.D. 2RCR BG, Weekly Assessment Rpt, 21 Apr 07.

9 Interview with Michael Callan, Nov 07.

CHAPTER 6

1 Michael Staples, "Five Soldiers From CFB Gagetown Killed," *The Daily Gleaner*, 9 April 2007.

2 Capt Christian Breede, e-mail message to author, 18 January 2008.

3 Interview with Capt John Hill, 13 November 2007.

4 Interview with MCpl Tracy Price, 28 November 2007.

5 Interview with MCpl Tracy Price, 28 November 2007.

6 Interviews with Maj Joe Hartson and Capt Christian Breede, 14 December 2006, and 31 October 2007.

7 Interview with Capt John Hill, 13 November 2007.

8 Interview with Shelly Hillier, 10 June 2008; Karen O'Keefe, "Centre offers support for military families," *The Daily Gleaner* (Military Families Supplement), 14 July 2007, pp. 2 and 9; Candice Robichaud, "Looking for the positive makes things easier," Ibid., pp. 16–17; Adam Bowie, "Being Separated from a partner is difficult, Ibid., pp. 25 and 27.

9 Interview with Capt. Mark Miliigan, 12 June 2008; Gillian Christie, "Deployment Support Centre assisting deployed soldiers by caring for their families," *The Post Gazette*, 28 April 2007, p. B3; Adam Bowie, "Deployment Support Centre an important part of GMFRC," *The Daily Gleaner*, (Military Families Supplement), 14 July 2007, pp. 7, 8, and 9.

10 Jennifer Dunville, "District 17 ready to help students cope with tragedy," *The Daily Gleaner*, 10 April 2007, p. A4; interview with Rev. Robert McDowell, 10 June 2008.

11 Michael Staples, "Community sends message to Armed Forces members," *The Daily Gleaner*, 19 January 2007, pp. A1–A2.

12 Sandra Carrier-Harquail, telephone interview, 3 June 2008; Jeffrey Bento-Carrrier, "'Support Our Troops' launched in Dalhousie," *The Tribune*, 14 February 2007, p. A1: Jeffrey Bento-Carrier, "Parcel program for those in Afghanistan," *The Tribune*, 4 April 2007, p. A8.

13 Interview with Rev. Robert McDowell, 10 June 2008; Heather Grattan, "Prayer rally held to comfort troops, families," *The Post Gazette*, 10 February 2007, p. A3; Gillian Christie, "Neighbours for Peace offers comfort, prayer for community in mourning," *The Post Gazette*, 21 April 2007, p. A1.

14 Jeremy Dickson, "Red Rally Day honours troops serving in Afghanistan," *The Daily Gleaner*, 18 June 2007, p. A3.

15 Interview with Rev. Robert McDowell, 10 June 2008.

16 Interview with Shelly Hillier, 10 June 2008.

17 For example, see Letters to the Editor of *The Daily Gleaner*, 22 February 2007, p. C7; 5 June 2007, p. C7; and 31 July 2007, p. C7.

18 Tim Jaques, e-mail message to author, 16 January 2008; Sandra Carrier-Harquail, telephone interview, 3 June 2008.

19 Chris Lambie and Christian Laforce, *On Assignment in Afghanistan: Maritimers at War*. (Halifax, NS: Nimbus and *The Chronicle Herald*, 2007).

20 Michael Staples, telephone interview, 4 June 2008.

21 Tim Jaques, e-mail message to author, 16 January 2008.

22 Michael Staples, "Covering soldiers' funerals helps Canadians grieve," *The Daily Gleaner*, 25 April 2007, p. B8.

23 Sgt. Terry Richardson, telephone interview, 5 June 2008; Sgt T. Richardson, "Postcard from Kandahar," *The Tribune*, 18 April 2007, p. C1.

24 Michael Staples, "Covering soldiers' funerals helps Canadians grieve," *The Daily Gleaner*, 25 April 2007, p. B8.

CHAPTER 7

1 B.R. Rubin, Abubaker Siddique, "Resolving the Pakistan – Afghanistan Stalemate." *US Institute for Peace Special Report* 176, (October 2006).

2 Rand Study (2008).

3 W.D. 2RCR BG, Spin Boldak District Report, Recce Squadron, 30 July 2007.

4 Interview with Geoff Marshall, Oct 2007.

5 Interviews with Steve Graham and Francis Conliffe, Nov 2007.

6 UN Report of the Secretary General on UNAMA 21 Sept 2007.

7 W.D. 2RCR, Operational Event Summary "A" Sqn LSH, 7 – 8 May 2007.

8 W.D. 2RCR, Post-Operation Report and Operational Event Summaries, 8 May 2007.

9 When LCol Walker returned from leave and found out about the video tape he asked to make it public to show Canada how careful his own troops were in using force and how the Taliban deliberately set up conditions for civilians to be killed. His request was denied. Public debate surrounding NATO use of force and the deaths of innocent civilians caught in the crossfire usually condemns ISAF troops. The spotlight is rarely cast the other way on an amoral enemy, much to the frustration of Canadian soldiers taking such great pains to use military force with care and precision. The Taliban seem tuned to the fact that media outlets are hungry for stories of ISAF airstrikes killing and maiming the very people ISAF was trying to protect.

10 W.D. 2RCR Weekly Assessment Report, 11 May 2007, Interview with Russell King, Oct 2007.

11 W.D. JTFA-3, KPRT Daily Situation Reports 7-10 May 2007.

12 Interviews with Russell King, David Sinclair April, Nov 2007, Tim Grant Dec 2007.

13 Two weeks mandatory leave out of the battle zone is a feature of Canadian tours of duty. The leave blocks are spread throughout the tour to limit the number of troops away at any one time.

14 W.D. 2RCR BG, Post Operations Report by Capt Mark Coté, Interviews with Dave Quick, Stephen Jeans, Eric Green, and Ed Jun, Nov 2007.

15 W.D. 2RCR BG, Hotel Coy Post-Operations Report 17 May 2007, Interview with Alex Ruff, Nov 2007.

16 W.D. 2RCR BG, *Operation Hoover* Report 17 – 25 May 2007.

17 Interviews with David Quick, Stephen Jeans, Nov 2007.

CHAPTER 8

1 W.D. 2RCR BG, Post Operations Report, 31 May 07, Message Logs 30–31 May, Interviews with Dave Quick and Stephen Jeans, Craig Volstad, November 07.

2 2RCR BG Post Operations Report, 4 June 07, Interviews with Dave Quick, Stephen Jeans, David Broomfield and Ryan Shepperd, Nov 2007.

3 W.D. 2RCR BG, India Company Combat Team Post Operations Report 20 June 07, Interviews with Dave Quick, Stephen Jeans, Ed Jun, and Craig Volstad Nov, 07.

4 W.D. 2RCR BG, Charles Company Consolidated Situation Report 29 May 2007, Post Operations Report 18 Jul 07, Mine Strike Report 20 June 07, Interview with Chris Henderson, Daman Dyer, Rob Walker Nov 07.

5 Interview with BGen Tim Grant, Col Mike Cessford Apr 2007, Michael Callan Dec 2006, Nov 2007.

6 W.D. 2RCR BG, Daily Situation Report, 11 June 2007.

7 W.D. 2RCR BG, *Operation Perserverance* Report, 7 Jul 2007, Interviews with David Broomfield Nov 2007, Michael Archibald Apr 2008.

8 W.D. 2RCR BG, *Operation Hiccup* Report 8 Jul 07, Interviews with Alex Ruff, and Chris Blencowe, Nov 07.

9 W.D. 2RCR BG, Recce Squadron Spin Boldak District Report, 31 July 2007.

10 Interviews with Steve Graham and Francis Conliffe, Nov 2007.

CHAPTER 9

1 WD 2RCR BG, Post Operations Reports 4 Jul 07, Interview with Rob Walker, Dave Quick, Nov 2007.

2 W.D. 2RCR BG, Weekly Assessment Report 20 July 07. Interview with Chris Henderson Nov 2007.

3 Serge Boudreau, telephone interview, 25 January 2008; interview with Fred Doucette, 10 June 2008.

4   Interview with Shelly Hillier, 10 June 2008.

5   Serge Boudreau, telephone interview, 26 January 2008.

6   Interview with Fred Doucette, 10 June 2008.

7   Interview with Shelly Hillier, 10 June 2008.

8   Jeff Ducharme, "Parents hope rally will help heal their wounds," *The Daily Gleaner*, 11 September 2007, p. A4.

9   Jeffrey Bento-Carrier, "Schoolbooks for Afghan children," *The Tribune*, 28 November 2007, p. C3.

10   W.D. KPRT, Daily Situation Report, 18 Jul 2007.

Bibliography

Primary Sources

Documents

B.R. Rubin, Abubaker Siddique, "Resolving the Pakistan— Afghanistan Stalemate" US Institute for Peace Special Report 176, October 2006.

Canadian International Development Agency. *Review of the Afghanistan Program*. Ottawa, May 2007.

Cold War International History Bulletin, Issues 8–9, Winter 1996/1997.

Gallis, Paul. *NATO in Afghanistan: A Test of the Trans-Atlantic Alliance. Congressional Research Service Report*. Washington, D.C.: Library of Congress, October 23 2007.

Independent Panel on Canada's Future Role in Afghanistan [Manley Report]. Ottawa, January 2008.

National Defence and Canadian Forces Ombudsman. "From tents to sheets: An analysis of the CF Experience with Third Location Decompression after Deployment," Ottawa: Department of National Defence, September 2004.

The 9/11 Commission Report. New York: W. W. Norton, 2004.

United Nations, Secretary General. *Report of the United Nations Secretary General on the Situation in Afghanistan*. New York, September 2007.

United Nations, Security Council. *Resolution 1333*. New York, 19 December 2000.

Zamorski, Mark A. "Evaluation of an Enhanced Post-Deployment Health Screening Program of Canadian Forces Members Deployed on Operation APOLLO (Afghanistan/SW Asia), Preliminary Findings and Action Plan," Ottawa: Department of National Defence, 1 June 2003.

War Diaries

These Canadian Forces Document Collections for units deployed on overseas missions include all documents recording administrative and operational activities including but not limited to:

Post Operations Reports
Weekly Assessment Reports
Intelligence Reports
Critical Incident Reports
Operational Event Summaries
Daily Situation Reports
Operational Plans and Orders
Honours and Award Recommendations
End Tour Reports

Unit or Formation War Diaries consulted:

Task Force Orion, 1PPCLI, January–August 2006.
Task Force 3–06, 1RCR BG, August–2006–January 2007.
Task Force 1–07, 2RCR BG, January–August 2007.
Task Force 1–07, Kandahar Provincial Reconstruction Team
Joint Task Force Afghanistan Headquarters

Interviews

Arbieter, Richard. Deputy Director, Public Policy and Advocacy Division, Afghanistan Task Force, Department of Foreign Affairs and International Trade, November 2007.

Archibald, Capt Michael. Second in Command Hotel Company TF 1–07. April 2007, April 2008.

Blencowe, Capt Chris. Operational Mentoring and Liaison Team TF 1–07 to 3rd Kandak, 1st Brigade 205th Corps Afghan National Army, April, November 2007.

Boudreau, Serge. Social Worker, Mental Health Department, Base Gagetown, Telephone Interviews, 25 and 26 January 2008.

Bowes, Col Stephan. KPRT Commander, Roto 0 2005–06, October 2007.

Breede, Capt Christian. Second-in-Command and Adjutant, TF 1–07 Rear Party, Base Gagetown, 14 December 2006 and 31 October 2007.

Broomfield, Maj David. Officer Commanding "A" Squadron, LSH TF 1–07. November 2006, April, November 2007.

Buchan, Gavin. Canadian Senior Foreign Affairs Officer, Kandahar, Afghanistan, April and November 2007.

Callan, Michael, Manager, Kandahar Unit, CIDA Afghanistan Task Force, December 2006, November 2007.

Camp, Sgt David, 41 Field Squadron RCE TF 1–07. April 2007.

Capstick, Col Michael. First Commander, Strategic Advisory Team—Afghanistan, 2005–06, Interviewed May 2007.

Carrier-Harquail, Sandra. 'Support Our Troops Group', Dalhousie, NB, Telephone Interview, 3 June 2008.

Cessford, Col Mike. Deputy Commander Joint Task Force Afghanistan — 3, November 2006, April 2007.

Conliffe, Capt Francis. Second in Command, Reconnaissance Squadron TF 1–07. April, November 2007.

Courty, Maj Sean. KPRT CIMIC Team Commander TF 1–07, November 2007.

Doucette, Fred. Peer Support Coordinator, Operational Stress Injury Social Support Network, 10 June 2008.

Dyer, Capt Damon. Adjutant, 2RCR Battlegroup TF 1–07. November 2006, April, November, December 2007, February 2008.

Fraser, BGen David. General Officer Commanding ISAF Regional Command South 2006, December 2007.

Gasparotto, Maj Mark. Officer Commanding 23 Field Squadron RCE, TF 3–06, December 2007.

Garwood-Filbert, Louise. Director, Correctional Services of Canada Detachment at KPRT TF 1–07. April 2007.

Gimby, Capt AJ. Staff Capt 2RCR Battlegroup HQ TF 1–07, November 2007.

Graham, Maj Stephan. Officer Commanding "A" Squadron RCDs TF 1–07, November 2006, April, Nov 2007.

Grant, MGen Tim. Former General Officer Commanding Joint Task Force Afghanistan, 2007, currently Deputy Commander, Canadian Expeditionary Force Command. April and December 2007.

Green, WO Eric. 7 Platoon Warrant Officer India Company TF 1–07, November 2007.

Hand, LCol Christopher. Commandant, Tactics School, Combat Training Centre, Base Gagetown, December 2007; Telephone Interview, 17 January 2008.

Hartson, Maj Joe. Officer Commanding, TF 1–07 Rear Party, Base Gagetown, 14 December 2006 and 31 October 2007.

Henderson, Maj Chris. Officer Commanding Charles Company 3PPCLI TF 1–07, April November 2007.

Hill, Capt John. Assisting Officer, Base Gagetown, 13 November 2007.

Hillier, Shelly. Deployment and Family Support Coordinator, Gagetown Military Family Resource Centre, 10 June 2008.

Hunter, WO William. KPRT Detachment Commander for Zharey District, April 2007.

Jeans, MWO Stephan. India Company Sgt-Maj TF 1–07, November 2007.

Jun, Lt Ed. 7 Platoon Leader, India Company, April, November 2007.

King, Maj Russell. Deputy Commanding Officer, 2RCR Battlegroup. November 2006, April, October, November 2007, February 2008.

MacDonald, Capt Brian. Former British Army Counter-Narcotics Liaison Officer at UK Embassy in Kabul, February 2007.

MacLean, WO Ken. KPRT CIMIC Detachment Commander for Panjwayi District, December 2007.

Marshall, Capt Geoff. KPRT CIMIC Detachment Commander for Spin Boldak District, October 2007.

McDowell, Rev Robert. Minister, Oromocto United Church, 10 June 2008.

Milligan, Capt Mark. Coordinator, Deployment Support Center, Base Gagetown, 12 June 2008.

Nixon, Capt David, Hotel Company LAV Captain TF 1–07, November 2006, April, November 2007.

O'Toole, MWO Wayne. Hotel Company Sgt-Maj TF 1–07, November 2007.

Price, MCpl Tracy, Hotel Company TF 1–07, Base Gagetown, 28 November 2007.

Quick, Maj David, SMV. Officer Commanding India Company TF 1–07, April, November 2007.

Rex, Kevin. CIDA Development Advisor at JTFA-3 HQ. November 2007.

Richardson, Sgt Terry. 2nd Battalion, Royal New Brunswick Regiment, Bathurst, NB, Telephone Interview, 5 June 2008.

Rogerson, Lt Ben. 5 Platoon Leader, Hotel Company TF 1–07, April, November 2007.

Ruff, Maj Alex. Officer Commanding Hotel Company TF 1–07, November 2006, April, November 2007.

Sheppard, Capt Ryan. Forward Observation Officer from "D" Battery 2nd RCHA attached to India Company Combat Team TF 1–07, November 2007.

Sinclair, Maj David. Judge Advocate General's Branch Advisor to 2 RCR Battlegroup TF 1–07, November 2006, April, November 2007.

Staples, Michael. Reporter/editor, *The Daily Gleaner*, (Fredericton, NB), Telephone Interview, 4 June 2008.

Thomson, Capt. Virginia. Mental Health Nurse, Mental Health Department, Base Gagetown, Telephone Interview, 26 February 2008.

Volstad, Capt Craig. Second in Command, "A" Squadron LSH TF 1–07, November 2006, April, November 2007.

Walker, LCol Rob, Commanding Officer 2RCR Battlegroup TF 1–07, November 2006, April, December 2007, March 2008.

Correspondence

Breede, Capt Christian. Second-in-command and Adjutant, TF 1–07 Rear Party, Base Gagetown, to Brent Wilson, e-mail, 18 January 2008.

Cross, Maj Dyrald, Royal Canadian Dragoons, to Brent Wilson, e-mail, 17 March 2008.

Jaques, Tim. Editor, *The Tribune* (Campbellton, NB), to Brent Wilson, e-mail, 16 January 2008.

Walker, LCol R.D., to David Charters, e-mail, 8 December 2006.

Presentations and Briefings

Alexander, Chris. UN Deputy Special Representative for Afghanistan, Presentation at "Afghanistan in Transition" conference. CIGI (Centre for International Governance Innovation), University of Waterloo, December 2006.

Comments by an official of the Privy Council Office. Centre for Conflict Studies annual conference, 2002.

Capstick, Col Michael. Commander, Strategic Advisory Team—Afghanistan, 2005–06, Presentation to Gregg Centre Fall Conference, October 2007.

Goodson, Larry. D.D. Eisenhower Chair in National Security Studies at the US Army War College, Presentation to "Afghanistan in Transition" conference. CIGI (Centre for International Governance Innovation), University of Waterloo, December 2006.

Grossman, Lt Col (Retd) Dave. "The Bullet Proof Mind," Base Gagetown, 26 January 2007.

Jalali, Ali A. Presentation to "Afghanistan in Transition" Conference. CIGI (Centre for International Governance Innovation), University of Waterloo, December 2006.

Military Family Briefing, Base Gagetown, 11 December 2006.

Olexiuk, Eileen. Remarks to "Afghanistan in Transition" Conference. CIGI, University of Waterloo, December 2006.

Thakur, Ramesh. Presentation to Symposium on Provincial Reconstruction Teams in Afghanistan. Wilfrid Laurier University, May 2007.

Stogran, LCol P. Presentation at the University of New Brunswick. May 2003.

Secondary Sources
Books and Theses

Arnold, Anthony. *Afghanistan's Two-Party Communism: Parcham and Khalq*. Stanford: Hoover Institution, 1983.

Blatchford, Christie. *Fifteen Days: Stories of Bravery, Friendship, Life and Death from Inside the New Canadian Army*. Toronto: Doubleday Canada, 2007.

Bradsher, Henry S. *Afghanistan and the Soviet Union*. Durham, NC: Duke University Press, 1983.

Byman, Daniel. *Deadly Connections: States That Sponsor Terrorism*. Cambridge: Cambridge University Press, 2005.

Caplan, Richard. *International Governance of War-Torn Territories: Rules and Reconstruction*. Oxford, UK: Oxford University Press, 2005.

Chayes, Sarah. *The Punishment of Virtue: Inside Afghanistan After the Taliban*. New York: Penguin, 2006.

Coll, Steve. *Ghost Wars: The Secret History of the CIA, Afghanistan, and Bin Laden, From the Soviet Invasion to September 10, 2001*. New York: Penguin, 2004.

Collins, Joseph J. *The Soviet Invasion of Afghanistan: A Study in the Use of Force in Soviet Foreign Policy*. Lexington, MA: Lexington Books, 1986.

Cooley, John K. *Unholy Wars: Afghanistan, America and International Terrorism*. London: Pluto Press, 1999.

Crile, George. *Charlie Wilson's War: The Extraordinary Story of the Largest Covert Operation in History*. New York: Atlantic Monthly Press, 2003.

Cuthbertson, Daniel Francis. "The U.S. Role in the Soviet-Afghan War and the Rise of Militant Islamism." Unpublished M.A. thesis, University of New Brunswick, July 2005.

Dallaire, Romeo. *Shake Hands with the Devil*. Toronto: Random House Canada, 2003.

Doucette, Fred. *Empty Casing: A Soldier's Memoir of Sarajevo under Siege*. Toronto: Douglas and McIntyre, 2008.

Dupree, Louis. *Afghanistan*. Princeton: Princeton University Press, 1973.

Durch, William J. *The Evolution of UN Peacekeeping: Case Studies and Comparative Analysis*. New York: St. Martin's Press, 1993.

Ghaus, Abdul Samad. *The Fall of Afghanistan: An Insider's Account*. London: Pergamon-Brassey's, 1988.

Goodson, Larry P. *Afghanistan's Endless War: State Failure, Regional Politics, and the Rise of the Taliban*. Seattle: University of Washington Press, 2001.

Grau, Lester W. *The Bear Went Over the Mountain: Soviet Combat Tactics in Afghanistan*. London: Frank Cass, 1998.

Grossman, Lt Col Dave. *On Combat: The Psychology and Physiology of Deadly Conflict in War and Peace*. PPCT Research Publications, 2004.

Kaldor, Mary. *New and Old Wars: Organized Violence in a Global Era*. Stanford: Stanford University Press, 1999.

Lambie, Chris and Christian Laforce. *On Assignment in Afghanistan: Maritimers at War*. Halifax, NS: Nimbus and The Chronicle Herald, 2007.

MacKenzie, Lewis. *Peacekeeper: the Road to Sarajevo*. Vancouver: Douglas and McIntyre, 1993.

Morrison, Alex, ed. *The New Peacekeeping Partnership*. Cornwallis Park, NS: The Lester B. Pearson Canadian International Peacekeeping Training Centre, 1995.

Piggot, Peter. *Canada in Afghanistan: The War So Far*. Toronto: Dundurn Press, 2007.

Rashid, Ahmed. *Taliban*. New Haven: Yale University Press, 2001.

Roy, Olivier. *Islam and Resistance in Afghanistan*. Cambridge: Cambridge University Press, 1986.

Stein, Janice Gross and Eugene Lang. *The Unexpected War: Canada in Kandahar*. Toronto: Viking Canada, 2007.

Talentino, Andrea Kathryn. *Military Intervention after the Cold War: the Evolution of Theory and Practice*. Athens, OH: Ohio University Press, 2005.

Van Creveld, Martin. *The Transformation of War*. New York: Free Press, 1991.

Wright, Lawrence. *The Looming Tower: Al-Qaeda and the Road to 9/11*. New York: Knopf, 2006.

Articles and Chapters

Charters, David A. "Out of the Closet: Intelligence Support for Post-Modernist Peacekeeping." in *Intelligence in Peacekeeping: The Pearson Papers Number 4*. Cornwallis Park, NS: The Lester B. Pearson Canadian International Peacekeeping Training Centre, 1999, pp. 33–70.

Dorn, A. Walter, and Jonathan Matloff. "Preventing the Bloodbath: Could the UN have Predicted and Prevented the Rwandan Genocide?" *Journal of Conflict Studies*. Vol. 20, no. 1, Spring 2000, pp. 9–52.

Jalali, Ali A. "The Legacy of War and the Challenge of Peace Building." in Robert I. Rotberg, ed., *Building a New Afghanistan*. Cambridge, MA and Washington, DC: World Peace Foundation and Brookings Institution, 2007.

Johnson, Thomas H. "The Taliban Insurgency and an Analysis of *Shabnamah* (Night Letters)." *Small Wars and Insurgency*. Vol. 18, no. 3 (September 2007), pp. 317–44.

Jukes, Geoffrey. "The Soviet Armed Forces and the Afghan War," in Amin Saikal and William Maley, eds. *The Soviet Withdrawal From Afghanistan*. Cambridge: Cambridge University Press, 1989.

Kaplan, Robert D. "The Coming Anarchy." *Atlantic Monthly*. February 1994, pp. 44–49, 52–54, 58–76.

Karzai, Hekmat. "Strengthening Security in Contemporary Afghanistan: Coping with the Taliban." in Rotberg, ed., *Building a New Afghanistan*, 2007.

Lizée, Pierre. "Peacekeeping, Peacebuilding and the Challenge of Conflict Resolution in Cambodia." in David A. Charters, ed. *Peacekeeping and the Challenge of Civil Conflict Resolution*. Fredericton, NB: Centre for Conflict Studies, University of New Brunswick, 1994, pp. 135–48.

Rotberg, Robert I. "Renewing the Afghan State," in Rotberg, ed., *Building a New Afghanistan*, 2007.

Rubin, Barnett. "Saving Afghanistan." *Foreign Affairs*, vol. 86, no. 1, January–February 2007, pp. 57–78.

"The Day the World Changed." *The Economist*, 15 September 2001. Cover and lead editorial.

Windsor, Lee. "Professionalism Under Fire: Canadian Implementation of the Medak Pocket Agreement, Croatia 1993." *Canadian Military History*. Autumn 2000, pp. 23–35.

Zabriskie, Phil. "That Other War." *Time*, 8 September 2003.

Newspapers

Bell, Stewart. "Al-Qaeda Warns Canada." *National Post*, 28 October 2006.

Bento-Carrrier, Jeffrey. "'Support Our Troops' launched in Dalhousie," *The Tribune* (Campbellton, NB), 14 February 2007, p. A1.

Bento-Carrier, Jeffrey. "Parcel program for those in Afghanistan," *The Tribune* (Campbellton, NB), 4 April 2007, p. A8.

Bento-Carrier, Jeffrey. "Schoolbooks for Afghan children," *The Tribune* (Campbellton, NB), 28 November 2007, p. C3.

Bowie, Adam. "Being separated from a partner is difficult," *The Daily Gleaner* (Military Families Supplement), 14 July 2007, pp. 25 and 27.

Bowie, Adam. "Deployment Support Centre an important part of GMFRC," *The Daily Gleaner* (Military Families Supplement), 14 July 2007, pp. 7, 8, and 9.

Canadian Press. "Military Worried About Tory failure to Defend Afghan Mission." *Globe and Mail*, 1 October 2006.

Christie, Gillian. "Neighbours for Peace offers comfort, prayer for community in mourning," *The Post Gazette* (Oromocto, NB), 21 April 2007, p. A1.

Christie, Gillian. "Deployment Support Centre assisting deployed soldiers by caring for their families," *The Post Gazette* (Oromocto, NB), 28 April 2007, p. B3.

Curry, Bill. "Time to Bring Troops Home, NDP Says." *Globe and Mail*, 11 September 2006.

Dickson, Jeremy. "Red Rally Day honours troops serving in Afghanistan," *The Daily Gleaner*, 18 June 2007, p. A3.

Ducharme, Jeff. "Parents hope rally will help heal their wounds," *The Daily Gleaner*, 11 September 2007, p. A4.

Dunville, Jennifer. "District 17 ready to help students cope with tragedy," *The Daily Gleaner*, 10 April 2007, p. A4.

Gannon, Kathy. "Taliban Reassert Themselves in Afghanistan." *Globe and Mail*, 3 April 2003.

Garcia, Malcolm. "Rise in Attacks in Afghanistan." *The Gazette*, (Montreal) 31 March 2003.

Grattan, Heather. "Prayer rally held to comfort troops, families," *The Post Gazette* (Oromocto, NB), 10 February 2007, p. A3.

Lamb, Christina. "Warlord Leads Bloody Return of the Taliban." *The Sunday Times*, (London) 2 February 2003.

Letters to the Editor of *The Daily Gleaner*, 22 February 2007, p. C7; 5 June 2007, p. C7; and 31 July 2007, p. C7.

Levitz, Stephanie. "Troops Discover Taliban Weapons," *The Sunday Herald,* (Halifax) 15 July 2007.

O'Keefe, Karen. "Centre offers support for military families," *The Daily Gleaner* (Military Families Supplement), 14 July 2007, pp. 2 and 9.

Richardson, Sgt Terry. "Postcard from Kandahar," *The Tribune* (Campbellton, NB), 18 April 2007, p. C1.

Robichaud, Candice. "Looking for the positive makes things easier," *The Daily Gleaner* (Military Families Supplement), 14 July 2007, pp. 16–17.

Salahuddin, Sayed. "Taliban Escalates Election Attacks." *National Post*, 28 June 2004.

Shah, Saeed. "Pakistani insurgents join forces on Afghan border." *Globe and Mail*, 17 December 2007.

Smith, Graeme. "Insurgents Melt Away From Battle." *Globe and Mail*, 12 September 2006.

Staples, Michael. "Community sends message to Armed Forces members," *The Daily Gleaner*, 19 January 2007, pp. A1–A2.

Staples, Michael. "Five Soldiers From CFB Gagetown Killed," *The Daily Gleaner*, 9 April 2007.

Staples, Michael. "Covering soldiers' funerals helps Canadians grieve," *The Daily Gleaner*, 25 April 2007, p. B8.

Strauss, Julius. "Marines Face Perils of Guerrilla Raids." *Daily Telegraph*, 21 March 2002.

Online Sources

"Afghan Election Results Finalized." *Radio Free Europe / RadioLiberty [RFERL] Afghanistan Report* 12 November 2005. www.rferl.org/featuresarticle/2005/11, accessed 29 January 2005.

"Afghanistan: A Chronology of Suicide Attacks Since 2001." 17 January 2006. *RFERL*
Afghanistan Report www.rferl.org/featuresarticle/2006/01, accessed 24 January 2008.

"Afghanistan's War: A Double Spring Offensive," *The Economist*, 22 February 2007, www.economist.com, accessed 30 January 2008.

"Analysts Expect Spring Assault on NATO Troops," *CBC News*, 21 December 2006, www.cbc.ca/world/story/2006/12/21, accessed 30 January 2008.

Associated Press. "Omar Regrouping Taliban Forces, Says Taliban Official." *CNN*, 5 May 2002. www.cnn.com, accessed 5 May 2002.

Blood, Peter R. *Afghanistan: A Country Study*. Washington, DC: United States, Library of Congress, 2001), at http://countrystudies.us/afghanistan/38.htm accessed 7 January 2008.

Bone, James and Zahid Hussain. "Taliban Fighters Regroup and Attack Coalition." *The Times* (London), 25 June 2003. www.timesonline.co.uk, accessed 25 June 2003.

Canadian Broadcasting Corporation. "Canadian-led Offensive May Have Killed 1,500 Taliban Fighters." *CBC News*, 20 September 2006. www.cbc.ca, accessed 20 September 2006.

Esfandiari, Golnaz. "Afghanistan: Violence Increasing in South, East." *RFERL*

Afghanistan Report. 11 July 2005, www.rferl.org/featuresarticle/2005/7, accessed 29 January 2008.

Gall, Carlotta. "In Pakistan Border Towns, Taliban Has a Resurgence." *New York Times*, 6 May 2003. www.nytimes.com, accessed 6 May 2003.

Gall, Carlotta. "Taliban Suspected in Killing of 11 Chinese Workers." *New York Times*, 11 June 2004. www.nytimes.com, accessed 11 June 2004.

Heber, Alexandra, Stephane Grenier, Donald Richardson, and Kathy Darte, "Combining Clinical Treatment and Peer Support: A Unique Approach to Overcoming Stigma and Delivering Care," in *Human Dimensions in Military Operations – Military Leaders' Strategies for Addressing Stress and Psychological Support*, Meeting Proceedings (2006), pp. 23-1–23-14, at http://www.rto.nato.int/abstracts.asp

Krulak, Gen. Charles C. "The Strategic Corporal: Leadership in the Three Block War." *Marines Magazine*. January 1999, at www.au.af.mil/au/awc/awcgate/usmc/strategic_corporal.htm

Lobjakis, Ahto. "Afghanistan: NATO's Top general Says Taliban Defeated." *RFE/RL Afghanistan Report*. 13 August 2004, www.rferl.org/featuresarticle/2004/08 , accessed 25 January 2008.

Lobjakis, Ahto "Afghanistan: UN Says Most of Country Safe for Refugees' Return." *RFERL Afghanistan Report*. 16 February 2005, www.rferl.org/featuresarticle/2005/01, accessed 26 January 2008.

Radio Free Europe/Radio Liberty. *Afghanistan Report*. [Daily and monthly reports] April–December 2004. www.rferl.org/featuresarticle/2004, accessed January 2008.

Reuters. "Taliban Offensive Kills 3 Afghans." *CNN*, 29 April 2003. www.cnn.com, accessed 29 April 2003.

Reuters/Agence France Presse. "Protest in Southeastern Afghan City Turns Violent." *RFERL Afghanistan Report*, 7 March 2005. www.rferl.org/featuresarticel/2005/03 accessed 26 January 2008.

Simon Robinson, "The World's Worst Suicide Bombers?" *Time*, 28 July 2007, www.time.com, accessed 28 July 2007.

Rohde, David. "Afghan Symbol for Change Becomes Symbol of Failure." *New York Times*, 5 September 2006. www.nytimes.com, accessed 5 September 2006.

Synovitz, Ron. "Afghanistan: Skeptics Urge Caution Over Purported Hekmatyar Cease-Fire." *Radio Free Europe / Radio Liberty Report*, 19 July 2007. www.refrl.org/featuresarticle/2007/07, accessed 18 January 2008.

"Taliban Form 'Resistance Force'." *CNN*, 24 June 2003. www.cnn.com, accessed 24 June 2003.

"U.S. Fights al Qaeda in Pakistan." *MSNBC News*, 25 April 2002. http://msnbc.com/news, accessed 25 April 2002.

Zabriskie, Phil. "Undefeated." *Time*, 21 July 2003. www.time.com, accessed 21 July 2003.

Acknowledgements

Writing a history of events that are still unfolding is an enormously difficult task. Historians normally know how the story ends, and enjoy a perspective that only time can bring. Nevertheless, the story of TF 1-07 needs telling, if only to inform a people divided and confused about their mission in Afghanistan. This task is also a key part of the Gregg Centre mandate, which is to understand the causes, course, and consequences of war and communicate what we find to the general public.

Weaving together the complex threads of Canada's effort in Kandahar was possible thanks to remarkably open access to DND and CIDA documents and incredibly candid interviews with diplomats, aid workers, Mounties, and especially with soldiers of all ranks. In particular we must thank MGen Tim Grant, Col Mike Capstick, LCol Chris Hand, Col Stephen Bowes, Col Mike Cessford, for piecing together the higher level whole-of-government approach and strategic picture. Wilfrid Laurier University Professor Terry Copp invited us to meet key decision makers and development specialists at a series of Afghanistan workshops in 2006 and 2007. Michael Callan, Kevin Rex, and Renata Pistone helped to unlock the largely unknown story CIDA's development effort. Gavin Buchan and Richard Arbietier did the same for Foreign Affairs. Louise Garwood-Filbert from Corrections Canada, and Superintendent Dave Fudge from the RCMP helped us with the justice reform story. PRT commander LCol Bob Chamberlain, his adjutant, Capt Mark Timms, and his CIMIC commander, Maj Sean Courty provided the window on the many functions of the Provincial Reconstruction Team. Maj Joe Hartson and Capt Christian Breede were invaluable for understanding the task force rear party and putting us in contact with other members of the CF's family support team. MCpl Sue Spracklin, manager of the 2RCR War Diary, like any archivist for any historian, was the most critical "enabler." Given our access to sensitive information, due consideration was paid to operational security so as not to endanger the safety of Canadians and Afghans still serving in harm's way in Kandahar. We are grateful to BGen Ian Poulter for vetting the manuscript with those concerns in mind.

The Gregg Centre gratefully acknowledges the support of the Security and Defence Forum (SDF) of the Department of National Defence. The SDF facilitated our work by helping us access people, materials and Afghanistan. In particular, our SDF grant made it possible for Lee Windsor to visit TF 1-07 during its training period in Canada and its tour in Afghanistan, as well as subsequent travel to interview participants. Special thanks to SDF Director Aaron Hywarren for his encouragement and assistance.

Once the story materialized all Gregg Centre staff and graduate students were "mobilized" to get the manuscript in shape for publication. Deb Stapleford and Charles Eddy ran the office as our attention focused on Kandahar. Our Director, Dr Marc Milner brought his skilled editorial eye and slashing pen to the project. Andrew Cogswell took on the task of combining our various components and revisions into one clean almost finished product. Our ever patient editor, Don Loney, and his colleagues at John Wiley & Sons took care of the rest.

This project would not have been possible without one of us going with Task Force 1-07 through training in Gagetown and Wainwright, and then to Kandahar. Only then could we see the terrain, troops and civilian officials in action, track reconstruction progress, observe the plight of the Afghan people and unfortunately even experience combat and death. Lee took on that task with the full support of the 2RCR Battlegroup and PRT. He is indebted to LCol Rob Walker and Maj "Rusty" King for giving him open access to the battlegroup in training and on operations, and for cutting through the administrative barriers necessary to get a former CF member-turned civilian historian into the midst of a war. Majors Dave Sinclair, Danny Bobbitt, and Damon Dyer and Capts Allan Best and Martell Thompson kept him fuelled with "Kandahar chicken" and introduced him to commanders, soldiers and aid workers from over a dozen NATO nations. Outside the wire Maj Jake Galuga, Lt George Williams, RSM Mark

Baisley, BSM Chad Wagar and their vehicle crews kept him alive and made certain he saw Kandahar's battlefields, its rebuilding successes and the ugly blemishes that remain to be dealt with. They and all of the men and women of Task Force 1-07 we encountered are brave, professional and proud Canadians.

Although the SDF and DND provided every possible encouragement and support for this project, they exercised no control whatever (beyond immediate concerns for operational security, which we shared) on content or opinion. Like many in the SDF community, the senior staff of the Gregg Centre argued strongly against a mission to Kandahar Province when the issue was being discussed. And like many others, once the decision was made to go in support of the international community and the Government of Afghanistan we shared the hope that the mission will succeed: that civil society will be restored to that trouble land. If this book reflects that bias, we make no apologies. Whatever it contains, its errors and its omissions are ours.

Fredericton, New Brunswick, July 2008

Index

Author Biographies

Lee Windsor, PhD, is Deputy Director of the Gregg Centre, a Canadian Army historian, and former soldier. In April 2007 he traveled to Afghanistan to directly observe the Kandahar mission as the regimental historian of the 2nd Battalion, Royal Canadian Regiment Battlegroup.

David Charters, PhD, is Professor of Military History and Senior Fellow of the Gregg Centre at the University of New Brunswick. He is an authority on insurgency, counter-insurgency and international terrorism.

Brent Wilson, MA, is the Gregg Centre's Executive Editor and Co-Director of the New Brunswick Military Heritage Project. He brings to this book his knowledge of the Canadian Forces' mental health and family support system, and the Atlantic region's militia heritage.